T0366739

*Constructions of Terrorism*

THE CONSTRUCTIONS OF TERRORISM PROJECT

This publication is part of the *Constructions of Terrorism* research project being carried out through a partnership between TRENDS Research & Advisory; Abu Dhabi, United Arab Emirates; and the Orfalea Center for Global and International Studies, University of California, Santa Barbara.

TRENDS Research & Advisory was established in 2014 as an independent think tank addressing a broad range of local and global forces impacting human security. TRENDS aims at further improvement of human security and peace through study, analysis, and the advancement of groundbreaking research. TRENDS strives to present policy alternatives designed to transform societies and improve the living standards of humanity. TRENDS is based in Abu Dhabi, UAE, with a network of Nonresident Fellows and institutional partners spanning the globe. For more information, visit http://trendsinstitution.org/.

The Orfalea Center for Global and International Studies was established in 2005 and works closely with instructional and research units across UCSB, and with partners around the world, on research and policy questions of global scope, implications, and relevance. The mission of the Orfalea Center for Global and International Studies is to provide an intellectual and programmatic focus for the University's activities in global, international, and area studies. For more information, visit http://www.orfaleacenter.ucsb.edu/.

# Constructions of Terrorism

*An Interdisciplinary Approach to Research and Policy*

Edited by

MICHAEL STOHL, RICHARD BURCHILL, AND SCOTT ENGLUND

University of California Press

University of California Press, one of the most distinguished university presses in the United States, enriches lives around the world by advancing scholarship in the humanities, social sciences, and natural sciences. Its activities are supported by the UC Press Foundation and by philanthropic contributions from individuals and institutions. For more information, visit www.ucpress.edu.

University of California Press
Oakland, California

Library of Congress Cataloging-in-Publication Data

Names: Stohl, Michael, editor, contributor. | Burchill, Richard, editor, contributor. | Englund, Scott, editor, contributor.
Title: Constructions of terrorism : an interdisciplinary approach to research and policy / [edited by] Michael Stohl, Richard Burchill, and Scott Englund.
Description: Oakland, California : University of California Press, [2017] | This publication is part of the Constructions of Terrorism Research Project being carried out through a partnership between TRENDS Research & Advisory, Abu Dhabi, UAE, and the Orfalea Center for Global and International Studies, University of California, Santa Barbara. | Includes bibliographical references and index.
Identifiers: LCCN 2017005897 (print) | LCCN 2017011096 (ebook) | ISBN 9780520294165 (cloth : alk. paper) | ISBN 9780520294172 (pbk : alk. paper) | ISBN 9780520967397 ()
Subjects: LCSH: Terrorism—Social aspects.
Classification: LCC HV6431 .C6527 2017 (print) | LCC HV6431 (ebook) | DDC 363.325—dc23
LC record available at https://lccn.loc.gov/2017005897

Manufactured in the United States of America

24  23  22  21  20  19  18  17
10  9  8  7  6  5  4  3  2  1

# Contents

# Illustrations

# Introduction

*Constructions of Terrorism*

Scott Englund, Michael Stohl, and Richard Burchill

Constructions of terrorism emanate from a wide range of sources. Governments and international organizations create criminal laws and administrative lists defining who is a terrorist or what acts constitute terrorism. In society, discussions among its members and the press play a major role in how the words *terrorism* and *extremism* are used and applied, which in turn influences public understanding and government policy. Terrorist groups themselves contribute to these constructions through the rationales and justifications they use for their actions. Today we are seeing the continual reference to terrorism in everyday language, government policy, news reporting, and international diplomacy and from various groups and uprisings.

With the term being used to describe a wide range of violence, it is difficult to formulate effective government responses aimed at prevention and eradication. It further makes things difficult in societal settings for creating conducive environments for reconciliation. This volume seeks to establish appropriate research frameworks for understanding how we construct understanding(s) of terrorism. From the perspective of countering terrorism and extremism, if there is not a well-developed understanding of the object of these frameworks, they will not be effective.

Assessments of the literature of terrorism have revealed consistent and troubling shortcomings. Lum, Kennedy, and Sherley and Andrew Silke carefully examined studies of terrorism published over the previous decades and the great explosion of terrorism research after 9/11.[1] The most germane findings about terrorism and counterterrorism research in their two studies help frame the contributions that have been reviewed here.

The first finding is that most of the publications on terrorism have been contributions by scholars who were relatively new to the subject. These scholars discovered terrorism as a problem, usually after a particularly spectacular and unexpected event, offered a solution for how to respond to terrorists and terrorism, and never returned to the study of terrorism. Indeed, Silke found that 83 percent of the publications on terrorism were authored by people who published just one article on the subject.[2] These scholars had not invested the time to discover what research had already been done—either by scholars engaged in the study or by previous groups of terrorists or policy makers responding to terrorism.

The second key finding is that most of the scholarly work on terrorism, reflecting the prevalent, one-off approach, has not been interested in the hard work of theory building. The vast majority of the scholars who have investigated terrorism have not approached their research with the purpose of developing theoretically grounded studies, and consequently they have not applied positivist research methods to its study. This has been a consistent finding of reviews of the "state of the art" for the past three decades. As Schmid and Jongman argued: "Perhaps as much as eighty percent of the literature is not research-based in any rigorous sense."[3] As a result, Schmid and Jongman concluded, "much of the writing in the crucial areas of terrorism research . . . is impressionistic, superficial, and at the same time also pretentious, venturing far reaching generalisations on the basis of episodal evidence."[4] Ariel Merari concurred: "By and large, terrorism literature is composed mainly of studies which rely on relatively weak research methods."[5] Ted Gurr also agreed, arguing that, "with a few clusters of exceptions there is, in fact, a disturbing lack of good empirically-grounded research on terrorism."[6] The consequence, as Merari wrote in 1991, is that terrorism research "resembles hearsay rather than twentieth century science"; and that, he added, "may well be an understatement."[7]

Writing in 2014 about the surge of money and research on terrorism since the September 11, 2001, terror attacks in New York and Washington, D.C., Marc Sageman commented: "After all this funding and this flurry of publications, with each new terrorist incident we realize that we are no closer to answering our original question about what leads people to turn to political violence. The same worn-out questions are raised over and over again, and we still have no compelling answers. It seems that terrorism research is in a state of stagnation on the main issues. How did this state of affairs arise?"[8] Sageman argues that the roots of the lack of progress lie both in the questions being asked and in the lack of data to pursue them. As he indicates, one set of questions centers on the psychological: Why do they hate us? What is the terrorist personality? Both questions eventually give way to a process approach to becoming a terrorist and searching for recruitment devices both in the new media and in personal charismatic figures. In addition to the shortcoming of these approaches, Sageman also bemoans the lack of appropriate data for studying these questions; much of the data that exist, he believes, is in the hands of government agencies whose analysts simply do not exploit them, because they lack the concepts, time, and ability necessary to do so. A serious impediment to scholars, whether fully dedicated to terrorism studies or only occasionally participating in them, is the lack of comprehensive and reliable data. We note that in what follows, scholars are now finding relevant and helpful data and are applying analytical methods to them.

In 2016 the journal *Terrorism and Political Violence* dedicated an issue to debating a recent modification of David Rapoport's "Four Wave" theory. Rapoport asserted, in an influential 2001 journal article and volume chapter, that modern terrorism can be collected into four "waves," the first of which began in Russia and Eastern Europe at the close of the nineteenth century; the fourth, religious wave predominates today.[9] Tom Parker and Nick Sitter advanced an alternative framework, according to which, rather than consecutive waves, each with a definable beginning and end, terrorism has come in four specific strains or "chains" that extend through its modern history.[10] The ensuing debate seriously challenged the "strain" model.[11] Perhaps confirming in part the criticisms made by Silke, Merari, and Gurr noted above, the discussion was entirely qualitative, and the theory Parker and Sitter introduced relied on selected anecdotal evidence; further, Parker and Sitter had published very little on terrorism prior to their "strains" theory. Separately, in 2010 Jeffrey Kaplan suggested his own modification of Rapoport's wave theory, arguing that presently a fifth wave of terrorism, which he called tribalism, is developing, and Rapoport's fourth, "religious" wave has crested and broken.[12]

Also in 2016, the journal *Studies in Conflict and Terrorism* dedicated an issue to data and measurement used in the study of terrorism. Introducing the special issue, Joshua Freilich and Gary LaFree observed:

> Recently, scholarly interest in terrorism has increased and systematic methods are now more commonly used. Importantly though, terrorism works continue to lag behind related fields of study in the analysis of data and the adoption of sophisticated research methods. The few terrorism works that do analyze data highlight substantive findings as opposed to measurement issues. A study's substantive findings are only meaningful though if it correctly addresses the measurement issues that invariably arise during the research process. In other words, while the quality of terrorism research has greatly improved in recent years, measurement issues have been under explored and researchers could do more in this area to further improve the field's rigor.[13]

Articles in the issue attack issues of measurement and data collection, from the use of official statistics, victim reports, interviews, and open-source databases such as International Terrorism: Attributes of Terrorist Events (ITATE) and the Global Terrorism Database (GTD). The collection of articles is a thorough catalogue of the state of the art in quantitative research in the study of terrorism.

One may conclude, therefore, that though the study of terrorism has benefited from increased rigor, greater access to reliable data, and more funding and attention, there is still work to be done. Indeed, the study of terrorism benefits from a wide variety of methods, different approaches by a diverse set of disciplines, and the attention of academics and policy makers alike. The chapters that follow represent a sample of that diversity.

## THE CONSTRUCTIONS OF TERRORISM PROJECT

TRENDS Research & Advisory, an Abu Dhabi–based independent research center, and the Orfalea Center for Global and International Studies at the University of California, Santa Barbara, announced a partnership in the summer of 2015 in order to focus on "constructions of terrorism." Occupying considerable space in the daily awareness of people across the globe, terrorism is nevertheless an elusive concept, falling prey to politicization, loose definition, and lack of context. In some ways terrorism has been described as whatever a person wants it to be, which often gives it an outsized role in public opinion and policy demands. The Constructions of Terrorism Project (COTP) seeks to approach this slippery concept from multiple directions, employing a variety of research methodologies emanating from many academic disciplines and policy-making perspectives.

The goal is to thoroughly explore the many ways in which terrorism is constructed by academics, political leaders, the public, and those who employ terror to get what they want. The COTP does not intend to solve the problem of defining terrorism by somehow exceeding the scholastic efforts of other research projects, or to fully reconcile divergent approaches to the theoretical concept. It does, however, seek to provide a forum in which the diversity of conceptual understandings of terrorism can be collectively interrogated, based on the belief that from the high ground of a more thorough, rigorously investigated understanding of terrorism, more effective means of confronting terrorism can be developed and implemented.

## STUDYING TERRORISM FROM MANY PERSPECTIVES

The scholars and their contributions assembled here are distinguished both within their own fields and within the community of scholars of terrorism.

Almost all have devoted a great deal of their scholarly attention to the problem, and most have done so for more than a decade and, in some cases, for much longer than that. The contributors differ in the ways they approach terrorism as a problem. They represent a number of very different scholarly fields and backgrounds: sociology, political science, communication, criminology, psychology, religious studies, history, and law. While there are many points of disagreement among these contributions (e.g., the construction of the problem and the various possible responses that policy makers and publics might have and make), there are also many points of overlap and agreement. All of the contributors reject a one-size-fits-all approach to the problem of characterizing those who use terrorism or those who are responsible for responding to terrorist violence. All are interested in exploring the similarities and differences among the perpetrators, the policy maker responses, and public reactions and assessments.

First, constructing terrorism is, in part, an introspective process, requiring an examination not just of terrorists and what they do but also of what is done to them before and after they decide to act. Acts of terror and terrorists themselves are embedded in both a local and a global political system. In chapter 1, Lisa Stampnitzky suggests that there would be no definition of terrorism without counterterrorism. Rather than a dearth of definitions for terrorism, there is actually a plethora, making selection the real problem. Stampnitzky suggests that the best definition of terrorism is how it is defined in practice; thus, counterterrorism "defines" terrorism.

Sometimes definitions of terrorism can be too inclusive, or constructed in such a way as to exaggerate its potential for damage. John Mueller and Mark G. Stewart have long held that the threat of terrorism has been exaggerated, with the consequence that phenomena like civil war and insurgency are being redefined as "terrorism." As a result, as they discuss in chapter 2, people overestimate their own risk of falling victim to terrorist violence, which in part fuels overreaction by government agencies. Central to Mueller and Stewart's argument is the widespread tendency to "overhype" the threat of terrorism.

Constructing terrorism means also constructing the institutional responses to terrorist violence. David H. Schanzer approaches the topic from a legal perspective in chapter 3. Terrorism is a tactic, one that can be used by anybody. Political expression can take many forms; even the use of violence to advance a political objective entails choices. What sets terrorism apart from other forms of violence is its intentional violation of the laws of war. Schanzer concludes that understanding terrorism as a tactic—akin to tactics like conventional warfare or murder for hire—and ridding us of particularly useless concepts like a "war on terror" or even "counterterrorism" will help bring clarity to the current sprawl of post-9/11 security policy.

In chapter 4, Ruth Blakeley challenges the commonly held position that widening the definition of terrorism to include state violence fruitlessly muddies an already murky phenomenon, making further study difficult. States can and do use terror in aid of their own political projects, she contends. She first interrogates scholarly and policy approaches to state terrorism, then moves to describe some incidents that, she claims, represent state terror, and concludes by advancing some consequences of excluding state terrorism from the study of terror more generally.

The best understanding of terrorism situates an act of violence within its unique political environment, in which there are multiple actors; to focus on the actions of terrorists alone is to perceive only part of the phenomenon. This is vividly described by Mark Juergensmeyer in chapter 5, where he explains that focusing on the perpetrators of violence alone is like trying to understand the moves of a boxer in a ring who is fighting an invisible opponent. One boxer's moves are comprehensible only with reference to the other boxer's actions. The suicidal act of flying airplanes into buildings, for example, can make sense only when one understands that the perpetrators and planners of that act believed themselves to be engaged in an apocalyptic cosmic battle of good versus evil.

In fact, terrorist violence may be conducted with the objective of eliciting a specific reaction. Clark McCauley, in chapter 6, argues that "jujitsu politics" is designed to use the overwhelming power of targeted states against themselves. According to his research, acts of terror elicit an anger emotional response that is stronger than fear and intimidation. As McCauley argues here: "Anger is associated with aggression and outgroup derogation; fear is associated with defensive strategies of surveillance and curtailed civil rights. Anger is the emotion sought by terrorists aiming to elicit overreaction to their attacks—using the enemy's strength against him in a strategy of *jujitsu politics.* The power of this strategy, and the importance of anger reactions in making the strategy successful, is hidden by definitions of terrorism that focus only on fear and coercion." The reaction itself is part of the larger strategy employed by terrorists. It is therefore impossible to disentangle the act of terrorist violence from the type of response it elicits; there are always at least two participants in an act of terrorism.

Benjamin Smith, Scott Englund, Andrea Figueroa-Caballero, Elena Salcido, and Michael Stohl provide in chapter 7 the results of a quantitative examination of more than 110,000 print newspaper articles. They find that "al-Qaeda" was the most symbolically meaningful name used to describe terrorism over the past eighteen years. In fact, in 60 percent of the articles, there was no reason for al-Qaeda to be mentioned, except as a way to help define some other terror group. The implication is that applying an "al-Qaeda" frame so broadly likely paints an erroneous veneer of solidarity over terrorist groups and actions that in fact belong to their own unique political milieus.

While terrorism is tricky to define, and different definitions lead to different responses, the concept of radicalization has become perhaps even thornier. Anthony Richards argues in chapter 8 that in the United Kingdom, the concepts of "terrorism, radicalization, and extremism" are being merged in unhelpful, and perhaps counterproductive, ways. He explains that in the United Kingdom, "there is an increased *wider* concern with the way citizens think ideologically—a broader view that if they believe in certain *nonviolent* dogmas said to be 'conducive' to terrorism, they are part of the 'terrorist problem,' even if they deplore the violent methods of al-Qaeda and ISIS."

In chapter 9, Richard Falk draws attention to the logically dangerous approach of using the term *terrorism* to signify a particular actor (usually one with whom one disagrees) rather than the nature of the violence itself. Focusing on actors invites selective use of the term; thinking about the act itself helps to situate it in its political context. By providing context, appropriate measures can be taken to provide durable security. The contemporary security environment requires new thinking. Falk concludes that "neither the war nor the crime paradigm is adequate to encompass the specific character of the security challenge posed by the 9/11 attacks on US targets or the Paris massacre of November 13, 2015, or any of the other kindred happenings since the year 2000." These new challenges require a nuanced approach that anticipates responses to counterterrorism efforts. "Reconfiguring a security paradigm that captures the distinctiveness of such events," Falk argues, "is needed to avoid policies that kill and devastate without contributing to improved security." Crafting such an innovative counterterrorism strategy is likely to present significant challenges to domestic civil liberties in Western societies, international legal traditions, intelligence collection and analysis, and even the institution of international sovereignty.

The traumatic events of September 11, 2001, and subsequent high-profile incidents of terrorist violence have resulted in an expanding body of law (both domestic and international) that addresses terrorism. Richard Burchill argues in chapter 10 that although a proliferation of laws concerning terrorism may allow governments to intervene earlier to disrupt terrorist planning, real improvements in security have not occurred:

> There is no doubt that states are required, and expected, to provide
> security for their citizens and others, but we have to ask if the legal
> regimes constructed for addressing terrorism are effectively achieving
> the objective of creating more security. Despite the fact that
> governments have been addressing the threat to security caused by
> terrorism for a considerable period of time, calls continue for more laws
> as the solution to improve security.

Burchill concludes that the expanding volume of law addressing the crime
of terrorism is itself a dangerous overreaction. Rather than producing more
security—a central duty of any state—terrorism law has become a symbolic act in response to an emotionally weighty crime. The result is to criminalize more and more behavior with no attending increase in security, and
to grant security services ever greater authority without producing more
effectiveness.

The multitude of ways one can define terrorism, including diverse sets of
actors and actions, can affect how one studies the phenomenon itself. Rachel
Levin and Victor Asal suggest in chapter 11 that although a great deal of
intellectual effort has been devoted to defining terrorism by focusing on
who is targeted in a particular act of violence, "this topic has not led to an
investigation of whether or not different constructs of the target would yield
different causes of terrorism." Levin and Asal suggest that the question may
be addressed by testing the Global Terrorism Database to determine whether
different operationalizations of the concept of terrorism (at least with respect
to who is targeted by terrorist violence) would produce different correlations
and causal relationships that would illuminate the dynamics of terrorism.
They conclude: "Different definitions of terrorism do not seem to be generating very different causal stories. This suggests that while the ethical arguments related to how we construct the definition of terrorism are important,
the basic explanations of extreme violent attacks at the country level of analysis are simply not that different, regardless of the target."

In chapter 12, Stefan Malthaner and Lasse Lindekilde present two alternative constructions of the "lone actor" terrorist. Rather than being isolated and entirely independent, they explain, these individuals are usually,
at least tangentially, part of a wider movement. In one construction, which
they label the peripheral drifter pathway, the individual is partially embedded in semi-radical friendship groups and weakly connected to wider
radical milieus. While never becoming a part of a radical group, the
peripheral drifter drifted in the margins, weakly considering but then
again dropping plans to join jihad abroad. In a second pathway, the failed
joiner tries to connect to radical groups, succeeds in making contact, but is

rejected or expelled. Thus forced to function outside the group, this individual decides to act alone.

Mia Bloom, in chapter 13, argues that to understand the construction of terrorism, we should examine how martyrdom is celebrated in the larger society and how youth are convinced that they can do far more with their death than they could with their life. Her chapter examines how the most vulnerable in a society take part in acts of terrorist violence and are convinced that martyrdom is an altruistic act. Bloom insists that so-called child terrorists "are not born; rather they are made and learn to *want* to be a part of a violent extremist group, either with or without the knowledge and support of their parents and families." This culture of martyrdom instills in young people an extreme appreciation for the afterlife and teaches them to value their own death more than life itself. Religious sanction for suicidal action comes with promises of religious reward for both martyrs and their families. The chapter examines various elements of "cultures of martyrdom" by comparing *jihadi* examples with *thatkodai* in Sri Lanka (among the Liberation Tigers of Tamil Eelam, or LTTE).

The Government Actions in Terror Environments (GATE) data set is introduced and discussed by Laura Dugan and Erica Chenoweth in chapter 14. Dugan and Chenoweth argue that government actions beyond what is explicitly described as counterterrorism can affect the behavior of terrorist groups. They conclude by arguing that counterterrorism analysis should "reconsider we can conceptualize counterterrorism to include more nuanced behavior by governments that could elicit a reaction from terrorist organizations or their constituencies. By expanding how we construct counterterrorism, we are better able to develop insight into what works and what does not work in different contexts."

Properly constructing a terror threat is essential to creating effective countermeasures. Englund and Stohl argue in chapter 15 that when distinct constructions, or facets, of the contemporary threat presented by Daesh are conflated, the response to that threat is bound to be muddled and ineffective. Fighting an insurgent army abroad may have little in common with detecting domestic terror threats. In fact, applying the wrong policy prescription to a particular facet of a complex problem may be counterproductive. "Bombing Daesh fighters in Raqqa," Englund and Stohl note, "will not make Parisians more secure; killing individual Daesh leaders is not likely to liberate Mosul; screening refugees more carefully will not solve the crisis that displaced them." They conclude that "properly demarcating the various distinguishable facets of a terrorist threat is a necessary, but not sufficient, step toward effectively countering that threat."

The purpose of this collection of essays is to further develop our understandings of terrorism through multidisciplinary approaches. While we do not wish to overstate the threat from terrorism, the scale of events around the world point toward the need for more effective understanding of the phenomena categorized as terrorism. There is no clear path to preventing and eradicating violence and extremism; however, more effective responses are needed globally. Our objective with this collection is to contribute to the formulation of more effective responses through a better understanding of how we construct understandings of terrorism.

## NOTES

1. C. Lum, L.W. Kennedy, and A.J. Sherley, "The effectiveness of counter-terrorism strategies: A Campbell systematic review," *Journal of Experimental Criminology,* 2:4 (2006): 489–516; A. Silke, "An introduction to research on terrorism," in A. Silke, ed., *Research on terrorism: Trends, achievements, and failures* (London: Frank Cass, 2004), 1–29; A. Silke, "The devil you know: Continuing problems with research on terrorism," *Terrorism and Political Violence* 13:4 (2001): 1–14.

2. Silke, "An introduction to research on terrorism."

3. A. Schmid and A. Jongman, *Political terrorism: A new guide to actors, authors, concepts, data bases, theories, and literature* (Amsterdam: North Holland, 1988), 219.

4. Ibid., 177.

5. Cited in ibid., 179.

6. T. Gurr, "Empirical research on political terrorism: The state of the art and how it might be improved," in R. Slater and M. Stohl, eds., *Current perspectives on political terrorism* (New York: St. Martin's Press, 1988), 2.

7. A. Merari, "Academic research and government policy on terrorism," *Terrorism and Political Violence* 3 (1991): 95, 220.

8. Marc Sageman, "The stagnation in terrorism research," *Terrorism and Political Violence* 26 (2014): 569.

9. David C. Rapoport, "The fourth wave: September 11 and the history of terrorism," *Current History* 100 (2001): 419–24; Rapaport, "The four waves of modern terrorism," in Audrey Kurth Cronin and James Ludes, eds., *Attacking terrorism: Elements of a grand strategy* (Washington, DC: Georgetown University Press, 2004), 46–73.

10. Tom Parker, and Nick Sitter, "The four horsemen of terrorism: It's not waves, it's strains," *Terrorism and Political Violence* 28:2 (2016): 197–216.

11. Jeffrey Kaplan, "A strained criticism of Wave Theory," *Terrorism and Political Violence* 28:2 (2016): 228–35; David C. Rapoport, "It is waves, not strains," *Terrorism and Political Violence* 28:2 (2016): 217–24; Charles Townshend, "Wave and strain," *Terrorism and Political Violence* 28:2 (2016): 225–27.

12. Jeffrey Kaplan, *Terrorist groups and the new tribalism* (New York: Routledge, 2010).

13. Joshua D. Freilich, and Gary LaFree, "Measurement issues in the study of terrorism: Introducing the special issue," *Studies in Conflict and Terrorism* 39 (2016): 569–79.

# 1. Can Terrorism Be Defined?

Lisa Stampnitzky

I've titled this chapter with the question "Can terrorism be defined?" But of course terrorism *can* be defined; the true problem is not a surfeit, but rather a *surplus,* of definitions. Yet neither experts, nor politicians, nor the lay public has been able to come to an agreement as to which of the many definitions circulating is correct, and the so-called problem of definition has been a central and enduring aspect of both public and expert debate on terrorism. In practice, this discussion most often takes the form of debate over how to differentiate "terrorism" from "not terrorism" and whether or not a particular act qualifies as such.

This chapter does not presume to resolve this dilemma. Rather, I suggest that the single-minded focus on defining terrorism has obscured a perhaps more interesting question: What does terrorism define? I argue in this chapter that if the problem of definition has not been resolved, it may be because struggles over its definition contain within them three questions even more central to contemporary politics:

1. Who is the enemy?
2. When is violence legitimate?
3. What is political?

Rather than presuming that we can resolve the problem of definition, I suggest that attempts to define terrorism, whether by the state or in the realm of public discourse, be understood as struggles over the answers to these questions. I begin this chapter with a brief overview of the emergence of the contemporary concept of terrorism, establishing that the problem of definition was a central feature of the discourse from the start. I then discuss each of the three questions above. I explicate what each of them means, why it is significant, and how its meaning can be read from the way terrorism is defined. I suggest that the answer to the question "What is terrorism?" then tells us (and depends on) the answer to these questions.

The concept of terrorism first began to take shape in its contemporary form in the early 1970s. Before that time, acts of political violence, including hijackings, assassinations, and other acts that we now consider terrorism, were instead most often understood through a discourse of insurgency.[1] Within the framework of insurgency, violence was generally understood to be rational, purposeful, sometimes even justifiable. With the emergence of a discourse dominated by the concept of terrorism, however, in which acts labeled as such came to be understood as fundamentally immoral, "terrorism" came to be understood as rooted in a terrorist *identity*, rather than as a tactic that any group might adopt. With these changes, the search for explanations of both "terrorism" as an act, and the "terrorist" as a type of person, took off, leading to the emergence of the new field of terrorism studies.[2] Since the discourse of terrorism has taken hold, with each new and subsequent incident, the key question has become "Is this an act of terrorism?"—with the answer guiding both the further questions to be asked and the answers needed to respond.

The problem of definition was thus present almost from the very start. Even terrorism experts have been unable to agree on how terrorism should be defined, and when I interviewed terrorism experts, they themselves often lamented this problem of definition. As Brian Jenkins, former head of terrorism research at the think tank RAND, told me in an interview, "Definitional debates are the great Bermuda Triangle of terrorism research. I've seen entire conferences go off into definitional debates, never to be heard from again."[3] Indicating that this is not a recent phenomenon, we may observe that a 1988 survey of the literature found more than one hundred different definitions in use among terrorism researchers; an observer at a mid-1980s Department of Defense symposium reported that there were "almost as many definitions as there were speakers"; and a 2001 article described a "perverse situation where a great number of scholars are studying a phenomenon, the essence of which they have (by now) simply agreed to disagree upon."[4] At the international level, attempts to develop an international counterterrorism response at the UN faltered throughout the 1970s, in large part because states were unable to agree on what constitutes terrorism (with countries from the Global South, in particular, arguing that the use of violence in national liberation struggles should be excluded).

I began by referencing the "problem of definition" in terrorism studies, characterized by a surplus of definitions and the lack of agreement on any one definition. In fact, the definitions circulating are often not just different but mutually contradictory. Competing definitions commonly suggest that states *can* or *cannot* commit terrorism, or that terrorism consists *only*, or *not only*, of violence against civilians.[5] Examples of these contradictions are easy to find, not just in abstract debates over definition but also in applications of the label in practice. For example, many will criticize the United States for following a "double standard"—pointing to US support for "terrorists" (violent insurgents who target civilians) such as the Contras in Nicaragua, Renamo in southern Africa, and even Osama bin Laden and his "mujahedeen" fighters in Afghanistan in the 1980s, while condemning the violence of those it deems enemies. As the saying goes, "One man's terrorist is another man's freedom fighter."

Given this essential contestation at the heart of defining terrorism, how have experts and others tried to resolve the problem of definition? Many (though by no means all) terrorism experts are highly disconcerted by this situation, and have sought (albeit with relatively little success) to "fix" or stabilize the definition of terrorism, sometimes suggesting that until this is accomplished, little progress can be made in the field, the "politicization" of the concept having commonly been pointed to as a key hindrance.[6] For example, Martha Crenshaw writes, "The task of definition . . . necessarily involves transforming 'terrorism' into a useful analytical term rather than a polemical tool."[7] Similarly, Schmid and Jongman, in their omnibus reference work, *Political Terrorism: A New Guide to Actors, Authors, Concepts, Data Bases, Theories, and Literatures,* suggest that there is a need for a neutral, stable, and universally accepted definition as a basis for scholarly progress:

> The search for a universalist definition of terrorism is one which scientists cannot give up. Without some solution to the definitional problem, without isolating terrorism from other forms of (political) violence, there can be no uniform data collection and no responsible theory building. . . . The search for an adequate definition of terrorism is still on . . . many authors seem fatigued about the need to still consider basic conceptual questions. This is a dangerous attitude as it plays into the hands of those experts from the operational antiterrorist camp who have a "we-know-it-when-we-see-it" attitude that easily leads to double standards which produce bad science and also, arguably, bad policies.[8]

What I refer to here as stabilization thus includes calls for the depoliticization of definitions of terrorism, for politically "neutral" definitions, and, often, for definitions that are agnostic with regard to moral judgment.

Furthermore, the problem of definition does not just trouble experts. Media coverage of terrorism, as well, has frequently been characterized by disputes over definition. Critiques of the conceptualization of terrorism in the media tend to highlight inconsistencies in the use of the term—particularly pointing out seeming double standards where the term is applied to one set of actors, but not another, engaging in similar acts. For example, Glenn Greenwald, of *The Intercept,* has repeatedly compared coverage of different incidents to argue that the misconceptualization and misapplication of the term *terrorism* is an ongoing problem. Referring to an incident in 2010 when a white American flew a small plane into an IRS building, he writes: "The attack had all of the elements of iconic terrorism, a model for how it's most commonly understood: down to flying a plane into the side of a building. But Stack was white and non-Muslim. As a result, not only was the word 'terrorism' not applied to Stack, but it was explicitly declared inapplicable by media outlets and government officials alike."[9] We can find similar examples of this form of critique in commentary on media coverage of the massacre of nine churchgoers in Charleston, South Carolina, in June 2015. For example, as an article on Salon.com stated:

> As many have pointed out, the media is unsure about what constitutes terrorism only when white people are the perpetrators. White men with guns are "lone wolves" or "mentally ill" or depraved criminals. Brown men with bombs are very obviously "terrorists." This is a double standard with consequences. "Terrorism" is a word that resonates; it inspires urgency and collective action, both of which are needed if we're to deal with the underlying problems. If white people can't, by definition, be terrorists, then the term has no practical meaning; it's about the actor, not the act. If terrorism is something only brown people do, then we should be honest and admit that. We should say that terrorism is about the color of the criminal, not the intent of the crime.[10]

Meanwhile, a piece in the *Washington Post* declared:

> But listen to major media outlets, and you won't hear the word "terrorism" used in coverage of Wednesday's shooting. You haven't heard the white, male suspect, 21-year-old Dylann Roof, described as "a possible terrorist" by mainstream news organizations (though some, including *The Washington Post,* have covered the growing debate about this discrepancy). And if coverage of other recent shootings by white men is any indication, he never will be. Instead, the go-to explanation for his alleged actions will be mental illness. He will be humanized and called sick, a victim of mistreatment or inadequate mental health resources.[11]

Each of these examples focuses upon forms of bias in the application of the "terrorism" label to events, illustrated by repeated inconsistencies in the use of the concept. In sum, there is significant contestation over the conceptualization of terrorism, both among experts and in the media. The debates tend to hinge on calls for stabilization of the concept, rooted in concerns either that it is inherently ambiguous or that it is applied inconsistently (i.e., there are double standards). For media critics, such stabilization would require making the concept fairer in its application, by removing bias—whether with regard to friend versus enemy, state versus nonstate, or race, religion, and ethnicity—and by applying definitions and moral judgments evenly to all perpetrators. Ultimately, many of these criticisms come down to making the point that the concept needs to be fixed, in two senses of the word: first, that it needs to be repaired, made more coherent, and applied in a more consistent way, and second, that it needs to be stabilized, prevented from being continually politicized or biased. These sorts of media critiques thus echo many of the calls for stabilization coming from the expert sphere.

If terrorism has not, and perhaps cannot, be pinned down to a fixed definition, how should we comprehend its continued centrality in political discourse? What I suggest is that rather than asking how terrorism should be defined, we instead ask, What is it that terrorism defines? I have argued that (debates over) definitions of terrorism tend to center on three central concerns: that it is illegitimate violence, perpetrated by enemies, with a political character. What the ongoing salience of the problem of definition suggests, however, is that none of these issues is self-evident, and, indeed, they indicate three of the most significant questions in contemporary political life. Who is the enemy? When is violence legitimate, and when is it illegitimate? (And relatedly, when is violence "out of place," and when is it expected, or even normal?) And which questions and concerns count as properly political? Where is the boundary between the "political" and the "nonpolitical"? What I argue here, then, is that struggles over the definition of terrorism are struggles over the correct (meaning culturally agreed upon or politically hegemonic) answers to these questions.

It is a commonplace in political science, most often attributed to Max Weber, that a key feature of the modern state is that it is the sole arbiter of legitimate violence. Terrorism, on the other hand, is most commonly understood as *illegitimate* violence. What my argument suggests, then, is that whatever is designated as terrorism is defined as illegitimate violence. Violence seen as legitimate, or as potentially justifiable, will face resistance in being labeled as terrorism. The most apt example here might be the question of "state terrorism" itself, and the struggle over whether or not this can even be a possibility. When critics attempt to apply the label to the state, they are likely to face pushback.[12] Similarly, we may cite the attempts of movements such as Black Lives Matter to label police violence as terror, and the strong responses that these claims can engender.

But of course not all illegitimate violence is designated as terrorism. What I suggest here, first, is that the core logic of the identification of terrorism "in practice" is that it is identified as *violence out of place*. The question, then, of course, is what counts as "out of place"? As one commentator has declared, "The promise of the 'war on terror' was that we would kill them 'over there' so they would not kill us 'over here.'"[13] Violence out of place is violence that moves beyond where it is "expected" to occur: in a site expected to be "peaceful" (i.e., Western or "civilized," not a war zone); in a place where those considered "representative" live (i.e., not the "inner city"); and further, when it is unexpected, on a site perceived as "innocent" and disconnected from explicit political causes or actions (thus attacks on an expressly "political" or "partisan" site are, ironically, less likely to be treated as terrorism than "random" or purely generic or civilian sites). The key thing here is what we might call the generalizability of those attacked: can they be seen as representative of the nation or our way of life, with all of the connotations of racial, class, and religious hierarchy and inequality that this entails?[14] The less this is seen to be the case, the less likely an incident is to be treated as terrorism. This also explains why terrorism is commonly described by politicians as "attacks on our way of life"—because this is a conclusion derived from those sorts of incidents to which the label is most likely to be applied, namely, those that target sites or groups most likely to be seen as representative of "us" (America or "the West"), usually committed by outsiders or those perceived as "out of place." And furthermore, I suggest that this is what leads to the definition of such violence as "illegitimate": it is not simply that "illegitimate" violence itself is considered terrorism, but rather, the reverse, that those acts labeled terrorism are illegitimate because they are "out of place," not because of anything inherent in the acts.

Second, the "application of terrorism" can be seen to define *the enemy*. What does this mean? As many critics have noted, the definition of acts as terrorism tends to depend upon the identity of the perpetrator, with, at the current moment, those perceived to be Arab or Muslim, or both, most likely to attract the label, while similar acts, when committed by those of differing backgrounds, are most likely to be categorized differently. An illustrative case here is the varying practical and discursive interpretation of the threat posed by (white, Christian, American) right-wing extremists. Despite a spreading consensus among both experts and police that this group represents the greatest potential threat of domestic mass violence in the United States,[15] this realization has not been translated into policy, and the labeling of right-wing violence as terrorism is still fairly contested by both politicians and the media. Following the release of a 2013 report from the Department of Homeland Security that highlighted the increasing danger from right-wing extremists, multiple politicians and commentators lashed out: "House Republican Leader, John Boehner, dismissed the report as 'offensive and unacceptable.' Republican Rep. Gus Bilirakis called it 'political and ideological profiling.' Conservative commentator Michelle Malkin wrote that it 'was one of the most embarrassingly shoddy pieces of propaganda I'd ever read.'"[16]

Third, designating an "act of violence" as *terrorism* defines that act as within the scope of the political, rather than the private, the personal, or the peculiar. For example, following the killing of nine black churchgoers in 2015, the director of the FBI initially discounted labeling this act as terrorism. "Terrorism," he said, "is [an] act of violence done or threatens to in order to try to influence a public body or citizenry so it's more of a political act and again based on what I know so more I don't see it as a political act."[17] The public debate following the mass shooting of patrons of the Pulse gay nightclub in Orlando, Florida, in June 2016 illustrates how conceptualizations of terrorism define what is political. Like other mass shootings in recent American history, debate following the event centered on the question of whether this was terrorism. Initial reports that the shooter, Omar Mateen, was a Muslim of Afghan heritage and had "pledged allegiance" to ISIS in a 911 call made from the scene of the attack convinced most observers that this was a straightforward case. And yet, after reports that Mateen had visited the club previously and may have harbored same-sex desires, experts and the media began to seem much less certain about the designation of the massacre as terrorism. I would suggest here that this shift tells us something about what sorts of violence count as political in the contemporary United States. If Mateen's motives were linked to his sexuality, the thinking goes, the shooting was best understood as nonpolitical.[18] This interpretation was contested by others, however, who pointed out that LGBTQ individuals and spaces have long been targets of violence stoked by homophobic currents in the dominant culture.[19] In other words, what is at stake here in the application of the label *terrorism* is whether violence against LGBTQ communities and individuals is understood as a *political* problem or as a more private form of violence, to be understood by reference to an individual's psychology, rather than broader political or cultural forces. The struggle over whether the Pulse massacre constitutes terrorism is not unique: we can see similar struggles at play in the attempts of some feminists to reinterpret domestic violence as a form of terrorism,[20] or the Black Lives Matter movement to reinterpret police killings of African Americans as a form of state terror. What all of these cases share is a struggle over whether categories of violence should be understood as primarily private or primarily public and political. And because terrorism has come to be seen as perhaps the ultimate form of political violence in contemporary American society, these struggles often take the form of attempts to reclaim that label.

Commentary from both academic and journalistic advocates of "fixing" the definition tend to suggest that a proper definition of terrorism would be neutral, both positionally (i.e., it would apply equally to those we consider enemies and those we view as friends) and morally (i.e., it would not take into account the question of whether we approve of the acts of violence in question). As to the question of the "political," the stabilizers tend to presume that the question of what is or is not political either is self-evident or, at the very least, can be held steady. While I have previously pointed to the weakly institutionalized character of the field of terrorism expertise,[21] I now return to my assertion that the problem of defining terrorism is a struggle over defining the enemy, the boundaries of legitimate violence, and the boundary of the political and the nonpolitical. In other words, advocates of the stabilizing impulse, both in academic and journalistic debates, tend to presume that these three concerns can be purged from the debate. Yet it may be that none of these assumptions are correct.

The difficulty with this project of "fixing" the concept—and perhaps one reason why it has yet to succeed—is that the "politicization" of (the concept of) terrorism is not primarily a corruption of an otherwise neutral term—in which case the solution would simply be the purification of the concept—the separation of the "core" essential bits from the extraneous, pasted-on, "politicized" pieces that bias it in one direction or another. Instead, "the political" is central to the concept from the start, and the question of what constitutes a "political" problem or motivation is itself contested. As I have suggested, the definition of terrorism may identify what is political, rather than the other way round. Similarly, the questions of who is "the enemy" and when violence is legitimate or illegitimate are both central to conceptualizing terrorism, and are themselves highly contested. Rather than trying to define terrorism, therefore, this chapter has suggested that we analyze the ways in which (struggles over) the definition(s) of terrorism act as conduits for struggles over three questions central to contemporary social and political life: Who is the enemy? When is violence (il)legitimate? And what is (and is not) political?

NOTES

1. Lisa Stampnitzky, *Disciplining terror: How experts invented terrorism* (Cambridge: Cambridge University Press, 2013).

2. Ibid.

3. Interview with Brian Jenkins, as quoted in ibid.

4. Alex P. Schmid and Albert J. Jongman, *Political terrorism: A new guide to actors, authors, concepts, data bases, theories, and literature* (New Brunswick, NJ: Transaction Books, 1988); Robert O. Slater, Michael Stohl, and Defense Academic Research Support Program, *Current perspectives on international terrorism* (New York: St. Martin's Press, 1988), 3; David Brannan, Phillip F. Esler, and N.T. Anders Strindberg, "Talking to 'terrorists': Towards an independent analytical framework for the study of violent substate activism," *Studies in Conflict and Terrorism* 24 (2001): 11.

5. This section draws on my book *Disciplining terror: How experts invented terrorism* (Cambridge: Cambridge University Press, 2013) and Lisa Stampnitzky, "Disciplining an unruly field: Terrorism studies and theories of scientific/intellectual production," *Qualitative Sociology* 34, no. 1 (2011).

6. Stampnitzky, "Disciplining an unruly field."

7. Martha Crenshaw, *Terrorism in context* (University Park: Pennsylvania State University Press, 1995).

8. Schmid and Jongman, *Political terrorism*, xxi, 3.

9. Glenn Greenwald, "Refusal to call Charleston shootings "terrorism" again shows it's a meaningless propaganda term," *The Intercept*, June 19, 2015, https://theintercept.com/2015/06/19/refusal-call-charleston-shootings-terrorism-shows-meaningless-propaganda-term/.

10. Sean Illing, "We must call him a terrorist: Dylann Roof, Fox News, and the truth about why language matters," *Salon*, June 21, 2015, http://www.salon.com/2015/06/21/we_must_call_him_a_terrorist_dylann_roof_fox_news_and_the_truth_about_why_language_matters/.

11. Anthea Butler, "Shooters of color are called 'terrorists' and 'thugs': Why are white shooters called 'mentally ill'?" *Washington Post*, June 18, 2015, http://www.washingtonpost.com/posteverything/wp/2015/06/18/call-the-charleston-church-shooting-what-it-is-terrorism/.

12. Richard Jackson, "The ghosts of state terror: Knowledge, politics, and terrorism studies," *Critical Studies on Terrorism* 1, no. 3 (2008); Jackson, "Unknown knowns: The subjugated knowledge of terrorism studies," *Critical Studies on Terrorism* 5, no. 1 (2012); Richard Jackson, Marie Smyth, and Jeroen Gunning, eds., *Critical terrorism studies: A new research agenda* (Abingdon, UK: Routledge, 2009); Joseba Zulaika, *Terrorism: The self-fulfilling prophesy* (Chicago: University of Chicago Press, 2009); Edward Said, "The essential terrorist," in Edward Said and Christopher Hitchens, eds., *Blaming the victims: Spurious scholarship and the Palestinian question* (1988; reprinted, New York: Verso, 2001).

13. Arun Kundnani, "Violence comes home: An interview with Arun Kundnani," *OpenDemocracy.com* (2015), https://www.opendemocracy.net/arun-kundnani-opendemocracy/violence-comes-home-interview-with-arun-kundnani.

14. And thus attacks on the state or on soldiers can also be included as terrorist attacks, in practice, as long as they fit this general schema.

15. "This month, the headlines were about a Muslim man in Boston who was accused of threatening police officers with a knife. Last month, two Muslims attacked an anti-Islamic conference in Garland, Tex. The month before, a Muslim man was charged with plotting to drive a truck bomb onto a military installation in

Kansas. If you keep up with the news, you know that a small but steady stream of American Muslims, radicalized by overseas extremists, are engaging in violence here in the United States. But headlines can mislead. The main terrorist threat in the United States is not from violent Muslim extremists, but from right-wing extremists. Just ask the police. In a survey we conducted with the Police Executive Research Forum last year of 382 law enforcement agencies, 74 percent reported anti-government extremism as one of the top three terrorist threats in their jurisdiction; 39 percent listed extremism connected with Al Qaeda or like-minded terrorist organizations. And only 3 percent identified the threat from Muslim extremists as severe, compared with 7 percent for anti-government and other forms of extremism." Charles Kurzman and David Schanzer, "The growing right-wing terror threat," *New York Times*, June 16, 2015, http://www.nytimes.com/2015/06/16/opinion/the-other-terror-threat.html?nytmobile=0&_r=0. See also Scott Shane, "Homegrown extremists tied to deadlier toll than jihadists in U.S. since 9/11," *New York Times*, June 25, 2015, http://www.nytimes.com/2015/06/25/us/tally-of-attacks-in-us-challenges-perceptions-of-top-terror-threat.html; and Maggie Ybarra, "Majority of fatal attacks on U.S. soil carried out by white supremacists, not terrorists," *Washington Times*, June 24, 2015, http://www.washingtontimes.com/news/2015/jun/24/majority-of-fatal-attacks-on-us-soil-carried-out-b/.

16. Illing, "We must call him a terrorist."

17. Andrew Husband, "FBI director says Charleston shooting not terrorism," *Mediaite*, June 20, 2015, http://www.mediaite.com/tv/fbi-director-says-charleston-shooting-not-terrorism/.

18. See, for example, Jay Weaver and David Ovalle, "What motivated Orlando killer? It was more than terrorism, experts say," *Miami Herald*, June 17, 2016, http://www.miamiherald.com/news/state/florida/article84511132.html.

19. See, for example, Greggor Mattson, "Post-Orlando truth for you: Gay bars aren't 'safe spaces,'" *Daily Beast*, June 18, 2016, http://www.thedailybeast.com/articles/2016/06/18/post-orlando-truth-for-you-gay-bars-aren-t-safe-spaces.html; and Mattson, "Interview: If Orlando wasn't terorrism, why do gays feel terrorized?" (2016), https://greggormattson.com/2016/06/16/interview-if-orlando-wasnt-terrorism-why-do-gays-feel-terrorized/.

20. Robin Morgan, *The demon lover: On the sexuality of terrorism* (New York: W.W. Norton, 1989).

21. Stampnitzky, "Disciplining an unruly field."

# 2. Misoverestimating Terrorism

John Mueller and Mark G. Stewart

While it is not true that 9/11 "changed everything," the tragedy did have a powerful impact in some areas. Terrorism's apparent incidence and intensity, and therefore its seeming importance, has been multiplied by effectively conflating it with insurgency. Accordingly, the category *civil war* may be going out of existence—and the same could even happen for much international war. In addition, extrapolating wildly from the apparent capacities of the 9/11 hijackers, some have greatly exaggerated the threat presented internationally by small bands of terrorists, sometimes even to the point of deeming it to be existential—a process that may be repeating itself with the vicious group called ISIS or the Islamic State. This chapter examines what might be called the misoverestimation of terrorism—playing on a verbal invention of George W. Bush. It also assesses the limited importance of the terrorism phenomenon more generally.

## EXAGGERATING TERRORISM'S INCIDENCE: CONFLATING TERRORISM AND WAR

The impact of 9/11 on language, on how terrorism has come to be understood and explained, has been substantial, in part because the pejorative use of the term *terrorism* increased so markedly with that dramatic event.

### The Distribution of Terrorism

Outside war zones, the number of fatalities caused by terrorists of all stripes has been, with very few exceptions (such as 9/11 of course), remarkably low. There were 3,372 fatalities from terrorist incidents within the United States during the forty-four-year period from 1970 to 2013. The attacks in 2001 represented almost all of these and most of the rest come from the attack by a domestic (non-Islamist) terrorist on the Murrah Federal Building in Oklahoma City in 1995. Even with 9/11 included in the count, this total equates to an annual fatality risk for the period of 1 in 4 million for the United States. The yearly rates for the period in other developed countries are also low: 1 in 1.2 million for the United Kingdom (including Northern Ireland), 1 in 4.3 million for Canada, and 1 in 8 million for Australia (including the Bali attack of 2002). By contrast, the yearly chance of dying in an automobile accident in the United States was 1 in 8,200 during the same period.[1]

One may also focus on the kind of terrorism that really concerns people in the developed world by restricting the consideration to violence committed by Muslim extremists anywhere in the world outside war zones, whether that violence is perpetrated by domestic Islamist terrorists or by those with international connections. Although these tallies make for grim reading, for most of the period since 9/11 the total number of people killed by Muslim extremists outside war zones comes to some 200 to 400 per year.[2] That, of course, is 200 to 400 too many, but it hardly suggests that the terrorists' destructive capacities are monumental. For comparison, during the same period more people—320 per year—drowned in bathtubs in the United States alone. Or there is another, rather unpleasant comparison: increased delays and added costs at US airports due to new security procedures provide an incentive for many short-haul passengers to drive to their destination rather than flying, and, since driving is far riskier than air travel, the resulting increase in automobile traffic has been estimated to result in 500 or more additional road fatalities per year.[3]

The vast majority, then, of what is now commonly being tallied as terrorism has occurred in war zones. This is especially true for fatalities. In 2014, 78 percent of all deaths from terrorism occurred in only five war zones: those in Iraq, Nigeria, Afghanistan, Pakistan, and Syria.[4] By comparison, the number of people killed by Islamist terrorists in the United States since 9/11 has averaged about six per year—a number so low that it might be wondered whether terrorism should be considered to constitute a "threat" to the country at all.

## Definitions of Terrorism

There are scores of definitions of terrorism, but the following seem to capture much of the variety.

1. LaFree et al. In a recent book discussing the Global Terrorism Database, which they have developed at the University of Maryland, Gary LaFree, Laura Dugan, and Erin Miller note that, although there are a great many definitions of terrorism, "most commentators and experts agree on several

key elements, captured in the definition we use here: 'the threatened or actual use of illegal force and violence by non-state actors to attain a political, economic, religious, or social goal through fear, coercion, or intimidation.'"[5]

2. Stohl. Michael Stohl, after extended consideration, defines terrorism as "the purposeful act or the threat of the act of violence to create fear and/or compliant behavior in a victim and/or the audience of the act or threat."[6]

3. Laqueur. Walter Laqueur, who has been studying terrorism for decades, has settled on defining terrorism as "the systematic use of murder, injury, and destruction, or the threat of such acts, aimed at achieving political ends."[7]

4. Hoffman. After several pages of assessment, Bruce Hoffman, in his well-known study *Inside Terrorism*, concludes that terrorism (1) is political in aims and motives; (2) is violent or threatens violence; (3) is designed to have far-reaching psychological repercussions beyond the immediate victim or target; (4) is conducted either by an organization or by individuals directly influenced, motivated, or inspired by ideological aims or example; and (5) is perpetrated by a subnational or nonstate entity. He then derives a definition of terrorism as "the deliberate creation of exploitation of fear through violence or the threat of violence in the pursuit of political change."[8]

5. Byman. Daniel Byman, another veteran terrorism scholar, defines terrorism as "political violence carried out by a nonstate group to achieve a psychological effect such as frightening or intimidating a government or a population."[9]

6. Burke. After acknowledging that there have been scores of definitions, journalist Jason Burke, who has reported on terrorism for decades, argues that the word "can be defined relatively easily" and that, "in its broadest sense, terrorism is a tactic which involves the use of violence against civilian targets to achieve political, social or religiously conceived aims through the provocation of fear."[10]

## Comparisons with War

There is some disagreement among these definitions, and that will be examined later. However, they generally agree on three components. They suggest that terrorism involves (1) the pursuit of a policy goal (2) by applying violence (3) in order to create fear and to create compliant behavior on the part of the enemy.

The problem is that these three elements do not differentiate terrorism from war. As Carl von Clausewitz stressed, the whole effort in war—at least in noncriminal ones—is to achieve political goals. According to his most famous formulation, "war is merely the continuation of policy with other means"—that is, war "is a true political instrument." Or, in the words of Mao Zedong, "politics is war without bloodshed; war is politics with bloodshed." And the means to attaining the goal, stresses Clausewitz, involve using violence to coerce and to inflict fear and intimidation in order to break the enemy's will. In battle, says Clausewitz, "the loss of morale" is the "major decisive factor."[11] Wars, then, do not involve the annihilation of the enemy, but the breaking of the enemy's will in order to generate surrender or policy change, something that may come quite quickly, as with the German invasion of France in 1940, or, as happened to the United States in Vietnam, may occur only after a long episode of attrition.[12]

Terrorism, then, differs from war not in its essential method or goal, not in its efforts to intimidate and create fear, and certainly not in the fact that it applies violence. Rather, terrorism differs from war in the frequency and probably the intensity with which violence is inflicted.

When violence is sporadic, it is called *terrorism* if the perpetrators are disciplined and have an ideological or policy goal. It is called *crime* when the perpetrators' goal is financial enrichment. If their violence becomes frequent and continuous, it is called *war*. If the perpetrators are disciplined and if they have a policy or ideological goal, the activity may then be called *disciplined war*: it can be either conventional or unconventional, depending on whether combat is characterized by tactics that might be called Clausewitzian or regimental, or is characterized by hit-and-run guerrilla (or primitive) tactics. If the perpetrators are primarily devoted to financial enrichment, the activity is called *criminal war*, and it is characterized by brigand or warlord bands, or by freebooting or mercenary behavior.[13] Thus, when either form of violence—disciplined or criminal—becomes frequent or sustained enough, it will look like, and traditionally has been called, *war*.

The goal for those engaged in countering such warfare is to reverse the process. Those countering disciplined warfare seek to reduce insurgent activities to more bearable terrorist levels and then to end it entirely if possible. Those combating criminal warfare seek to reduce the frequency of the violence that criminal bands commit, to the point that "war" ceases to exist and any remaining violence and predation are indistinguishable from ordinary crime.

Analyst John Horgan is certainly correct to suggest that "terrorism is fundamentally a form of psychological warfare."[14] But so is war.

## 9/11 as a Potential Game Changer

Before 9/11, terrorism was generally seen to be a limited phenomenon, and terrorism was often called the weapon of the weak. If terrorists began to engage in disciplined violence that was neither fitful nor sporadic, the enterprise was relabeled war or insurgency.

That definitional condition could change if terrorists became capable of visiting substantial destruction with episodic attacks. Under our approach, the activity would still be considered terrorism because it would remain sporadic, but the damage inflicted could hardly be deemed limited.

That is, if 9/11 had become typical—had that tragedy proved a harbinger—it would be reasonable to conclude, as was commonly held in the aftermath of that terrible day, that "everything has changed." In the early months and years after 9/11, many feared that was going to come about.[15] But it didn't, and the tragic event seems increasingly to stand out as an aberration, not as a harbinger.[16] A decade and a half after the event, 9/11 remains an extreme outlier—scarcely any terrorist act before or since, even those so designated that take place in war zones, has inflicted even one-tenth as much total damage.

## Civil War and Insurgency

Since 9/11, there has been a marked exaggeration in the perceived frequency and importance of terrorism. To a considerable degree, this has been the result of a more expansive application of standard definitions of terrorism to the point that virtually any violence perpetrated by rebels in civil wars is now being called terrorism.

In the past, when terroristic violence by substate actors (or elements) became extensive within a country, the activity was no longer called terrorism but rather civil war or insurgency. The Irish Republican Army, for example, was generally taken to be a terrorist enterprise, while fighters in Sri Lanka in the 1990s were considered combatants or insurgents in a civil war. And the violence that Vietnamese Communists were inflicting on the civilian population in the early to mid-1960s—assassination, ambush, harassment, sabotage, assault—was generally considered part of an insurgent or guerrilla war, not terrorism, because the violence was so sustained.[17]

Even after 9/11, the US military applied the distinction to the war in Iraq. In the early days of the war when violence was sporadic, those opposing the American presence were called "terrorists." When the violence became more continuous, they became "insurgents." Byman describes the process in his discussion of the rise and fall of the Zarqawi organization in Iraq: it "began as a small terrorist group" using "high-profile attacks" to "undermine the Iraqi government and make a name for itself." Then, "it came to embrace insurgency, destabilizing and eventually replacing local governments." But when its efforts to rule in Iraq failed, "it returned to insurgency and then survived using terrorism."[18]

In the wake of 9/11, *terrorism,* already a pejorative word, became far more so. The result was that the word has increasingly been slung around in an effort to discredit enemies.

The rather confusing process could be seen in 2016 when ISIS was commonly labeled a band of terrorists, even though it occupied territory, ran social services, and regularly confronted armed soldiers in direct combat. In any armed conflict before the current century, that would have been called an insurgency.[19] In the civil war in Syria, the United States has branded those fighting the government of Bashar al-Assad to its own convenience. ISIS fighters are "terrorists," while those approved by the United States are labeled the "moderate opposition." Assad himself has been more consistent, if equally self-serving: any violent opposition to a sitting government, he says, is "terrorism."[20]

Assad's perspective, one that has become increasingly popular since 9/11, would allow us to retire the concept of civil war just about entirely. That is, if one wishes to embrace the broader definition of terrorism that substantially took hold after 9/11, a huge number of violent endeavors that had previously been called civil wars would have to be recategorized, and the amount of terrorism in the world in years past would accordingly mushroom.

After LaFree and his colleagues took into account various problems with the data set, including those concerning what they call "data collection artifacts," they found a rough trend pattern for terrorism worldwide: a persistent rise from the 1970s to the early 1990s, a somewhat abrupt decline thereafter (which they say has yet to be "adequately explained"), and then a rise again a few years into the new century.[21] But that pattern rather closely mirrors trends for the amount of civil warfare going on in the world.[22] Even at that, the Global Terrorism Database in its present form seems to severely undercount the number of "terrorist" deaths during civil wars in Algeria, Liberia, and Bosnia in the 1990s. And it finds that there were no terrorist deaths at all in Vietnam during the tumultuous war years of 1970–75.

## Interstate War

This can be taken a step further. Stohl's definition is, in his words, "actor-neutral," and he points out that terrorism, as he sees it, is very frequently committed by states, as well as by "non-state actors."[23] In this spirit, much of the bombing by the United States in World War II, including that of Hiroshima, would be designated as state terrorism. Burke's definition, too, does not require that terrorism must be carried out by substate actors, and he points out that "lots of different actors" apply terrorism, "state and substate, local and international."[24]

If that element of the definition is adjusted, the entire category of "war," including those of the international variety, could substantially vanish. Almost all violence, at whatever level, that has a policy or ideological goal would become "terrorism."

## Targeting: Civilian versus Military

Burke's definition, unlike the others, makes a distinction about targets. By his definition, only violence against civilians counts as terrorism.

This is a distinction that has some substantive weight in evaluating the success of terrorists and insurgents in accomplishing their policy goals. A considerable body of research suggests that it is important to distinguish violence directed at military targets from that directed at civilians when attempting to assess the effectiveness of terrorism and insurgency.

Thus, in her analysis of civil wars, Virginia Page Fortna pointedly notes that many definitions of terrorism "are so broad as arguably to encompass all rebel groups in all civil wars." Indeed, she continues, "much of the terrorism literature could substitute *rebellion* or *insurgency* for *terrorism*." In civil wars, "civilian targeting is ubiquitous; almost all rebel groups (and almost all governments involved in civil wars) target individuals as a form of 'control' to force cooperation and deter civilians from providing aid to the opponent." For her approach she contrasts insurgencies that use terrorism as a tactic—which she differentiates as the employment of "a systematic campaign of indiscriminate violence against public civilian targets to influence a wider audience"—from those that do not.[25] She finds that insurgents who use terrorism as she defines it pretty much *never* win. Similarly, Max Abrahms finds that terrorists, including those operating outside a war situation, who target civilians tend to fail in their policy goal: the targeting of civilians by terrorists is "highly correlated with political failure."[26]

However, if, following Burke, murderous activities are considered terrorism only if they are visited upon civilians, this scarcely differentiates terrorism from war. Like Fortna, military historian Matthew Waxman points out that, in war, "punishment of civilians is a commonly used strategy of coercion."[27]

## The Results of the Definitional Inflation

The definitional issue developed here can be seen in operation in the interpretation of the ISIS-related terrorist attacks that killed 130 in Paris on the night of November 13, 2015. French president François Hollande immediately labeled this an "act of war" that was "committed by a terrorist army" against "France, our values, who we are."[28] He is on the same page as an ISIS sympathizer quoted in the *Washington Post* about how to label the attacks—although the two disagree on the essential motive for them: "The brothers launched the attack in Paris to prove that we are a strong state and we can fight our enemies anywhere. . . . Since they are fighting us in our land, we are going to fight them in their lands."[29] However, a "strong state" or a "terrorist army" would have engaged France with direct warfare. ISIS instead used sporadic attacks in Europe—terrorism, the weapon of the weak.[30]

Whatever the definition, the post-9/11 conflation of insurgency (or even of all warfare) with terrorism makes it seem that the world is awash in terrorism, something that stokes unjustified alarm outside war zones where, as discussed earlier, terrorism remains a quite limited hazard.

For example, applying data from the Global Terrorism Database, it is possible to argue that there has been a "staggering" increase in terrorism deaths during the twenty-first century.[31] However, as suggested earlier, that is the result of designating much of the violence from what would previously have been considered civil wars—as in Iraq, Afghanistan, Syria, and Nigeria—as terrorism while failing to apply a similar approach to such wars in earlier decades.[32]

It is certainly true that there are several terrible civil wars going on. But in decades past, civil war was often much more frequent. As noted earlier, civil wars reached a peak in the late 1980s and early 1990s. By this century, the number declined to a half dozen or so in most years. Insurgents in those previous wars, like those today, often used massacre, random violence, dismemberment, assassination, propaganda barrages, sabotage, ambush, torture, rape, ethnic cleansing, summary execution, and even genocide. They just weren't commonly called terrorists.

The post-9/11 terrorism obsession has had many consequences, some quite bizarre. Early in the Syrian civil war, for example, President Bashar al-Assad released jihadists from his jails so that they could join the insurgency against him in order to "convince the world that we are facing Islamic terrorism."[33] This rather resembles the Cold War phenomenon in which Third World potentates found it greatly to their advantage to portray local insurgents as communists. There is also the pattern in which lone-wolf attackers, many of them clearly mentally disturbed or at least severely disconnected from reality, become "terrorists" (and generate massive additional publicity) if they manage to mutter or tweet something about al-Qaeda or ISIS when carrying out their deed. And perhaps the ultimate expansion of the term has been to rebrand the Holocaust or domestic violence as terrorism.

## EXAGGERATING TERRORIST CAPACITIES

The reaction to 9/11 led not only to definitional mischief but also to the exaggeration of terrorist capacities. In 2009, for example, the US Department of Homeland Security (DHS) issued a lengthy report on protecting the United States. Key to achieving such an objective, it would seem, should be a careful assessment of the character, capacities, and desires of potential terrorists targeting that homeland. The report does contain a section dealing with what its authors call "the nature of the terrorist adversary." However, it devotes only two paragraphs to this important concern, and both are decidedly one-dimensional and fully preoccupied with the dire end of the spectrum of the terrorist threat. Within that section, it devotes but two sentences to an assessment of the actual nature of the "adversary" it is so concerned about: "The number and high profile of international and domestic terrorist attacks and disrupted plots during the last two decades underscore the determination and persistence of terrorist organizations. Terrorists have proven to be relentless, patient, opportunistic, and flexible, learning from experience and modifying tactics and targets to exploit perceived vulnerabilities and avoid observed strengths."[34]

In stark contrast, when seeking to describe their subjects, the authors of a set of case studies of terrorists who have focused on the United States since 9/11 chiefly apply different descriptors: incompetent, ineffective, unintelligent, idiotic, ignorant, inadequate, unorganized, misguided, muddled, amateurish, dopey, unrealistic, moronic, irrational, foolish, and gullible.[35] Brian Jenkins's assessment of domestic terrorists is apt: "Their numbers remain small, their determination limp, and their competence poor."[36] And Michael Kenney finds that would-be terrorists in Europe and other Western locations, like their counterparts in the United States, tend to be operationally unsophisticated, short on know-how, prone to make mistakes, poor at planning, and limited in their capacity to learn.[37]

There have been widespread worries that, because the 9/11 terrorists were successful with box cutters, they might soon be able to turn out and detonate nuclear weapons. For example, in 2004, Graham Allison found a large receptive audience when he alarmingly relayed his "considered judgment" that "on the current path, a nuclear terrorist attack on America in the decade ahead is more likely than not."[38] Not only has such an attack not happened, but it seems clear, in the words of William Langewiesche, who has assessed the process in detail, that no terrorist group "has gotten any-where near this."[39]

Since 2001, in fact, al-Qaeda Central's record of accomplishment has been rather meager even taking into consideration that it has been isolated and under siege. Bin Laden's tiny group of perhaps one hundred or so operatives does appear to have served as something of an inspiration to some Muslim extremists, may have done some training, may have contributed a bit to the Taliban's far larger insurgency in Afghanistan, may have participated in a few terrorist acts in Pakistan, and has delivered a considerable number of empty, deluded, self-infatuated threats.[40] Only two of the major terrorist plots against the West since 9/11 could be said to be under its "command and control," and both of these, as it happens, failed miserably.[41] And, although *billions* of for-eigners have been admitted legally into the United States since 2001, not one of these, it appears, has been an agent smuggled in by al-Qaeda.[42]

It is possible to argue, of course, that the damage committed by jihadists in the United States since 9/11 is so low because "American defensive measures are working," as Peter Bergen puts it.[43] Although these measures should be given some credit, however, it is not at all clear that they have made a great deal of difference.

To begin with, one may look at the dozens of plots by Islamist extrem-ists, many of them inspired by al-Qaeda, seeking to commit terrorism in the United States. A few of these have been carried out, but most have been rolled up by authorities. In general, as noted earlier, the capacities of the people involved are singularly unimpressive. Indeed, most of these plots were at best embryonic or facilitated by infiltrating FBI operatives. Left on their own, it is certainly possible that a few of the plotters would have gotten their acts together and actually done something, but it seems unlikely that the total damage would have increased by much.[44]

In addition to those prosecuted on terrorism charges, authorities have encountered a considerable number of loud-mouthed aspirational terrorists within the United States, and, lacking enough evidence to convict them on terrorism charges, the authorities have levied lesser ones in order to jail or deport them. For the most part, these plots or aspirations were even less likely to lead to notable violence than the ones that have led to terrorism tri-als. Further, the bulk of people who have been jailed on terrorism-associated prosecutions have served short terms and, accordingly, have soon been set free to commit terrorism if they so choose. Yet none have attempted to do so.

Nor is it likely that security measures have deterred much terrorism. Extensive and costly security measures may have taken some targets—

commercial airliners and military bases, for example—off the list for just about all terrorists. However, no dedicated would-be terrorist should have much difficulty finding other potential targets if the goal is to kill people or destroy property to make a statement—the country is filled with these.

There has been a tendency to exaggerate not only the terrorists' skills but also the importance and potential destructiveness of their plots. Thus, although the efforts of the Times Square bomber of 2010 are sometimes held to have "almost succeeded," the bomb was reported from the start to be "really amateurish" with a hopeless array of design flaws.[45]

There has also been a concerted effort to identify evil "masterminds" dominating the show. Chief among these is the "mastermind" of 9/11, Khalid Shaikh Mohammed, who has since declared himself to be the power behind dozens of other schemes as well.[46] What is impressive is that just about *all* these other schemes either failed or did not even begin to approach fruition.[47] Overall, he has a fertile mind but a feeble record of accomplishment, one characterized by fanciful scheming and stunted execution. In this context, 9/11 clearly stands out as an aberration.

The exaggeration of capacities can also be seen in the reaction to the rise of ISIS. According to one poll, by 2016, 77 percent of Americans had come to see the group as a threat to their country's existence and survival.[48] The Islamic State burst into official and public attention with some military victories in Iraq and Syria in 2014—in particular, taking over Iraq's second largest city, Mosul. In fact, the conquest of Mosul was essentially a fluke. The plan was to hold part of the city for a while in an effort, it seems, to free some prisoners. The defending Iraqi army, "trained" by the American military at enormous cost to US taxpayers, simply fell apart in confusion and disarray, abandoning weaponry, and the city, to the tiny group of seeming invaders.[49]

In contrast to the popular view, Middle East specialist Ramzy Mardini argued in 2014 that "the Islamic State's fundamentals are weak"; that "it does not have a sustainable endgame"; that its "extreme ideology, spirit of subjugation, and acts of barbarism prevent it from becoming a political venue for the masses"; that its foolhardy efforts to instill fear in everyone limits "its opportunities for alliances" and makes it "vulnerable to popular backlash"; that "its potential support across the region ranges from limited to nonexistent"; and that the group "is completely isolated, encircled by enemies."[50] Mardini's observations proved prescient: ISIS soon went into considerable decline, both in the Middle East and in its appeal to would-be jihadists around the world.[51]

## CONCLUSION

Even knuckleheads can occasionally do damage. But there is something quite spooky about expanding the definition of terrorism so that it threatens to embrace all violent behavior directed at an ideological or policy goal, about imagining terrorists to be everywhere, about extrapolating wildly from 9/11 to conclude that many are omnicompetent masterminds, and about acting like their press agent by flaunting and exaggerating their often pathetic schemes to do damage. The result has been an exaggeration of terrorism's importance and impact.

When properly differentiated from insurgency, terrorism has had a quite limited effect on human affairs—indeed, any significant historical impact seems to have derived much more from the reaction or overreaction it inspired or facilitated than from anything the terrorists accomplished on their own.[52] Moreover, the persistent exaggeration of the capacities of terrorists has the perverse effect of glorifying the terrorist enterprise in the minds of many of its practitioners.[53]

Nonetheless the process will likely continue to flourish. The incentives are to play to the galleries and to inflate the threat: if 77 percent of the American people appear to be convinced that ISIS presents "a serious threat to the existence or survival of the US," there is likely to be considerably more purchase in servicing the notion than in seeking to counter it. Officials seem incapable of pointing out that an American's chance of being killed by a terrorist is one in 4 million per year, and to suggest that terrorism might pose an acceptable risk (or even to discuss the issue) appears utterly impossible. Accordingly, the misoverestimation of terrorism will likely long be with us.

## NOTES

1. For additional data on annual fatality risks, see Mueller and Stewart 2016a, 138.

2. For the derivation of this number, see Mueller and Stewart 2016a, 306n4. The rise of ISIS and of ISIS affiliates and sycophants has raised this number in the last few years, a phenomenon discussed below.

3. Mueller and Stewart 2016a, 161.

4. Institute for Economics and Peace 2015, 4. See also LaFree, Dugan, and Miller 2015, 54 and, more generally, chs. 3 and 4.

5. LaFree, Dugan, and Miller 2015, 13; but compare 22–23. See also Stohl 1988, 14–15.

6. Stohl 1988, 3. See also Stohl 2012, 46; Grabosky and Stohl 2010, 5.

7. Laqueur 2003, 238.

8. Hoffman 2006, 40. See the original text for the full wording of the five points.

9. Byman 2016, 129n6.

10. Burke 2015, 216.

11. Clausewitz 1976, 87, 231. Mao quoted in Griffith 1978, 26. On the importance of a key preposition in the Clausewitz formulation, see Holmes 2014.

12. On the search for a Clausewitzian "breaking point" in Vietnam, see Mueller 1980.

13. On these distinctions, see also Mueller 2004, 18–20.

14. Pérez-Peña, Healy, and Medina 2016.

15. Mayer 2008, 3; Mueller and Stewart 2016a, 13–17.

16. As Russell Seitz put it in 2004, "9/11 could join the Trojan Horse and Pearl Harbor among stratagems so uniquely surprising that their very success precludes their repetition," and accordingly, "al-Qaeda's best shot may have been exactly that." See also Diab 2015; Mueller 2002, 2003.

17. Pike 1966, ch. 8; Karnow 1991, 254–55.

18. Byman 2016, 146. The shifting definitional process is discussed in detail in Warrick 2015, 115–22.

19. On this issue, see also Cronin 2015; and Byman 2016, 144.

20. "An hour with Syrian President Bashar Al-Assad," charlierose.com, March 31, 2015.

21. LaFree, Dugan, and Miller 2015, 28–34.

22. Mueller 2004, 87. Pinker 2011, 303.

23. Stohl 2012.

24. Burke 2015, 216. The same seems to hold for Laqueur's definition.

25. Fortna 2015, 522. One study seeks to differentiate "battle deaths" from deaths from terrorism, though it is not clear what mechanism is being used, and the distinction is not included in its definitions discussion. Institute for Economics and Peace 2015, 6–7, 20, 24.

26. Abrahms 2006, 2012, 2016. Abrahms and Potter 2015.

27. Waxman quoted in Watts 2015, 157.

28. Vinocur 2015.

29. Morris 2015. However, the *Post* suggested, ISIS had been in decline in its core area, and may have been motivated to lash out abroad in order "to divert attention from its territorial losses." See also Mueller and Stewart 2016b.

30. See also Byman 2016, 145.

31. For example, Dixon and Sahi 2016; Alcantara 2016.

32. Similarly, before 2003, the US State Department's count of terrorist events included only international ones (i.e., events in which terrorists attack somebody from or in another country). After that year, however, the definition was changed so that much domestic terrorism—including much of what was happening in the war in Iraq—was included in the terrorism count. Later numbers, therefore, are not comparable to earlier ones. See National Counterterrorism Center 2006, ii–iii.

33. Byman 2016, 134.

34. Department of Homeland Security 2009, 11.

35. Mueller 2017.

36. Jenkins 2011, 1. See also Mueller and Stewart 2016a, ch. 3; Jenkins 2010; Schneier 2007; Brooks 2011; Friedman, Harper, and Preble 2010; LaFree, Dugan, and Miller 2015, 99, 173.

37. Kenney 2010. See also Sageman 2008, 141.

38. Allison 2004, 15. On alarmism about atomic terrorism, see Mueller 2006, 45–46; Mueller 2010, 181–83; and Diab 2015.

39. "Browsing the 'Atomic Bazaar,'" *Morning Edition*, National Public Radio, May 15, 2007, http://www.npr.org/templates/story/story.php?storyId=10175622.

For an extended discussion of the difficulties facing the would-be atomic terrorist, see Mueller 2010, chs. 12–15; Jenkins 2008; and Diab 2015.

40. See Sageman 2008. On threats, see Mueller and Stewart 2011, 36.
41. Silber 2012. See also Sageman 2008, 139; Mueller 2017, cases 1, 20.
42. Mueller 2006, 177.
43. Bergen 2016, 218.
44. Mueller 2017; Aaronson 2013.
45. Mueller and Stewart 2016a, 33; Mueller 2017, case 34.
46. McDermott and Meyer 2012, 310–13.
47. Ibid., 241–42, 268.
48. Poll data and expressions of alarm are from Mueller and Stewart 2016b, 32–34. See also Morell 2014, 305.
49. Parker, Coles, and Salman 2014.
50. Mardini 2014.
51. Mueller and Stewart 2016b.
52. For an extended discussion, see Mueller 2011.
53. Sageman 2008, 153–54; Mueller and Stewart 2016a, 130.

## REFERENCES

Aaronson, Trevor. 2013. *The Terror Factory*. Brooklyn, NY: Ig.
Abrahms, Max. 2006. "Why Terrorism Does Not Work." *International Security* 31:2 (Fall): 42–78.
———. 2012. "The Political Effectiveness of Terrorism Revisited." *Comparative Political Studies* 20:10: 1–28.
———. 2016. "Does Terrorism Work as a Political Strategy? The Evidence Says No." *Los Angeles Times*, April 1. http://www.latimes.com/opinion/op-ed/la-oe-0403-abrahms-strategic-model-terrorism-20160403-story.html.
Abrahms, Max, and Philip B. K. Potter. 2015. "Explaining Terrorism: Leadership Deficits and Militant Group Tactics." *International Organization* 69:3 (Spring): 311–42.
Alcantara, Chris. 2016. "45 Years of Terrorist Attacks in Europe, Visualized." washingtonpost.com, December 19.
Allison, Graham T. 2004. *Nuclear Terrorism: The Ultimate Preventable Catastrophe*. New York: Times Books.
Bergen, Peter. 2016. *United States of Jihad: Investigating America's Homegrown Terrorists*. New York: Crown.
Brooks, Risa A. 2011. "Muslim 'Homegrown' Terrorism in the United States: How Serious Is the Threat?" *International Security* 36:2 (Fall): 7–47.
Burke, Jason. 2015. *The New Threat*. New York: New Press.
Byman, Daniel. 2016. "Understanding the Islamic State." *International Security* 40:4 (Spring): 127–65.
Clausewitz, Carl von. *On War*. 1976. Princeton, NJ: Princeton University Press.
Cronin, Audrey. 2015. "ISIS Is Not a Terrorist Group." *Foreign Affairs*, March–April.
Department of Homeland Security. 2009. *National Infrastructure Protection Plan: Partnering to Enhance Protection and Resiliency*. Washington, DC.

Diab, Robert. 2015. *The Harbinger Theory: How the Post-9/11 Emergency Became Permanent and the Case for Reform.* New York: Oxford University Press.

Dixon, Robyn, and Aoun Sahi. 2016. "Diary of Terror." *Los Angeles Times,* June 24. latimes.com.

Fortna, Virginia Page. 2015. "Do Terrorists Win? Rebels' Use of Terrorism and Civil War Outcomes." *International Organization* 69:3 (Summer): 519–56.

Friedman, Benjamin H., Jim Harper, and Christopher A. Preble. (eds.) 2010. *Terrorizing Ourselves.* Washington, DC: Cato Institute.

Grabosky, Peter, and Michael Stohl. 2010. *Crime and Terrorism.* Los Angeles: Sage.

Griffith, Samuel B., II. 1978. *Mao Tse-Tung: On Guerrilla Warfare.* Garden City, NY: Anchor.

Hoffman, Bruce. 2006. *Inside Terrorism.* Revised and Expanded Edition. New York: Columbia University Press.

Holmes, James R. 2014. "Everything You Know about Clausewitz Is Wrong: A Botched Translation of Clausewitz Has Had an Enduring Impact on Our Thinking on Warfare." *The Diplomat,* November 12. http://thediplomat.com/2014/11/everything-you-know-about-clausewitz-is-wrong/.

Institute for Economics and Peace. 2015. *Global Terrorism Index 2015: Measuring and Understanding the Impact of Terrorism.* New York.

Jenkins, Brian Michael. 2008. *Will Terrorists Go Nuclear?* Amherst, NY: Prometheus.

———. 2010. *Would-Be Warriors: Incidents of Jihadist Terrorist Radicalization in the United States since September 11, 2001.* Santa Monica, CA: RAND.

———. 2011. *Stray Dogs and Virtual Armies: Radicalization and Recruitment to Jihadist Terrorism in the United States Since 9/11.* Santa Monica, CA: RAND.

Karnow, Stanley. 1991. *Vietnam: A History.* New York, Penguin.

Kenney, Michael. 2010. "'Dumb' Yet Deadly: Local Knowledge and Poor Tradecraft among Islamist Militants in Britain and Spain." *Studies in Conflict and Terrorism* 33:10 (October): 911–22.

LaFree, Gary, Laura Dugan, and Erin Miller. 2015. *Putting Terrorism in Context: Lessons from the Global Terrorism Database.* London: Routledge.

Laqueur, Walter. 2003. *No End to War: Terrorism in the Twenty-First Century.* New York: Continuum.

Mardini, Ramzy. 2014. "The Islamic State Threat Is Overstated." *Washington Post,* September 12.

Mayer, Jane. 2008. *The Dark Side: The Inside Story on How the War on Terror Turned into a War on American Ideals.* New York: Doubleday.

McDermott, Terry, and Josh Meyer. 2012. *The Hunt for KSM: Inside the Pursuit and Takedown of the Real 9/11 Mastermind, Khalid Sheikh Mohammed.* New York: Little, Brown.

Morell, Michael. 2015. *The Great War of Our Time: The CIA's Fight against Terrorism from al Qa'ida to ISIS.* New York: Twelve.

Morris, Loveday. 2015. "Islamic State Is Losing Ground: Will That Mean More Attacks Overseas?" *Washington Post,* November 19. washingtonpost.com.

Mueller, John. 1980. "The Search for the 'Breaking Point' in Vietnam: The Statistics of a Deadly Quarrel." *International Studies Quarterly* 24:4 (December): 497–519.

———. 2002. "Harbinger or Aberration? A 9/11 Provocation." *National Interest* (Fall): 45–50.

———. 2003. "Blip or Step Function?" Paper presented at the Annual Convention of the International Studies Association. politicalscience.osu.edu/faculty/jmueller/ISA2003.PDF.

———. 2004. *The Remnants of War.* Ithaca, NY: Cornell University Press.

———. 2006. *Overblown.* New York: Free Press.

———. 2010. *Atomic Obsession: Nuclear Alarmism from Hiroshima to Al Qaeda.* New York: Oxford University Press.

———. 2011. "Action and Reaction: Assessing the Historic Impact of Terrorism." In *Terrorism, Identity, and Legitimacy: The Four Waves Theory and Political Violence,* 112–22. Edited by Jean E. Rosenfeld. New York: Routledge.

———. (ed.) 2017. *Terrorism since 9/11: The American Cases.* Columbus: Mershon Center, Ohio State University. politicalscience.osu.edu/faculty/jmueller/since.html.

Mueller, John, and Mark G. Stewart. 2011. *Terror, Security, and Money: Balancing the Benefits, Risks, and Costs of Homeland Security.* New York: Oxford University Press.

———. 2016a. *Chasing Ghosts: The Policing of Terrorism.* New York: Oxford University Press.

———. 2016b. "Misoverestimating ISIS: Comparisons with al-Qaeda." *Perspectives on Terrorism* 10:4 (August): 32–41.

National Counterterrorism Center. 2006. *Report on Incidents of Terrorism 2005.* April 11. https://fas.org/irp/threat/nctc2005.pdf (accessed February 19, 2017).

Parker, Ned, Isabel Coles, and Raheem Salman. 2014. "Special Report: How Mosul Fell—An Iraqi General Disputes Baghdad's Story." *Reuters,* October 14. http://www.reuters.com/article/us-mideast-crisis-gharawi-special-report-idUSKCN0I30Z820141014 (accessed February 19, 2017).

Pérez-Peña, Richard, Jack Healy, and Jennifer Medina. 2016. "Shooting Scares Show a Nation Quick to Fear the Worst." *New York Times,* August 29. https://www.nytimes.com/2016/08/30/us/shooting-scares-show-a-nation-quick-to-fear-the-worst.html?_r=0.

Pike, Douglas. 1966. *Viet Cong.* Cambridge, MA: MIT Press.

Pinker, Steven. 2011. *The Better Angels of Our Nature: Why Violence Has Declined.* New York: Viking.

Sageman, Marc. 2008. *Leaderless Jihad.* Philadelphia: University of Pennsylvania Press.

Schneier, Bruce. 2007. "Portrait of the Modern Terrorist as an Idiot." *schneier. com*, June 14.

Seitz, Russell. 2004. "Weaker Than We Think." *American Conservative*, December 6.

Silber, Mitchell D. 2012. *The Al Qaeda Factor: Plots against the West.* Philadelphia: University of Pennsylvania Press.

Stohl, Michael. 1988. "Demystifying Terrorism: The Myths and Realities of Contemporary Political Terrorism." In *The Politics of Terrorism*, 1–28. Edited by Michael Stohl. New York: Marcel Dekker.

———. 2012. "State Terror: The Theoretical and Practical Utilities and Implications of a Contested Concept." In *Contemporary Debates on Terrorism*, 43–50. Edited by Richard Jackson and Samuel Justin Sinclair. London: Routledge.

Vinocur, Nicholas. 2015. "'An Act of War.'" *Politico,* November 13. http://www .politico.eu/article/paris-attacks-multiple-dead/ (accessed February 19, 2017).

Warrick, Joby. 2015. *Black Flags: The Rise of ISIS.* New York: Doubleday.

Watts, Clint. 2015. "Let Them Rot: The Challenges and Opportunities of Containing Rather Than Countering the Islamic State," *Perspectives on Terrorism* 9:4 (August): 156–64.

# 3. Terrorism as Tactic

David H. Schanzer

Terrorism is the illegal use of highly visible and well-publicized violence against civilian targets to achieve some political purpose. The key defining feature of terrorism is its inherently political nature. No matter who uses it, terrorism is a tactic used to influence politics.

Popular discourse makes three mistakes when conceptualizing terrorism. The first is the idea that terrorism creates fear because of the violent impact it has on the public. The second is that *terrorism* is used almost exclusively to characterize actions of individuals and nonstate actors—not states. Finally, and probably most controversially, labeling certain organizations "terrorist groups" gives the inaccurate perception that these groups exist and are motivated primarily by the use of violence.

All of these popular misconceptions of terrorism flow from the same flaw, the belief that terrorism is a definable, distinct social phenomenon. It is not. Rather, terrorism is a tactic used by a broad range of actors—including individuals, groups, insurgencies, proto-states (such as ISIS/Daesh), and states—to bring about a political result. Conceptualizing terrorism by focusing on the type of violence that is used—that is, often spectacular or extreme forms of violence against civilians—causes us to ask all the wrong questions: Why do people use this form of violence? What psychological factors led to this result? How can we dissuade them from becoming violent? All of these questions distract society from the far more uncomfortable and intractable problem of understanding and addressing the political grievances that are causing the violence. Using a conception of terrorism that explains and emphasizes the role of politics would help to undo a great deal of the public misunderstanding about this form of political violence and bring more clarity to discussions about how to combat it.

## TERRORISM: THE COMBINATION OF VIOLENCE AND POLITICS

Media coverage and popular discussions of terrorism often focus on the bloody impact of the violence—that is, how the violence has "terrorized" the public. But many things can terrorize the public—serial killers, a rampaging virus, or a violent criminal drug gang. Violence motivated by nonpolitical concerns, in contrast, is not terrorism. What gives terrorism salience is the connection to politics. Indeed, this connection (and the public's genuine fear of violence motivated by political grievances) is perhaps the only way to explain why so much attention and resources are dedicated to preventing terrorism when the total harm to society caused by terrorism often pales in comparison to the societal damage caused by other (nonpolitical) phenomena (such as car accidents, street crime, or infectious disease).[1] Political motivation, not the quantum of harm, is what distinguishes terrorism from nonpolitical forms of violence.

There can be no dispute that crime, for example, has a much greater impact on American society than terrorism. But crime is generally pursued for pecuniary benefit. This profit motive impacts how the potential dangerousness of crime is perceived by society in comparison to terrorism in at least four ways.

First, society understands that criminals want to enjoy the fruits of their illegal conduct. So criminals have a built-in incentive to minimize the violence they cause in order to reduce their risk of being killed or injured. Likewise, they have incentives not to cause murder and mayhem, so as to reduce the amount of attention their criminal activities receive from law enforcement. Most robberies are not solved; a much higher percentage of murders are.

The second reason why society perceives crime as less dangerous than terrorism is that criminals are seen as less dedicated to, and certainly less willing to die for, their cause. Terrorists are feared more than criminals because they seem more capable of causing unrestrained, large-scale violence than criminals. Fear is generated by terrorists despite the fact that all forms of terrorism caused only about 182 deaths between 9/11 and the end of 2014, whereas the United States has experienced approximately 210,000 non-terrorism-related homicides over that same period.[2]

Third, the societal fear of terrorism stems from the perception that any random civilian can possibly be a victim, whereas a majority of society perceives that victims of crime are generally those who, themselves, are involved in or connected in some way to criminal activity, like organized crime or narcotics trafficking. This tendency varies in many cases based on economic circumstance. Those who live in disorganized neighborhoods with large amounts of violent street crime may well feel far more vulnerable to criminal victimization than to terrorism as compared to those who live in affluent neighborhoods where crime is less prevalent.

Finally, compared to terrorism, crime does not present the same level of threat to the underlying principles of democratic society. Crime is not conducted to seek a change in law or policy. Terrorism is. Terrorists seek to force political change upon society by changing the public will through fear. Fear distorts normal politics. In democratic societies, terrorism pressures political actors to take steps to mollify public fear that, absent such fear, would not be taken. Autocratic governments have less popular legitimacy than democratic ones, but terrorism still represents a challenge to normal politics, and thus a far greater affront to society than crime.

It is worth noting that widespread, highly organized criminal enterprises—such as drug cartels operating in Central and South America—may present such a challenge to the established political order that they should be considered a form of political violence despite the fact that their motivation is, at its root, monetary gain. These drug-trafficking organizations seek not simply to run their businesses without state interference but to subvert the states in which they operate through intimidation and fear, in some cases co-opting, or rendering inert, state functions such as the police and justice systems. When these criminal enterprises are killing civilians to intimidate them into acquiescing to the enterprises' dominance over public institutions, their activities are more properly labeled a form of terrorism—perhaps narco-terrorism rather than crime.

Other emotions besides greed may motivate crime, but these too are distinguishable from the political phenomenon of terrorism. Domestic violence in the United States is deeply troubling—but it usually involves relations between small numbers of people. The fear it produces is confined within a social group or family and is not directed at fomenting political change in society. (To be sure, violence against women—often backed by legal frameworks and cultural norms—is so deeply pervasive in some societies that it is a tool of political power. In these cases, it would not be inaccurate to consider targeted violence against women to be a form of terrorism.)

Violence committed by mentally ill individuals is another category of violence that falls outside the category of terrorism. To be sure, the "serial killer on the loose" can definitely cause widespread fear in a community, but again, this panic is isolated to the area where the victimization is occurring. A terrorist incident in one location can often cause widespread fear in another, sometimes a continent away.

In the United States, there is a disturbing tendency to presume that mental illness is a cause when certain violent acts are perpetrated by racists or other extremists, but is not a factor when the perpetrator is a Muslim American, especially when the Muslim's social media accounts indicate some affinity with radical ideologies. For example, the issue of mental disturbance was directly discussed with respect to the shooter in the Lafayette, Louisiana, movie theater and the shooter at the Planned Parenthood clinic in Colorado Springs. With all of these so-called lone wolves, who do not have direct connections with violent organizations, it is difficult to determine if they are terrorists or to evaluate the role that mental illness may have played in their violent conduct. Yet the same standards of evaluation should be applied regardless of the identity or political inclinations of the perpetrators.

Hate crimes, however, constitute a category of criminal activity that ought to be considered acts of terrorism. In the United States, acts of violence arising from religious, ethnic, or racial animus are often categorized as "hate crimes," which are either separate criminal offenses or are sentencing enhancements that can be applied after a conviction for certain violent crimes. Yet, if we are to regard violence directed at civilians for a political cause as terrorism, it is very difficult to distinguish between terrorism and many hate crimes. Because of the political effects of their violence, hate crime perpetrators may receive more severe criminal punishment than perpetrators motivated by other factors. As the US Supreme Court has stated, "Bias motivated crimes are more likely to provoke retaliatory crimes, inflict distinct emotional harms on their victims, and incite community unrest."[3] These are clearly political impacts and are similar to harms caused by terrorism. The shooter who killed nine African American parishioners in Charleston, South Carolina, was charged with a hate crime, but it seems equally plausible that he could have been prosecuted for "domestic terrorism," which federal law defines as violent crimes that "appear to be intended to intimidate or coerce a civilian population."[4] Indeed, Attorney General Loretta Lynch noted during her announcement of the indictment of the Charleston shooter that "racially motivated violence . . . is the original domestic terrorism."[5] Regardless of the technical legal charge, most hate crimes are forms of terrorism.

As this review demonstrates, society is more fearful of terrorism than other forms of violence and chooses to impose greater levels of punishment on terrorists than other criminals. The reason is the connection between violence and politics.

## A TACTIC USED BY STATES, ORGANIZATIONS, AND INDIVIDUALS

The second common misperception that colors public understanding of terrorism is the idea that acts of terrorism are committed only by nonstate actors or individuals connected or inspired by those organizations. However, excluding violence against civilians committed by state actors from the concept of terrorism makes no sense from a descriptive, historical, or theoretical perspective.[6] Understanding terrorism as a tactic used by a full range of political organizations cures these difficulties.

### Entities That Use Terrorism as a Tactic

The historical record is full of examples of states, nonstate actors, and individuals who have used violence against civilians for a political purpose. Use of such violence most frequently arises as the by-product of a contest for political power.[7] The size and strength of the entity using terrorism often reflects the level of popular support for the perpetrators' political cause.

Individual terrorism (sometimes referred to with the misnomer "lone-wolf" terrorism)[8] is most frequently perpetrated by individuals whose ideology has little or no popular support or who are psychologically ill-equipped to interact with other people. The fact that they are single individuals limits their level of dangerousness, but they can still cause significant harm, as demonstrated by Ted Kaczynski, the "Unabomber," and Nidal Hasan, the Fort Hood shooter. Domestically, pairs of terrorists have been more successful in executing spectacular attacks, such as the Oklahoma City and Boston Marathon bombings. Still, in these cases and many others in the United States, the violent individuals were not integrated into larger groups, because hardly anyone supports the substance of their political views or the belief that these political views will be advanced by the use of violence against civilians.

Small groups of individuals engage in terrorist activity. These groups can be a structured cell of an organization, such as the 9/11 attackers, who received direct funding, planning, and technical assistance from the core al-Qaeda organization, or a more loosely associated group of friends or associates who join together, adopt a common radical ideology, and ultimately plot violence against civilian targets. A large cell of radicals linked to ISIS/Daesh wreaked carnage and havoc in Paris and Brussels in 2015 and

2016; some of them had formally joined ISIS, while others were family, friends, or associates. Scholars Clark McCauley and Sophia Moskalenko note that the psychology of small-group dynamics can promote radicalization of group members to violence.[9] Similarly, Marc Sageman has posited that small groups of like-minded, disaffected men—what he labels a "bunch of guys"—have the potential to radicalize themselves to violence without any connection to highly organized groups or terrorist networks.[10]

Structured, named, and branded organizations are the archetypal perpetrators of terrorist acts, ranging from ethno-nationalist groups like the IRA or PLO, to violent, radical Middle Eastern extremists like al-Qaeda, to domestic groups such as the Ku Klux Klan or the Weather Underground. These groups can be large enough to cause large-scale violence over an extended period that requires a response by state actors or, in the case of globally networked organizations like al-Qaeda, an international response.

Some violent political organizations that use terrorist tactics also engage in other forms of violence, such as irregular warfare, or become formal political opposition forces within a state. Hezbollah in Lebanon is the best example of an organization that plots violent actions against civilians as part of its political opposition to the state of Israel, but also has military units that have been mobilized in southern Lebanon and the Syrian civil war. Hezbollah has also evolved into a political party that runs candidates for office and holds a substantial share of political power in the Lebanese government. Categorizing Hezbollah as a terrorist group, as many do, poorly describes the multiple roles that it plays and the ways it uses violence to pursue its political agenda.

Violent political groups that grow in size and organization advance to the level of insurgencies against the state or an occupying power. They attack civilians to advance their political cause, but often have sufficient size and scope to engage in formalized military activities akin to irregular warfare or, if they get larger and more sophisticated, conventional warfare. Boko Haram is an insurgency against the Nigerian government that uses terrorist tactics like kidnappings, bombings, and assassinations, but also has engaged in large-scale killing and taken control of large swaths of territory. Some estimate that Boko Haram has killed as many as 17,000 people and displaced 2.6 million from their homes.[11] Similarly, ISIS/Daesh is an insurgent organization that has grown to take absolute control of a large area of territory spanning an international border and to assert governmental authority over millions of civilians. It uses horrific forms of terrorist violence against civilians such as beheadings and gang rape, but also deploys hierarchical military units to wage irregular and even conventional warfare. ISIS/Daesh uses abusive police powers to force its ideology on the civilian population, but also performs classic governmental functions like tax collection and business regulation. It is most accurately described as a proto-state.

Finally, there are states that use terrorist tactics. First, states sponsor terrorism executed by nonstate actors. Iran, instead of using its own operatives directly, uses proxy groups to pursue its political agenda through violence, including Palestinian groups in Gaza, Hezbollah in Lebanon (which is also active in Syria), and various Shia militia groups active in Iraq.[12]

While state-sponsored terrorism was a national security concern of the United States in the 1970s and 1980s, direct use of violence against civilians by states has been far more common in modern history. The reasons for state violence against civilians are often wrapped in historical complexity, but the use of this violence is, nonetheless, unmistakable and well known. Examples include use of violence by Russian czars in the nineteenth century to quell revolt by organized anarchists, mass violence against Native Americans during their forced removal from their homelands in the southeastern United States, violence against civilians by the Red Army to consolidate Bolshevik power, and the Nazis' use of terror to crush dissent as they seized state control and then perpetrated world war, mass extermination, and genocide.[13]

## State Terrorism: Illegal Use of Force against Civilians for a Political Purpose

Of course, not all uses of violence by states constitute terrorism. Indeed, as Max Weber noted, the condition of statehood depends on having a monopoly on the use of physical force over the state's own citizens. The law of armed conflict and international human rights law help to define the boundary between legitimate state use of force and illegal, immoral use of violence against civilians (that is, terrorism).

The use of violence by a state during an armed conflict, if in compliance with the law of war, is legally authorized state conduct. Armed conflicts can occur between two states (an international armed conflict), or between a state and nongovernmental armed groups, or between multiple nongovernmental armed groups.[14] In all such conflicts, the core law-of-war principles are as follows:

1. Civilians may not be intentionally targeted.

2. Force may be used only to further a military necessity.

3. Incidental civilian damage from attacks may not be excessive in relation to the military advantage expected to be gained.

4. Weapons that cause excessive human suffering may not be used.[15]

Violations of these principles can rise to the level of a war crime, but not all war crimes are acts of terrorism. For example, if a state uses a banned munition, such as a chemical weapon, against an opposing army on the battlefield, that is a war crime. If civilian populations are unaffected, terrorism has not occurred. States that knowingly violate the laws of war by intentionally targeting civilians for a political purpose are engaging in terrorism.

Objective application of the law of war is critical to sorting the wheat from the chaff in public discourse on whether a state's use of force constitutes an act of terrorism. This very issue arose in the White House press room in 2013 when a reporter asked if US drone strikes were acts of terrorism.[16] Applying principles of international law, the United States argued that it is engaged in an armed conflict against al-Qaeda and may use lethal force against belligerents in this conflict. The United States claims that its drone strikes are intended to hit legitimate military targets (though mistakes are sometimes made) and therefore it complies with the mandate against targeting civilians. The Assad regime uses similar, but far less persuasive, arguments concerning its uses of force in regions populated by civilians. The regime labels all rebel opposition fighters as terrorists and claims it has a right to use force against them. What distinguishes US drones from the barrel bombs dropped on civilians by Assad is the care with which efforts are made to minimize civilian casualties. Extensive measures are taken to avoid unnecessary civilian casualties during drone strikes, such as aerial surveillance of the target to determine if innocent civilians are present and use of precision weaponry to minimize casualties of nontargets. Assad does not conduct prestrike surveillance, consistently drops munitions on densely populated areas, and uses such crude weaponry that the regime knows large numbers of civilians will be killed.[17] Assad's use of barrel bombs is undoubtedly state terrorism. The United States' use of drones is not (in my view, though I recognize the controversy over this point).

States may also commit terrorism through abusive use of domestic police forces against civilians. Of course, the police have legal authority to use force to enforce domestic law and provide security for the civilian population. But human rights standards require that police use force only if nonviolent means are ineffective and any force used is proportional to the seriousness of the criminal conduct. Use of lethal force is even more highly regulated. It may be used only in self-defense, in defense of others in imminent danger, to avert serious crimes involving grave threat to life, or to prevent the escape of a highly dangerous person.[18]

Violation of these standards by individual police officers may lead to punishment ranging from loss of employment to potential criminal liability, as we have seen in controversies stemming from police shootings of African Americans in multiple US cities since the summer of 2014. Police agencies that violate human rights standards relating to the use of force en masse, however, are engaging in terrorist activity. If police shoot indiscriminately into a crowd of political protestors or use violent coercive power outside the rule of law to arrest and detain political opponents of the ruling regime, such activities are part and parcel of terrorist activity by a state against its own citizens.

## TERRORISM AND INSURRECTION

Terrorism is thus the intentional use of violence against civilians for a political purpose used by a range of actors, from single individuals to a nation-state. It is in all instances illegal and in all instances immoral.

Terrorism committed by individuals or groups is particularly illegitimate in democratic societies that have institutional mechanisms to bring about political change through peaceful, consensual means. In such circumstances, terrorism is truly the weapon of the weak—not weak in resources or weaponry, but weak in political power. Even small political minorities have some means at their disposal to influence political outcomes in democratic societies. Terrorism, however, is resorted to by minorities whose ideas have so few advocates that they cannot influence the political process to any extent, other than through the use of terrorist tactics. Terrorists' unwillingness to accept that their views are politically unpalatable to the vast majority of people and to abide by democratic norms is part of what makes their use of terrorist tactics so deeply troubling and immoral.

The use of terrorism by individuals and nonstate actors against autocracies has greater moral ambiguity. When the state has closed all avenues of political dissent and minorities have few, if any, means to influence political outcomes, the resort to violence by political minorities has greater legitimacy than it does in a democracy. In brutal autocracies, violent rebellion may be the only way to bring about positive political change. Nonviolent peaceful protest is a preferable means to confront an unjust regime, such as the Tahir Square revolution in Egypt or the protest movement leading to the disintegration of the East German government. Yet, over the course of history, violent revolutions have also successfully removed oppressive rulers (albeit, with mixed results).

Even in the context of popular uprisings against oppression, there is a difference between legitimate violent rebellion and terrorism. The legitimate tactics available to rebels include the use of violence against military installations, government infrastructure and troops, and top political leaders.

Rebellions that use violence against civilians as a means for undermining the legitimacy of the state, however, are themselves illegitimate. Killing civilians for a political purpose elevates the political cause over innocent human life—treating civilians as mere means to an end. This is the essence of the moral wrong of terrorism, even when pursued in opposition to an oppressive state.

This distinction helps to undercut the moral relevancy argument, often made by individuals and organizations that resort to terrorism, that "one man's terrorist is another man's freedom fighter." Freedom fighters have legitimacy if they fight for their cause through legitimate means of armed revolt against government forces and facilities. Rebels who use the illegitimate means of pursuing political change by intentionally targeting civilians are not freedom fighters, but rather are terrorists.

This distinction has been recognized to some extent in modern developments of international law. The Additional Protocol I to the Geneva Conventions provides that "armed conflicts in which people are fighting against colonial domination and alien occupation, and against racist regimes in the exercise of self-determination," are international armed conflicts in which combatants are entitled to humanitarian protections.[19] These protections are triggered, however, only if the combatants operate in units with a command structure, wear a distinctive insignia identifying their status as combatants, carry weapons openly, and comply with the laws of war. Combatants who comply with these rules are privileged belligerents who may not be prosecuted for taking part in combat and, if captured, must be treated as prisoners of war. However, participants in these conflicts who intentionally blend into the civilian populations, ignore the prohibition on preventing civilian casualties, and blatantly violate other laws of war are committing acts of terrorism, regardless of the justness of their cause. They are merely insurgents who use terrorism as a tactic.

## "TERRORIST GROUPS" ARE POLITICAL GROUPS USING THE TACTIC OF TERRORISM

The third error of popular discourse in constructing the term *terrorism* is the widespread use of the phrase *terrorist group*, but consistent failure to use parallel terms such as *terrorist state* or *terrorist insurgency*. Scholar Louise Richardson goes so far as to argue that "if we want to have any analytical clarity in understanding the behavior of terrorist groups," we cannot even consider violence carried out by states against civilians to be terrorism.

I disagree.

First, as the preceding descriptive sections demonstrate, cabining the use of the term *terrorism* to refer only to the activities of nonstate actors deeply distorts the true nature of modern political violence. Individuals, groups, insurgencies, and states have all at times used violence against civilians for political purposes. It is simply impossible to maintain the moral claim that such violence is illegitimate if the pejorative term *terrorism* is applied to nonstate actors (even those who fight against unjust regimes), but called something entirely different when the violence is used by the state.

Second, the term *terrorist group* is inapt because it emphasizes a group's use of immoral violence while underplaying the fact that the violence is generated by a set of political grievances. It is too comfortable, in my view, for the public to conceptualize terrorist groups as a collection of aberrant sociopaths who kill the innocent primarily out of bloodlust rather than as part of complex political phenomena. Public disregard of the political component of the violence leads to the assumption that if the violent actors can be eliminated or constrained, the violence will end. What we have seen in Iraq puts the lie to this assumption with al-Qaeda in Iraq (AQI) having been virtually destroyed in 2007–9, only to have ISIS/Daesh arise in its place based on the exact same set of unresolved political grievances that gave rise to AQI in the first place.

Similarly, use of terminology emphasizing the means that groups use to advance their aims (that is, "terrorism"), rather than the substantive grievances that have activated the group (that is, "politics"), leads to the development of "counterterrorism" strategies that focus on physically confronting and destroying the groups instead of trying to address the underlying political conflict. The Syrian civil war is a perfect example of this phenomenon. ISIS/Daesh has gained territory in Syria by fashioning itself as the protector of Syrian Sunni Muslims against the use of mass terrorist violence by the Bashar al-Assad regime. Like it or not, ISIS/Daesh is a political oppositional movement, not a mere "terrorist group."[20] Simplistic solutions such as mass-bombing campaigns may degrade the group, but the violence and use of terrorist tactics by ISIS/Daesh, or whatever successor group arises to represent disenfranchised Syrian and Iraqi Sunni Muslims, will continue until the political conflict with the Assad regime and the Shia-dominated Iraqi government ends.

Richardson is simply wrong that we cannot understand or analyze non-state actors that use terrorist tactics (what she calls terrorist groups) if state use of violence against civilians also falls within the definition of terrorism. Indeed, the exact opposite is true. We cannot truly understand why groups use violence as a tactic for political causes unless we also consider the consequences of states using violence against civilians to pursue their political agendas. States and nonstate actors are often engaged in a battle over political power. Understanding this contest for political power is the key to preventing the violence. Characterizing state violence against civilians differently than nonstate actor violence against civilians is likely to muddle public understanding and frustrate the search for solutions. We would be far better off if we got rid of the term *terrorist groups* altogether.

## THE INCOHERENCE OF COUNTERTERRORISM

An additional indicator that the popular conceptualization of terrorism is wrong is that the field of "counterterrorism" is totally incoherent. This should not be the case. Think about the problem of infectious disease. The problem of disease is well defined and understood, as are the countermeasures used to combat infectious disease, which constitute the field of public health. Preventing the spread of infectious disease involves the same strategies whether undertaken by an individual, within a community, or around the world: diligent hygiene, minimizing contact with infected individuals, vaccination, quarantine, and so on. Pretty much the same strategies would apply no matter what the infectious disease is and no matter where the outbreak occurs.

The field of counterterrorism, however, does not have a consistent, uniform set of practices. Consider three incidents that took place in late 2015—all of which were labeled as terrorism in public discourse and would be included in most academic databases that catalog terrorist attacks:

- The mass shooting by an American and his immigrant wife in San Bernardino, California, apparently inspired by radical Islamist ideology.

- The shooting and siege at the Radisson Blu Hotel in Bamako, Mali, apparently planned and executed by the group al-Mourabitoun, in conjunction with al-Qaeda in the Islamic Maghreb.

- The bombing of a Russian jetliner that departed from Sharm el Sheik, Egypt, apparently conducted by individuals and groups affiliated with the so-called Islamic State in Iraq and Syria (ISIS/Daesh).

The countermeasures that can best address these three terrorist incidents, however, have little or nothing in common.

- *San Bernardino:* Addressing violent extremists with marginal or no connections to organized groups requires either surveillance by local law enforcement agencies or tips from community members who know the perpetrators. In the long run, community-based programs can try to build resilience against violent ideologies or establish trusting relationships that will enhance the flow of information about potentially dangerous individuals. Immigration controls could, if their predictive judgments are exceptionally sharp, preclude such individuals from admission, but such measures would have no impact on "homegrown" terrorism.

- *Radisson Blu Hotel:* Violent political organizations like al-Mourabi-toun can be targeted through a decapitation strategy to kill or arrest group leaders; measures to cut off sources of financing; coordinated national-level intelligence collection, sharing, and analysis to thwart plots and arrest perpetrators; and training foreign special forces or paramilitaries to conduct targeted operations against organization members. Improved governance and enfranchisement of political minorities in Mali are needed to undercut the support for insurgent groups like al-Mourabitoun.

- *Russian airliner:* ISIS/Daesh is a pseudo- or proto-state that holds territory and can also be characterized as a large-scale insurgency against the governments of Iraq and Syria. As such, it can be defeated only by coordinated action of nation-states through a combination of military, economic, and diplomatic action. In the end, some form of armed conflict on the ground will be necessary to recapture the territory it now holds. A political solution that provides protection to Sunni Muslims in Syria and Iraq is necessary to relieve the grievances giving rise to this violence.

The diversity and range of these actions demonstrate that counterterrorism does not hold together as a coherent concept. Incoherence results because the only commonality between the three events is that the perpetrators used the tactic of terrorism to attempt to achieve their objectives. But their use of terroristic tactics tells us little about the sociopolitical problems that led to violence and, therefore, provides scant insight into the types of countermeasures necessary to address those problems.

## TERRORISM AS A TACTIC—NOT A SOCIAL PHENOMENON

Widespread use of terrorism by a range of political actors is really a barometer of social and political dysfunction. The dysfunction may involve a set of individuals, larger groups, organizations, insurgencies, mass insurrections, and, often, the state itself. These parties use terrorist tactics for a variety of reasons that are contextual and derive from their history, experience, and psychology. The reasons the Tsarnaev brothers bombed the Boston Marathon has little or no connection to the bombings that take place in cities throughout the Middle East on virtually a daily basis. Likewise, the IRA bombing of civilian targets to confront UK rule in Northern Ireland provides minimal insight into the reasons Hamas shoots rockets into civilian cities in Israel. The nature of the political conflicts is often masked by labeling a nonstate actor as a terrorist group and then deploying a set of tools against the nonstate actor to disrupt, degrade, defeat, and then destroy it. But as we have seen in very recent history, these tools do not effectively address the political conflict that gave rise to the terrorist violence, which frequently involves a contest over state power and reactions by individuals and groups to the illegitimate use of violence against civilians by the state itself. We will not reduce the prevalence of terrorism until we get much better at finding ways to eliminate, or at least mitigate, the political conflicts that motivate these atrocious acts.

## NOTES

1. John Mueller and Mark G. Stewart, *Terror, Security, and Money* (New York: Oxford University Press, 2011), 182–85.

2. For the number of deaths resulting from homegrown violent extremism, see National Consortium for the Study of Terrorism and Responses to Terrorism, "Islamist and Far-Right Homicides in the United States," https://www.start.umd .edu/pubs/START_ECDB_IslamistFarRightHomicidesUS_Infographic_Feb2017.pdf (accessed March 2, 2017). For the number of homicides in the United States since 9/11, see "Crime in America 2015," Federal Bureau of Investigation, Table 1, https:// ucr.fbi.gov/crime-in-the-u.s./2015/crime-in-the-u.s.-2015/tables/table-1 (accessed March 2, 2017). The estimate was obtained by adding one-third of the homicides in 2001 and the total homicides in 2002–14.

3. *Wisconsin v. Mitchell*, 508 U.S. 47 (1993).

4. 18 U.S.C. §2331.

5. Lynch quoted in Catherine E. Shoichet and Evan Perez, "Dylan Roof Faces Hate Crime Charges in Charleston Shooting," CNN.com, July 22, 2015, http:// www.cnn.com/2015/07/22/us/charleston-shooting-hate-crime-charges/.

6. On this point, I have been strongly influenced by Martin A. Miller, *The Foundations of Modern Terrorism* (New York: Cambridge University Press, 2012).

7. Miller, *The Foundations of Modern Terrorism*, 3.

8. There is virtually no commonality between the behavior of wolves who leave their packs (genuine lone wolves) and individual human terrorists. All wolves start out life in a pack. Some become lone wolves because they voluntarily leave or are kicked out by the dominant wolves in the pack. Most individual terrorists, in contrast, do not leave a violent political group, but rather radicalize to violence all on their own. Moreover, the lone wolf is not particularly dangerous as it lacks the advantages of hunting in a group. Individual terrorists, however, have caused almost all of the terroristic violence in the United States since 9/11. Terrorism is often

referred to as animalistic behavior, but this too is wildly inaccurate. Animals expend only the energy and resources they need to kill the amount of prey they can efficiently eat. Mass killings for the purpose of sending a message is, unfortunately, quintessentially human behavior.

9. Clark McCauley and Sophia Moskalenko, *Friction: How Radicalization Happens to Them and Us* (New York: Oxford University Press, 2011).

10. Marc Sageman, *Leaderless Jihad* (Philadelphia: University of Pennsylvania Press, 2008).

11. "At Least 50 Killed as Boko Haram Attacks Nigerian Village," *The Telegraph*, January 31, 2016, http://www.telegraph.co.uk/news/worldnews/africaandindian-ocean/nigeria/12133052/At-least-50-killed-as-Boko-Haram-attacks-Nigerian-village.html (accessed February 16, 2017).

12. United States Department of State, "Country Reports on Terrorism 2014, Chapter 3—State Sponsors of Terrorism Overview," http://www.state.gov/j/ct/rls/crt/2014/239410.htm.

13. Miller, *The Foundations of Modern Terrorism*, 181.

14. International Committee of the Red Cross, "How Is the Term 'Armed Conflict' Defined in International Humanitarian Law?" March 2008, https://www.icrc.org/eng/assets/files/other/opinion-paper-armed-conflict.pdf.

15. "4 Basic Principles," Law of Armed Conflict Blog, https://loacblog.com/loac-basics/4-basic-principles/.

16. Geoffrey Ingersoll, "A Reporter Asked Jay Carney If Air Strikes That Kill Civilians Are 'Considered Terrorism,'" *BusinessInsider*, April 18, 2013, http://www.businessinsider.com/reporter-asks-jay-carney-are-us-strikes-that-kill-civilians-acts-of-terror-2013-4.

17. United Nations Security Council, Resolution 2139, para. 3, February 22, 2014 (demanding all parties to cease "indiscriminate employment of weapons in populated areas . . . such as the use of barrel bombs").

18. United Nations High Commissioner for Human Rights, *Basic Principles on the Use of Force and Firearms by Law Enforcement Officials* (1990).

19. Protocol Additional to the Geneva Conventions of 12 August 1949, and Relating to the Protection of Victims of International Armed Conflicts (Protocol I), June 8, 1977, Article I(4).

20. Audrey Kurth Cronin, "ISIS Is Not a Terrorist Group," *Foreign Affairs*, March–April 2015; David Schanzer, "Iraq Is Not a 'Terrorism' Problem," *Huffington Post*, June 17, 2014, http://www.huffingtonpost.com/david-schanzer/iraq-is-not-a-terrorism-problem_b_5500861.html.

# 4. The Construction of State Terrorism
Ruth Blakeley

The literature on terrorism is dominated by work that examines the use of terrorism by nonstate actors. While some of the literature acknowledges that states can also be perpetrators of terrorism, it is usually assumed that states that use and sponsor terrorism are so-called rogue states or states governed by authoritarian regimes. Since 9/11 and the subsequent wars in Afghanistan and Iraq, there has been growing interest in the terroristic effects of state responses to terrorism, with dozens of scholars engaging with the arbitrary detention, torture, and cruel treatment that occurred at the Abu Ghraib prison in Iraq, at the US Department of Defense facility in Guantánamo Bay, Cuba, and in the network of secret CIA prisons that operated across Europe, the Middle East, and Asia. Yet even these studies tend not to consider the historical roots of terroristic violence by Western states. Just as Schmid and Jongman and Gurr have observed, much scholarship on terrorism is impressionistic and not grounded in rigorous historical, empirical analysis.[1] This is true in relation to both state and nonstate terrorism; while recent manifestations of Western state terrorism have attracted attention, few consider the rather long and illustrious history of the use and sponsorship of state terrorism by Western states—historically as part of their imperial projects, and more recently to deal with a range of perceived threats to their strategic and material interests. The limited engagement, not only within the literature but also in policy circles and among the public, has important implications both for our ability to theorize and analyze terrorism and for our capacity to develop the most effective ways to tackle terrorism in all its forms, whether perpetrated by state or nonstate actors.

In common with other contributors to this volume, including Lisa Stampnitzky, Mark Juergensmeyer, and Clark McCauley, I contend in what follows that a symbiotic relationship exists between terrorism and counter-terrorism. Furthermore, counterterrorism campaigns more often than not involve practices that ought to be understood as state terrorism. The aim of the chapter is to explore the consequences of that relationship. I begin by examining the ways in which state terrorism is constructed in the scholarly literature and by the governments of powerful liberal democratic states. These constructions have the effect of hiding from view the widespread use and sponsorship of terrorism by those powerful liberal democratic states. I then examine when, how, and why states use or sponsor terrorism. I argue that when states have used terrorism against their own populations, they have tended to do so as a means of curtailing political opposition and maintaining power. I show that it was also central to the imperial projects of powerful Western states, both during colonization and to thwart decolonization, and more recently, to the neo-imperial projects of such states, especially the United States, aimed at opening access to resources and markets across the Global South. It has also been part of the response to threats emanating from al-Qaeda–inspired terrorism. In all cases, the use of state terrorism has been directed at groups or movements considered a threat to the strategic and material interests of the states in question. It has also often been accompanied by efforts to construct those targeted in particular ways—as insurgents or terrorists, or those who harbor them—so as to delegitimize them and justify the violence directed at them. I show that the violence is deliberately intended to have a terrorizing effect on a population wider than those directly targeted by the violence, with a view to curtailing support for them. In closing, I explore the consequences that arise when states resort to terrorism to deal with threats to their interests, and when publics fail to engage with what is being done in their name. I show that such violent and terroristic approaches to dealing with perceived threats are largely counterproductive and tend to have far-reaching, detrimental consequences for democracy, human rights, and the liberalizing international projects of powerful liberal democratic states.

## SCHOLARLY AND POLICY CONSTRUCTIONS OF STATE TERRORISM

In policy and academic circles, there has been a tendency to resist the notion that states can be perpetrators of terrorism. Yet the vast majority of state violence, particularly when directed against domestic populations, is intended to have a terrorizing effect. This is because it involves extreme human rights violations, including torture and other cruel, inhuman, and degrading treatment, and assassination, often on an industrial scale. It also tends to result in far higher numbers of casualties than nonstate terrorism does.

States are especially reluctant to recognize state terrorism since doing so would leave them vulnerable to accusations that they are perpetrators. Evidence of this reluctance can be traced through debates between member states of the United Nations. In 1972 the UN General Assembly established the Ad Hoc Committee on International Terrorism. Among its tasks has been the elaboration of a comprehensive convention on international terrorism. The initial Resolution 3034 (XXVII), passed in 1972, referred explicitly to "the continuation of repressive terrorist acts by colonial, racist and alien regimes." The inclusion of this clause was a response to the extremely violent struggles for decolonization that characterized the 1950s and 1960s, discussed below. Despite the fact that this clause recognizes the role that state forces often play in perpetrating terrorism, a sticking point that for decades halted the adoption of the draft convention on international terrorism was whether it should address state terrorism. Israel, the United States, and most Western states opposed such a clause, whereas a number of Arab states insist on its inclusion, singling out Israel for its use of state terrorism within the Occupied Palestinian Territories.[2] When in 1994 the General Assembly adopted the Declaration of Measures to Eliminate International Terrorism, the term *state terrorism* was simply avoided, and instead the formula "by whomever committed" was adopted.[3]

Among those states that are opposed to the condemnation of state terrorism within the UN convention, on occasion they nevertheless acknowledge the role that states do play in terrorism, mainly to condemn state-sponsored terrorism by other, "rogue" states. Shortly after the terrorist attacks of September 11 2001, for example, during his State of the Union address, US president George W. Bush declared, "We will pursue nations that provide aid or safe haven to terrorism. . . . From this day forward, any nations that continue to harbor or support terrorism will be regarded by the United States as a hostile regime. . . . We condemn the Taliban regime. It is not only repressing its own people; it is threatening people everywhere by sponsoring and sheltering and supplying terrorists."[4] The president made similar assertions during his January 2002 State of the Union address: "Our second goal is to prevent regimes that sponsor terror. . . . Iran exports terror. . . . States like these, and their terrorist allies, constitute an axis of evil. . . . We will work closely with our coalition to deny terrorists and their state sponsors the materials, technology, and expertise to make and deliver weapons of mass destruction."[5]

Two slightly contradictory approaches are at play here. On the one hand, policy makers resist acknowledging that states can be perpetrators of terrorism. On the other, they are willing to point the finger at states much more repressive than their own and accuse them of using or sponsoring terrorism. This latter approach reinforces the assumptions underlying the former; that is, liberal democratic states do not use terrorism—that is the preserve of more repressive regimes.

There is a similar reluctance among scholars to engage with state terrorism, particularly as perpetrated by liberal democratic states, with scholars making forceful arguments for precluding actions of state agents from our understanding and analysis of terrorism. In the scholarly literature, it tends to be assumed that because the existence of the state is based on its monopoly of coercive power, there is a fundamental difference between terrorism perpetrated by nonstate actors and violence perpetrated by state agents. Leading terrorism scholars have argued that because states are permitted to use violence in self-defense, we should not refer to these acts as terrorism. Walter Laqueur, for example, claims that those who argue state terrorism should be included in studies of terrorism ignore the fact that "the very existence of a state is based on its monopoly of power. If it were different, states would not have the right, nor be in a position, to maintain that minimum of order on which all civilised life rests."[6] He also suggests that "there are basic differences in motives, function and effect between oppression by the state (or society or religion) and political terrorism. To equate them, to obliterate them is to spread confusion."[7] Including state terrorism in the study of terrorism, he insists, "would have made the study of terrorism impossible, for it would have included not only US foreign policy, but also Hitler and Stalin."[8]

Bruce Hoffman has made similar claims. He argues that if we do not distinguish between state and nonstate violence, and we equate the innocents killed by states to those killed by nonstate actors, we "ignore the fact that, even while national armed forces have been responsible for far more death and destruction than terrorists might ever aspire to bring about, there nonetheless is a fundamental qualitative difference between the two types of violence."[9] For Hoffman, this distinction is based on the historical emergence of "rules and accepted norms of behavior that prohibit the use of certain types of weapons" and "proscribe various tactics and outlaw attacks on specific categories of targets." He adds that "terrorists" have by contrast "violated all these rules."[10] The reality, however, is that states frequently violate these rules, as set out in the Geneva Conventions, particularly when they resort to violence to curtail political opposition. The monopoly of violence enjoyed by the state is not a reason for us to exclude state terrorism from analysis.[11] Neither is it a reason to legitimize the use of violence in all ways that a state may choose to deploy it.

The failure by policy makers and academics to engage with state terrorism in any consistent way has significant consequences for the quality of our analysis and for our ability to fully understand the causes and consequences of terrorism, whoever the perpetrator. The remainder of this chapter explores how and why states use terrorism and then assesses the consequences of state terrorism for democracy, human rights, and the liberalizing international projects of powerful democratic states.

## THE USE AND SPONSORSHIP OF STATE TERRORISM

The regimes of Stalin, Hitler, and Pol Pot were responsible for terroristic state violence on a massive scale, perpetrating genocide but also terrorizing the population at large into submission to the regime.

The academic literature that does engage with state terrorism does so often with reference to those regimes. Far less is said of the use of state terrorism by liberal democratic states, though there are some important exceptions.[12] Such states have an inglorious history of using and sponsoring state terrorism, and this practice can be traced back to their colonial legacies, through World War II, and into the Cold War period and most recently in the "War on Terror." When we get beyond the legitimizing rhetoric that enshrouds the use of state terrorism by powerful liberal democratic states, it is possible to provide a more honest analysis of the centrality of state terrorism to the imperial and neo-imperial projects of those states.

States have long deployed violence to coerce populations into acquiescing to the agendas of political and economic elites, particularly where those elites perceive a threat to their interests. This threat may emanate from groups using terrorism, but the historical record shows that more often than not, the state tends to target groups that have aims that contrast with those of the elites. (Indeed there is a small but growing body of work that seeks to explore the relationships between state power, capitalist elite interests, and the use of terroristic violence by the state.[13]) States then construct the threat from these groups in particular ways, such as declaring that they pose a threat and imposing labels on opposition groups such as "guerrillas," "insurgents," or "terrorists" to justify the state's subsequent coercive response. Initially, states may target a limited number of individuals, but the number then tends to grow. A deliberate intent of the use of coercion is to instill fear in wider populations in order to deter them from supporting the "insurgents," "guerrillas," or "terrorists." This approach often has the effect of eroding support for the state and driving more people into the arms of the opposition. The state then responds by extending the use of force in an effort to maintain power and control. Frequently, states deploy paramilitary and private security forces to conceal the state's involvement in the violence. As Stohl has argued, this tactic can also increase the degree of terror experienced by the target audience, since it involves the "extensive use of groups who appear to be virtually 'uncontrolled' and who are notoriously unrestrained in their use of vicious methods."[14] In this sense, there is a symbiotic relationship between state terrorism and terrorism by nonstate actors, in terms of both the rhetoric surrounding the use of state terrorism and the actual interplay between states and political movements that challenge them.

State terrorism underpinned the conquest of large swathes of the world's territory by the European colonial powers. The aim of these expansionist endeavors was the domination of trade and resource extraction, all realized through the mass exploitation of indigenous labor, cowed into submission through extreme violence and terror.[15] When Brazil was colonized by Portugal, for example, 80 percent of the indigenous population was wiped out, while in territories occupied by Spanish colonizers, an initial wave of violence terrified surrounding populations into supplying resources to the colonizers.[16] Across Africa, the British, French, Belgians, and Germans took a very similar approach. Where resistance arose, houses and even whole villages would be razed to the ground if labor and taxes were not forthcoming.[17] By the twentieth century, the same effects could be achieved through aerial bombardment, and this the British did in response to a rebellion in Iraq in 1920, when the British air force was instructed to fly over 4,000 missions to conduct "terror" raids against supposed rebels, with one official describing the mission as "relentless and unremitting and carried on continuously by day and by night, on houses, inhabitants, crops and cattle."[18]

As the sun set on the European empires, and movements emerged within colonized states for national self-determination, they were met with further state terrorism by the colonial powers and their proxies. Caroline Elkins has shown in some depth the lengths Britain went to, in collaboration with elite allies in Kenya, to crush the Mau Mau insurgency in the 1950s. After Britain declared a state of emergency in 1952, indiscriminate detention and torture characterized the British response. Targets had their livestock seized, were forced into slave labor, and were subjected to torture, simulated drowning, beatings, and further threats of violence. Women were living under siege, effectively interned in their villages, and subjected to widespread violence and rape.[19] France's response to the liberation movement in Algeria was equally brutal. Mass internment of three million people in *auto-défense* villages was accompanied by a systematic campaign of state terrorism, led by the French military, intended to deter support for the liberation movement.[20] Of 24,000 arrested in the Battle of Algiers, 3,000 disappeared in detention,[21] with many subject to torture that was justified by military commanders, such as General Jacques Massu, as a military necessity in order to identify the insurgency's leaders, though Massu later admitted the torture was ineffective for securing intelligence.[22]

Decolonization for Britain and France coincided with the extension of US hegemony. US interventions around the world during the Cold War were frequently justified as necessary to contain communism, but there was also an underlying material imperative, with coercion aimed at ensuring US primacy. Officials would emphasize the economic threats posed when left-wing governments were elected, and the United States frequently shored up right-wing authoritarian regimes to protect US capital.[23] This was the case in the CIA's involvement in the coup in Guatemala in 1954, which ousted the Arbenz government after it became clear that economic reforms would involve the expropriation of lands occupied by the United Fruit Company. Declassified documents tell a similar story in relation to the 1973 coup against Chile's President Salvador Allende, in which the threat to US material interests was a key driver in US support for the Pinochet regime and the systematic campaign of state terrorism that followed the coup. The CIA had been planning such a coup as early as 1970, and cables following the coup indicate satisfaction at the highest levels of the US government.[24] In the following years, 2,279 people were killed or disappeared: 815 of whom were victims of execution or death by torture, 957 disappeared following arrest, and the remainder were killed as a result of war tribunals, during political protests, or in attempting to escape gun battles.[25] The coup also ushered in a period of intense economic restructuring, including the privatization of state assets, all supported with considerable financial and other aid from the US government.[26]

The Chilean case is indicative of US foreign policy priorities during the Cold War. US support for counterinsurgency campaigns was funded to confront the rise of left-wing movements and governments that would hinder unfettered access to resources and markets and would otherwise pose a challenge to US primacy. These counterinsurgency campaigns, initiated in the first instance in Vietnam, were extended to the Philippines and across Central and South America. They were executed by local military and paramilitary groups, with heavy backing from Washington in the form of security assistance, including hardware and military training.[27] The emphasis was on identifying indicators of insurgency and taking out insurgents in ways that would send a clear signal to other would-be insurgents, intimidating them into desisting. Operation Phoenix, a CIA-led program in Vietnam aimed at strengthening intelligence so that the Vietcong could be wiped out, provided a blueprint for subsequent counterinsurgency campaigns across Latin America—in Guatemala, El Salvador, Chile, Argentina, Uruguay, Paraguay, and Brazil. The Phoenix program resulted in widespread violations of human rights against tens of thousands of people, including torture, rape, and disappearances.[28] Subsequent campaigns of terror waged by US-backed regimes in Guatemala led to the disappearance of 20,000 between 1966 and 1976 alone, and many more thousands by the time the conflict finally ended in 1994.[29] In Argentina, the number was 10,000 disappearances just within the dictatorship's first three years.[30] Across Latin America, those targeted included politicians, trade unionists, clergy and nuns, human rights workers, students, and activists. Torture and disappearances were widespread and specifically intended to create fear among targeted populations. Indeed, as research by Amnesty International shows, whenever counterinsurgency campaigns of this sort are initiated, those targeted are initially limited to a few suspected insurgents, after which the regime always becomes much more indiscriminate, with individuals from numerous communities singled out to send a message to a much broader audience.[31]

These counterinsurgency methods also found their way into US efforts to deal with the terrorist threat posed by al-Qaeda and affiliated groups. Within days of the 9/11 terror attacks, President George W. Bush authorized the CIA director to establish a "terrorist detention and interrogation program." Within two months, Bush issued his Executive Order on the Detention, Treatment, and Trial of Certain Non-citizens in the War against Terrorism,[32] granting authority to the US Department of Defense to indefinitely detain any non-US nationals anywhere in the world, if they were considered a threat to US interests. A subsequent memo, sent to the president's senior staff in February 2002, declared that al-Qaeda and Taliban captives were "unlawful combatants" and did not therefore enjoy status as "prisoners of war" under the Geneva Conventions. He also denied their protections under Common Article 3 to protection under International Humanitarian Law.[33] The public justifications for these moves consisted of a rhetoric that dehumanized the targeted, referring to them as subhuman, evil, dangerous parasites, even though the incarcerations were devoid of any process for charge, prosecution, and trial in a public court.[34]

These moves laid the ground for the establishment of the military detention facilities in Afghanistan, Iraq, and Guantánamo Bay, Cuba, which saw the imprisonment of thousands of suspected insurgents, as well as a secret network of prisons, operating at numerous locations on four continents, in which 119 terror suspects were detained between 2001 and 2008 by or on behalf of the CIA.[35] The CIA's rendition, detention, and interrogation (RDI) program was facilitated by the transfer of prisoners on dozens of aircraft owned by private companies and hired by the CIA through a series of shell companies that provided the particular logistics necessary to kidnap and transfer each of the prisoners. The primary purpose of these secret detentions was to extract intelligence from prisoners by means of torture and to hold them incommunicado for months or years. By analyzing flight data relating to the dozens of aircraft involved in rendition operations, and triangulating these data with declassified documents, human rights investigations, and victim testimonies, the Rendition Project has mapped the contours of the CIA's rendition program,[36] and has shown the extent of the involvement of dozens of other collaborating states.[37] Britain played a key role and even orchestrated some of the rendition operations.[38] The publication of the 499-page executive summary of the Senate Select Committee on Intelligence's investigation of CIA torture provided excruciating evidence of the agency's use of torture, corroborating the evidence gathered by the Rendition Project. It also concludes that the torture was of little use in securing intelligence that had not already been obtained through legitimate means.[39] By contrast, US-led state terrorism through the RDI program certainly did achieve its secondary aim of terrorizing and dehumanizing the prisoners and of intimidating and terrifying those connected to them.

## CONCLUSION: THE COUNTERPRODUCTIVE EFFECTS OF STATE TERRORISM

The use of state terrorism is not purely a weapon of authoritarian regimes. It has played a significant role in the imperial and neo-imperial projects of powerful Western liberal states that have used and sponsored it in their efforts to subdue populations that might otherwise resist their ambitions. Yet it tends to be framed in policy, media, and even academic circles as counterterrorism, and thereby gains legitimacy, because its purpose is to deal with the apparently greater, more pernicious and ubiquitous threat of nonstate terrorism. The use of state terrorism, however, has significant and far-reaching consequences, many of which undermine the very purposes it is intended to serve. First, it tends to fuel the cycle of violence, resulting in mass atrocities. In each of the cases discussed above, it is clear that when states resorted to state terrorism to quell political opposition, its use quickly spiraled. Nowhere is this more evident than in the case of Guatemala, where, following the coup in 1954, the state fought a forty-year protracted civil conflict that resulted in hundreds of thousands of deaths and disappearances, widespread use of torture, and millions internally displaced. The Guatemalan Truth Commission concluded that every institution of the state was controlled by the military, rendering it incapable of implementing any kind of justice. With military intelligence units infiltrating every aspect of society, the militarization of the state was exacerbated. The police, too, were co-opted as a counterinsurgent force. Victims of the violence were criminalized. Social institutions were incapacitated.[40] Terror reigned, and with no effective independent judiciary, the conflict was further prolonged. The commission found that the United States' support for the regime further prolonged the conflict and played a role in the extent of the violence.

Second, the use and sponsorship of state terrorism undermines democracy and human rights, and in particular impairs the legitimacy of liberalizing projects that powerful liberal states have championed since the end of World War II. The use of torture and arbitrary detention against terror suspects in the US-led "War on Terror" clearly illustrates this point. In its findings on the CIA's RDI program, the Senate Select Committee on Intelligence concluded that the United States' use of torture and other human rights violations had eroded cooperation with the United States by other states through concerns over the legality and oversight of the CIA's activities. Furthermore, the program "caused immeasurable damage to the United States' public standing, as well as to the United States' longstanding global leadership on human rights in general and the prevention of torture in particular."[41] A further cost was the capacity it gave al-Qaeda and its affiliates to use US human rights violations as a propaganda tool in their recruitment of supporters. This reinforces the point that the relationship between terrorism and counterterrorism is a symbiotic one, and that ill-judged counterterrorism measures that result in terroristic violence and human rights abuses can do untold and lasting damage to any effort to effectively counter the threat from nonstate terrorism.

One way in which state terrorism has been challenged through the decades is by sustained scrutiny and activism by human rights organizations, litigators, and, sometimes, scholars. As I have argued elsewhere, critiques of the illicit use of state power are important for developing improved analysis and more informed publics.[42] The transnational human rights agenda has been and should continue to be a powerful force in challenging state terrorism and the abuse of state power. This endeavor involves identifying the contradictions between states' rhetoric on human rights and their coercive actions on the ground and bringing these contradictions to public attention. But efforts to contain and halt state terrorism ought to go far beyond analyzing the discourse surrounding it. They should involve collective political and social action to change state behavior by identifying those mechanisms and institutions that can best be deployed to this end, as well as identifying and supporting those agents best placed to take action. Engaging seriously with historically grounded analyses of state violence and terrorism, and of the social struggles that have most effectively challenged it, is an excellent starting point for changing how states respond to terrorism in ways that will both be effective and help advance the universalization of democracy and human rights.

## NOTES

1. A. Schmid and A. Jongman, *Political Terrorism: A New Guide to Actors, Authors, Concepts, Data Bases, Theories and Literature* (Amsterdam: North Holland, 1988), 219; T. Gurr, "Empirical Research on Political Terrorism: The State of the Art and How It Might Be Improved" in *Current Perspectives on Political Terrorism*, ed. R. Slater and M. Stohl (New York: St. Martin's Press, 1988), 2.

2. Thalif Deen, "U.N. Remains Divided over Domestic and State Terrorism," 1 July 2015, http://www.ipsnews.net/2015/07/u-n-remains-divided-over-domestic-and-state-terrorism/.

3. United Nations, "A/Res/49/60: Measures to Eliminate International Terrorism," 9 December 1994, http://www.un.org/documents/ga/res/49/a49r060.htm.

4. George W. Bush, "State of the Union Address," 21 September 2001, https://www.theguardian.com/world/2001/sep/21/september11.usa13.

5. George W. Bush, "State of the Union Address," 29 January 2002, http://stateoftheunionaddress.org/2002-george-w-bush.

6. Walter Laqueur, *No End to War: Terrorism in the Twenty-First Century* (New York: Continuum, 2003), 237.

7. Walter Laqueur, "Reflections on Terrorism," *Foreign Affairs* 65 (1986): 89.

8. Laqueur, *No End to War*, 140.

9. Bruce Hoffman, *Inside Terrorism* (New York: Columbia University Press, 1998), 34.

10. Ibid.

11. Michael Stohl, "The State as Terrorist: Insights and Implications," *Democracy and Security* 2 (2006): 4–5.

12. Noam Chomsky and Edward Herman, *The Political Economy of Human Rights*, Vol. 1: *The Washington Connection and Third World Fascism* (Boston: South End Press, 1979); Chomsky and Herman, *The Political Economy of Human Rights*, Vol 2: *After the Cataclysm: Postwar Indochina and the Reconstruction of Imperial Ideology* (Nottingham, UK: Spokesman, 1979); Edward Herman, *The Real Terror Network*, 2nd ed. (Montreal: Black Rose Books, 1985); Michael Stohl and George Lopez, eds., *The State as Terrorist: The Dynamics of Governmental Violence and Repression* (Westport, CT: Greenwood Press, 1984); Stohl and George A. Lopez, *Terrible beyond Endurance? The Foreign Policy of State Terrorism* (New York: Greenwood Press, 1988); Christopher Mitchell et al., "State Terrorism: Issues of

Concept and Measurement," in *Government Violence and Repression: An Agenda for Research,* ed. Michael Stohl and George Lopez (New York: Greenwood Press, 1986); Ruth Blakeley, *State Terrorism and Neoliberalism: The North in the South,* Routledge Critical Terrorism Studies (London: Routledge, 2009); Sam Raphael, "In the Service of Power: Terrorism Studies and US Intervention in the Global South," in *Critical Terrorism Studies: A New Research Agenda,* ed. Richard Jackson, Marie Breen Smyth, and Jeroen Gunning, Routledge Critical Terrorism Studies (Abingdon, UK: Routledge, 2009); "Paramilitarism and State Terror in Colombia," in *Contemporary State Terrorism: Theory and Cases,* ed. Eamon Murphy, Scott Poynting, and Richard Jackson (London: Routledge, 2009); Alexander George, *Western State Terrorism* (Cambridge: Polity Press, 1991).

13. Lee Jarvis and Michael Lister, "State Terrorism Research and Critical Terrorism Studies: An Assessment," *Critical Studies on Terrorism* 7, no. 1 (2014); Eric Herring and Doug Stokes, "Critical Realism and Historical Materialism as Resources for Critical Terrorism Studies," *Critical Studies on Terrorism* 4, no. 1 (2011); Anthony McKeown, "The Structural Production of State Terrorism: Capitalism, Imperialism, and International Class Dynamics," *Critical Studies on Terrorism* 4, no. 1 (2011); Blakeley, *State Terrorism and Neoliberalism.*

14. Stohl, "The State as Terrorist," 10.

15. Leslie Bethell, *The Cambridge History of Latin America,* Vol. 2 (Cambridge: Cambridge University Press, 1984), 8–43; Caroline Elkins, *Britain's Gulag: The Brutal End of Empire in Kenya* (London: Jonathan Cape, 2005); John Gallagher and Ronald Robinson, "The Imperialism of Free Trade," *Economic History Review* 6, no. 1 (1953); David Killingray, "The Maintenance of Law and Order in British Colonial Africa," *African Affairs* 85, no. 340 (1986); Killingray, *A Plague of Europeans: Westerners in Africa since the Fifteenth Century* (London: Penguin, 1973); Jean Suret-Canale, *French Colonialism in Tropical Africa, 1900–1945,* trans. Till Gottheiner (1964; reprinted, London: C. Hurst, 1971); M.P.K. Sorenson, *Origins of European Settlement in Kenya* (Nairobi, Kenya: Oxford University Press, 1968).

16. Bethell, *Cambridge History of Latin America,* 2:8–10.

17. Barbara Bush and Josephine Maltby, "Taxation in West Africa: Transforming the Colonial Subject into the 'Governable Person,'" *Critical Perspectives on Accounting* 15 (2004).

18. Jonathan Glancey, "Our Last Occupation: Gas, Chemicals, Bombs; Britain Has Used Them All before in Iraq," *The Guardian,* no. 19 (April 2003), http://www.guardian.co.uk/world/2003/apr/19/iraq.arts.

19. Elkins, *Britain's Gulag,* 33–74, 327–28.

20. Pierre Vidal-Naquet, *Torture: Cancer of Democracy* (Middlesex, UK: Penguin Books, 1963), 40–44.

21. Ian Beckett, *Modern Insurgencies and Counter-insurgencies: Guerrillas and Their Opponents since 1750* (London: Routledge, 2001), 165.

22. Neil MacMaster, "Torture: From Algiers to Abu Ghraib," *Race and Class* 46, no. 2 (2004): 167–68.

23. For a detailed account, see Blakeley, *State Terrorism and Neoliberalism.*

24. US Central Intelligence Agency, "Report on CIA and Chilean Task Force Activities, 15 September to 3 November 1970," declassified document obtained by the National Security Archive, George Washington University, Washington, DC, NSA Electronic Briefing Book 8, 18 November 1970, http://www.gwu.edu/~nsarchiv/NSAEBB/NSAEBB8/ch01–01.htm; Patrick Ryan, "Navy Section, United States Military Group, Chile, Situation Report Number 2," declassified document obtained by the National Security Archive, George Washington University,

Washington, DC, NSA Electronic Briefing Book 8, 1 October 1973, http://www.gwu.edu/~nsarchiv/NSAEBB/NSAEBB8/ch21–01.htm.

25. CNCTR, "Report of the Chilean National Commission on Truth and Reconciliation," (1991), United States Institute of Peace, http://www.usip.org/files/resources/collections/truth_commissions/Chile90-Report/Chile90-Report.pdf (accessed February 19, 2017).

26. William Robinson, *Promoting Polyarchy: Globalisation, US Intervention, and Hegemony* (Cambridge: Cambridge University Press, 1996), 165–66.

27. Ruth Blakeley, "Still Training to Torture? US Training of Military Forces from Latin America," *Third World Quarterly* 27, no. 8 (2006); Dana Priest, "Army Instructed Latins on Executions, Torture Manuals Used 1982–1991, Pentagon Reveals," *Washington Post*, September 21, 1996.

28. Douglas Valentine, *The Phoenix Program*, 2nd ed. (Lincoln, NE: Authors Guild BackinPrint.Com, 2000), 85.

29. Christian Tomuschat, Otilia Lux-de-Cotí, and Alfredo Balsells-Tojo, "Guatemala: Memory of Silence; Report of the Commission for Historical Clarification," 26 February 1999, https://www.aaas.org/sites/default/files/migrate/uploads/mos_en.pdf.

30. US Embassy Argentina, "Airgram from US Embassy in Argentina to the US Department of State: Human Rights Case Reports," declassified document obtained by the National Security Archive, George Washington University, Washington DC, Document 8 of NSA Electronic Briefing Book 73, Part One, 19 June 1979), http://nsarchive.gwu.edu/NSAEBB/NSAEBB73/790619d0s1.pdf.

31. Amnesty International, "Torture and Ill-Treatment: The Arguments" (2006).

32. George W. Bush, "Executive Order: Detention, Treatment, and Trial of Certain Non-Citizens in the War against Terrorism," The White House, Washington, DC, *Federal Register*, vol. 66, no. 222 (2001).

33. The White House, "Memorandum for the Vice President, the Secretary of State, the Secretary of Defense, the Attorney General, Chief of Staff to the President, Director of Central Intelligence, Assistant to the President for National Security Affairs, and Chairman of the Joint Chiefs of Staff. Subject: Humane Treatment of Al Qaeda and Taliban Detainees," 7 February 2002, http://nsarchive.gwu.edu/NSAEBB/NSAEBB127/02.02.07.pdf.

34. Richard Jackson, "Constructing Enemies: 'Islamic Terrorism' in Political and Academic Discourse," *Government and Opposition* 42, no. 3 (2007); Richard Devetak, "The Gothic Sense of International Relations: Ghosts, Monsters, Terror, and the Sublime after September 11," *Review of International Studies* 31, no. 4 (2005).

35. Senate Select Committee on Intelligence, "Committee Study of the Central Intelligence Agency's Detention and Interrogation Program: Declassified Executive Summary" (2014).

36. See the Rendition Project's website, www.therenditionproject.org.uk.

37. Sam Raphael et al., "Tracking Rendition Aircraft as a Way to Understand CIA Secret Detention and Torture in Europe," *International Journal of Human Rights* 20, no. 1 (2015).

38. Ruth Blakeley and Sam Raphael, "British Torture in the War on Terror," *European Journal of International Relations* (2016), http://ejt.sagepub.com/content/early/2016/05/26/1354066116653455.full.pdf.

39. Senate Select Committee on Intelligence, "Committee Study of the Central Intelligence Agency's Detention and Interrogation Program."

40. Tomuschat, Lux-de-Cotí, and Balsells-Tojo, "Guatemala," 24–27.

41. Senate Select Committee on Intelligence, "Committee Study of the Central Intelligence Agency's Detention and Interrogation Program," 15–16.

42. Ruth Blakeley, "Human Rights, State Wrongs, and Social Change: The Theory and Practice of Emancipation," *Review of International Studies* 39, no. 3 (2013).

# 5. Killing before an Audience

*Terrorism as Performance Violence*

Mark Juergensmeyer

Are "lone-wolf" terrorists really lone wolves? Some of the most striking terrorist attacks in recent years have been perpetrated by one or two individuals who do not appear, at first glance, to be part of an organized group. Yet, as I explain in this chapter, in each case there is an audience in mind and a larger network of imagined supporters whom the act is meant to impress. Even lone-wolf terrorist acts, I contend, are examples of public violence.

Let us take the case of the horrific massacre at an Orlando gay nightclub that killed fifty innocent people enjoying a night out on the town during the wee hours of June 12, 2016. "ISIS inspired" is one way of describing it. And yet it seems to me that this is a complicated case. It may have been one where the action was not so much inspired by ISIS but *branded* as ISIS related, both by the killer and by the ISIS press agency, both of which had reasons to want to have this act perceived by the wider public as an ideological act, whether or not it was primarily inspired by the ideology.[1]

Branding an event is a way of speaking to a particular audience and framing the event as a public statement. The term *inspired* implies a more personal act, an allegiance to the ideology of a movement such as the Islamic State in Iraq and Syria (also known as the Islamic State in Iraq and the Levant, or ISIL) regardless of the event's impact on the wider audience. It also implies that the primary intention of undertaking an act of terrorism is to carry out the broad directive of the movement—in this case, attacking unbelievers and enemies of the ISIS cause. Earlier in 2016 an ISIS spokesman, Abu Mohammad al-Adnani, had urged followers around the world to make the month of Ramadan that year "a month of calamity everywhere." Individuals were told that they did not need to check with ISIS headquarters in Raqqa but should attack unbelievers in the name of ISIS wherever they were. In other words, he wanted these acts to be not only inspired by ISIS but also branded with the ISIS name.

The perpetrator of the Orlando attack, Omar Mateen, did exactly this: he declared his allegiance to the head of ISIS, Abu Bakr al-Baghdadi, by telephone to 911 emergency operators minutes into his rampage. He was said to have been surfing ISIS sites online in the weeks before the attack. And the ISIS news agency quickly proclaimed him a "fighter for ISIS."

That sounds as if his act was ISIS inspired as well as ISIS branded. But there is evidence that he harbored motives that were more personal than ideological, and that he was pursuing a homophobic cause. His ex-wife thought he was violent and mentally unstable, and his father said his motives had nothing to do with religion—he had seen two men kissing in Miami and went into a rage. Some members of the gay community in Orlando claimed that he had frequented the bar before—and may even have dated some men online through a gay dating service—indicating that the violence may have been an act of self-hatred as much as homophobia directed toward others.

Moreover, his ideological affiliation seemed to be confused. In the same statement in which Mateen allegedly swore his allegiance to ISIS, he also praised the Tsarnaev brothers for their attack on the Boston Marathon; yet they were not ISIS fighters, but supporters of Chechen separatism. Mateen in the past had also praised the al-Nusra movement in Syria and Hezbollah in Lebanon, both of which are in competition with ISIS and have fought against it. So his allegiance seems to be somewhat thin—not so much to a particular organization but to Islamic radicalism in general. Yet he chose to brand his event as an ISIS act and to broadcast that connection to the wider world.

The attack on the Boston Marathon is an interesting parallel to the Orlando massacre. On April 15, 2013, during the final moments of the Boston Marathon, two backpacks were casually placed along the curbside near the finish line. When they were ignited in a pair of horrific blasts, three innocent bystanders were killed and 264 others were injured. In the days that followed, surveillance camera photographs identified the culprits, who turned out not to be agents of some foreign terrorist force, but two local young athletes: twenty-six-year-old Tamerlan Tsarnaev and his nineteen-year-old brother, Dzhokhar. As in the case of Mateen, the motives of the Tsarnaev brothers seemed confused. Were they on a rampage because of personal problems and a sense of being socially marginalized, or were they in fact true believers in the Chechen separatist cause? They wanted the world to see this as the latter and to brand their action as ideological.

The Orlando and Boston cases appear similar to many of the other lone-wolf terrorist attacks in the United States in recent years. Before Boston, there was the August 2012 attack on the Milwaukee Sikh Gurdwara by Wade Michael Page, and before that, the July 2011 Oslo bombings and youth camp massacre by Anders Breivik, the 2010 Times Square bombing attempt by Faisal Shahzad, the 1996 Atlanta Olympic park bombing by Eric Robert Rudolph, and most spectacular of all, the 1995 Oklahoma City federal building bombing carried out by Timothy McVeigh.

Some of these were committed by Christians and others by Muslims, but in almost all cases, lonely, alienated individuals raged against a society that they thought had abandoned them, and they then branded their actions in ideological terms. These lone-wolf events are different from other instances in recent years, in which organized radical religious groups such as the Christian Militia or Muslim *jihadi* organizations have plotted attacks and recruited participants to be involved in them. In the lone-wolf cases, religious ideas, when they appeared at all, seemed more of an excuse than a reason for the violence. Yet in each of these cases the perpetrators had a larger audience in mind and an imagined community of supporters to encourage them. The ideological branding linked their actions to these larger imagined audiences.

For such people as the Tsarnaev brothers, Mateen, Breivik, and the many other soldiers of fortune undertaking lone-wolf terrorist attacks, the idea of warfare is exciting, and the imagined wars of great religious conflict are more than exhilarating. They offer the promise of opportunity, the hope of victory and triumph, and an ennobling role as a soldier within that cosmic war. Perhaps most directly, such imagined wars provide a justification for violence, including revenge against the society that they think has shunned them. The ideological branding offers legitimation for undertaking the most vicious of acts and a moral rationale for vengeance.

Hence the defense of religion provides a cover for violence. It gives moral license to commit something horrible that the perpetrators have longed to do, to show the world how powerful they really can be, and to demonstrate their importance in one terminal moment of violent glory. Religion doesn't cause violence, but branding it that way often provides the legitimation for it.

Prior to Orlando, the two most devastating acts of terrorism perpetrated by lone-wolf killers in recent years were both branded with ideologies related to religion—in both cases, to the defense of an imagined Christian civilization that was under attack by forces of secularism and what the actors regarded as alien religion. These were the 1995 bombing of the

Oklahoma City federal building by Timothy McVeigh and the 2011 attack on the youth camp near Oslo by Anders Breivik. The similarities between Norway's mass killer Anders Breivik and Oklahoma City bomber Timothy McVeigh are striking. Both were good-looking young Caucasians and self-imagined soldiers in a cosmic war to save Christendom. Both thought their acts of mass destruction would trigger a great battle to rescue society from liberal forces of multiculturalism that allowed non-Christians and non-whites positions of acceptability. Both regretted the loss of life but thought their actions were "necessary." For that they were staunchly unapologetic. Their similarities even extend to the kind of explosive used in their actions. Both used a mixture of fuel oil and ammonium nitrate fertilizer, which Breivik said he needed for his farm operations. The farm, it turned out, was rented largely because it was a convenient place to test his car bombs.

And then there is the matter of dates. McVeigh was fixed on the day of April 19, the anniversary of the Waco siege. Breivik chose July 22, the day in 1099 that the Kingdom of Jerusalem was established during the First Crusades. The title of Breivik's manifesto, which he posted on the day of his attacks, is "2083." This is the date that Breivik suggested would be the culmination of a seventy-year war that was to have begun with his actions. Yet seventy years from 2011 would be 2081—why did he date the final purge of Muslims from Norway to be two years later, in 2083? I found the answer on page 242 of Breivik's manifesto, where he explains that in 1683 at the Battle of Vienna, the Ottoman Empire's army was defeated in a protracted struggle, thereby insuring that most of Europe would not become part of the Muslim empire. The date in Breivik's title is the four hundredth anniversary of that decisive battle, and in Breivik's mind he was re-creating the historic efforts to save Europe from what he imagined to be the evils of Islam. The threat of Islam is a dominant motif of his fifteen-hundred-page manifesto, "2083: A European Declaration of Independence."[2]

The writing of a manifesto is a major difference between Breivik and McVeigh, who was not a writer; instead McVeigh copied and quoted from his favorite book, the novel *The Turner Diaries,* written by neo-Nazi William Pierce under the pseudonym Andrew Macdonald.[3] But the novel McVeigh loved explains his motives in a matter eerily similar to the writings of Breivik in "2083": McVeigh thought that liberal politicians had given in to the forces of globalization and multiculturalism and that the "mudpeople" who were nonwhite, non-Christian, non-heterosexual, non-patriarchal males were trying to take over the country. To save the country for Christendom, the righteous white, straight, nonfeminist Christian males had to be shocked into reality by the force of an explosion that would signal to them that the war had begun. These were McVeigh's ideas from *The Turner Diaries,* but they were also Breivik's.

"The time for dialogue is over," Breivik writes on page 811 of his manifesto. "The time for armed resistance has come." The enemy in Breivik's imagined war consisted of "the cultural Marxist/multiculturalist elites" whom he regarded as the "Nazis of our time," intent on "leading us [i.e., white Europeans] to the cultural slaughterhouse by selling us into Muslim slavery." Breivik says, threateningly, to the "multiculturalist elites" that "we know who you are, where you live and we are coming for you."

Perhaps the most interesting section of Breivik's manifesto is the chronology, day by day, of the weeks preceding his bombing and massacre on July 22. He ends the chronology with this matter-of-fact statement: "I believe this will be my last entry. It is now Fri July 22nd, 12.51." Moments later he emailed the fifteen-hundred-page book to more than a thousand addresses on his email contact list. Then, ninety minutes later, he drove to downtown Oslo to detonate the bomb that killed seven and shattered major buildings housing offices of the ruling political party. Within an hour afterward he donned his policeman's uniform to gain entrance to the liberal party's youth camp, where he coldly murdered more than eighty of the young people in a rampage that lasted over an hour.

Like McVeigh, he thought that this horrible dramatic action would bring a hidden war into the open. Like many modern terrorists, his violent act was a form of performance violence, a symbolic attempt at empowerment to show the world that for the moment he was in charge. The terrorist act was a wake-up call, and a signal that the war had begun. Behind the earthly conflict was a cosmic war, a battle for Christendom. As the title of Breivik's manifesto indicates, he thought he was re-creating that historical moment when Christianity was defended against the hordes and Islam was purged from what he imagined as the purity of European society.

Was this a religious vision, or was religion simply used to justify and give a more legitimate branding to Breivik's racist ideology? It is true that Breivik—and McVeigh, for that matter—were much more concerned about politics and history than about scripture and religious belief. And much the same can be said about Osama bin Laden, Ayman al-Zawahiri, and many other Islamist activists. Bin Laden was a businessman and engineer, and al-Zawahiri a medical doctor; neither were theologians or clergy. Their writings show that they were much more interested in Islamic history than theology or scripture, and imagined themselves as re-creating glorious moments in Islamic history in their own imagined wars. Tellingly, Breivik writes of al-Qaeda with admiration, as if he would love to have created a

Christian version of their religious cadre. If bin Laden is a Muslim terrorist, Breivik and McVeigh are surely Christian ones, though none is strictly interested in the theological aspects of religion. Breivik was fascinated with the Crusades and imagined himself to be a member of the Knights Templar, the crusader army of a thousand years ago. But in an imagined cosmic warfare, time is suspended and history is transcended as the activists imagine themselves to be acting out timeless roles in a sacred drama. The tragedy is that these religious fantasies are played out in real time, with real and cruel consequences.

## PERFORMANCE VIOLENCE

How do we make sense of such theatrical forms of violence? What were the perpetrators trying to accomplish? These are questions that I have pondered in my book *Terror in the Mind of God*, from which many of the following insights have been taken.[4] The traditional way of answering these questions is to view dramatic violence as part of a strategic plan. This viewpoint assumes that terrorism is always part of a political strategy—and, in fact, some social scientists have defined terrorism in just this way: "the use of covert violence by a group for political ends."[5] In some cases this definition is indeed appropriate, for an act of violence can fulfill political ends and have a direct impact on public policy.

Yet the situation is more complicated than that traditional view admits. Many acts of terrorism do not seem to have a direct political result. When I asked the political leader of Hamas, Dr. Abdul Aziz Rantisi, about his group's political motives, he said that their attacks were not aimed at Israeli internal politics.[6] Similarly, the 9/11 attacks on the World Trade Center provided no immediate political benefits to those who caused them. When I interviewed a jihadi activist convicted for his part in the 1993 World Trade Center bombing, he told me that assaults on public buildings did have a kind of strategic value in that they helped to "identify the government as enemy." But the political and economic ends for which these acts were committed were distant indeed.[7]

Political scientist Martha Crenshaw has shown that the notion of "strategic" thinking can be construed in a broad sense to cover not just immediate political achievements but also the internal logic that propels a group into perpetrating terrorist acts.[8] My investigations indicate that Crenshaw is right—acts of terrorism are usually the products of an internal logic and not of random or crazy thinking—but I hesitate to use the term *strategy* for all rationales for terrorist actions. *Strategy* implies a degree of calculation and an expectation of accomplishing a clear objective that do not jibe with such dramatic displays of power as the destruction of the World Trade Center towers. These creations of terror are done not to achieve a strategic goal but to make a symbolic statement. By calling acts of religious terrorism "symbolic," I mean that they are intended to illustrate or refer to something beyond their immediate target: a grander conquest, for instance, or a struggle more awesome than meets the eye. The point of the 9/11 attack was to produce a graphic and easily understandable object lesson, a grand event intended to impress for its symbolic significance. As such, terrorist acts such as these can be analyzed as one would any other symbol, ritual, or sacred drama.

I can imagine a continuum with "strategic" on the one side and "symbolic" on the other, with various acts of terrorism located in between. When Boko Haram took hostages in attempts to leverage power in order to win the release of members of its movement held prisoner, these acts might be placed closer to the political, strategic side. The choreographed videos of ISIS beheadings might be closer to the symbolic theatrical side. Each was the product of logical thought, and each had an internal rationale. In cases such as the ISIS killings that were more symbolic than strategic, however, the logic was not focused on an immediate political acquisition, but aimed at a larger goal, the projection of an image of terrifying strength.

The very adjectives used to describe acts of religious terrorism—*symbolic, dramatic, theatrical*—suggest that we look at them not as tactics but as performance violence. The spectacular assaults of the Orlando massacre and the multiple ISIS attacks in Paris were not only tragic acts of violence; they were also spectacular theater. In speaking of terrorism as "performance," however, I am not suggesting that such acts are undertaken lightly or capriciously. Rather, like religious ritual or street theater, they are dramas designed to have an impact on the several audiences that they affect. Those who witness the violence—even at a distance, via the news media— are therefore a part of what occurs. Moreover, like other forms of public ritual, the symbolic significance of such events is multifaceted: they mean different things to different observers. This suggests that it is possible to analyze comparatively the performance of acts of religious terrorism.

In addition to referring to drama, the term *performance* also implies the notion of "performative"—as in the concept of "performative acts." This is an idea developed by language philosophers regarding certain kinds of speech that are able to perform social functions: their very utterance has a transformative impact.[9] Like vows recited during marriage rites, certain words not only represent reality but also shape it: they contain a certain power of their own. The same is true of some nonverbal symbolic actions, such as the gunshot that begins a race, the raising of a white flag to show defeat, or acts of terrorism. Terrorist acts, then, can be both performance events, in that they make a symbolic statement, and performative acts, insofar as they try to change things. When Omar Mateen entered the nightclub in Orlando, he was undoubtedly aware that he was about to create an enormous spectacle. He probably also hoped that his actions would make a difference—if not in a direct, strategic sense, then in an indirect way as a dramatic show so powerful as to change people's perceptions of him and of the world.

But the fact that Mateen hoped that his act would make such a statement does not mean that it in fact did. Public symbols mean different things to different people, and a symbolic performance may not achieve its intended effect. The way the act is perceived—by both the perpetrators and those affected by it—makes all the difference. In fact, the same is true of performative speech. A leading language philosopher, J.L. Austin, has qualified the notion that some speech acts are performative by observing that the power of the act is related to the perception of it. Children, for example, playing at marriage are not wedded by merely reciting the vows and going through the motions, nor is a ship christened by just anyone who gives it a name. The French sociologist Pierre Bourdieu, carrying further the idea that statements are given credibility by their social context, has insisted that the power of performative speech—vows and christenings—is rooted in social reality and is given currency by the laws and social customs that stand behind it.[10] Similarly, an act of terrorism usually implies an underlying power and legitimizing ideology. But whether the power and legitimacy implicit in acts of terrorism are like playacted marriage vows or are the real thing depends in part on how the acts are perceived. It depends, in part, on whether their significance is believed.

This brings us back to the realm of faith. Public ritual has traditionally been the province of religion, and this is one of the reasons that performance violence comes so naturally to activists from a religious background. In a collection of essays on the connection between religion and terrorism published some years ago, one of the editors, David C. Rapoport, observed— accurately, I think—that the two topics fit together not only because there is a violent streak in the history of religion but also because terrorist acts have a symbolic side and in that sense mimic religious rites. The victims of terrorism are targeted not because they are threatening to the perpetrators, Rapoport wrote, but because they are "symbols, tools, animals or corrupt beings" that tie into "a special picture of the world, a specific consciousness" that the activist possesses.[11] The street theater aspect of performance violence forces those who witness it directly or indirectly into that "consciousness"—that alternative view of the world. This gives the perpetrators of terrorism a kind of celebrity status and their actions an illusion of importance. When we who observe their acts take them seriously—are disgusted and repelled by them, and begin to distrust the peacefulness of the world around us—the purposes of this theater are achieved.

## KILLING FOR AN AUDIENCE

As the novelist Don DeLillo once wrote, terrorism is "the language of being noticed."[12] Without being noticed, in fact, terrorism would not exist. The sheer act of killing does not create a terrorist act; what makes an act terrorism is that someone is terrified by it. The acts to which we assign that label are deliberate events, bombings and attacks performed at such places and times that they are calculated to be observed. Terrorism without its horrified witnesses would be as pointless as a play without an audience, and for many who have been involved in plotting terrorist attacks, the ability to seize the attention of the public through the news media is precisely the point.

In a collection of essays on contemporary culture, Jean Baudrillard described the terrorism of the late twentieth century as "a peculiarly modern form" because of the impact that it has had on public consciousness through electronic media. According to Baudrillard, terrorist acts have emerged "less from passion than from the screen: a violence in the nature of the image."[13] Baudrillard went so far as to advise his readers "not to be in a public place where television is operating, considering the high probability that its very presence will precipitate a violent event." His advice was hyperbolic, of course, but it does point to the reality that terrorist events are aimed at attracting news media exposure and perhaps would not happen so frequently, or in the same way, if the enormous resources of the news media were not readily at hand to promote them. The worldwide media coverage of the attacks on the nightclub in Orlando, the World Trade Center, the US embassies in Africa, and the Oklahoma City federal building illustrates a new development in terrorism: the extraordinary widening of terror's audience. Throughout most of history the audiences for acts of terrorism have been limited largely to government officials and their supporters, or members of rival groups. What makes the terrorism of recent years significant is the breadth of its audience, a scope that is in many cases virtually global.

When television does not adequately report the ideas and motivations behind their actions, many activist groups have found the Internet, Facebook, and Twitter to be effective alternatives. Movements such as Hamas and Aryan Nations have well-established websites. Other groups, including ISIS and Christian militias, protect their sites with passwords that allow only their members to gain access, change their Twitter accounts frequently to keep them from being closed down, or disseminate their information on the "dark web" such as TOR, The Onion Router, rather than the World Wide Web. Thus, even when the audience is selective, the message is projected through a public medium. In some cases an act of violence sends two messages at the same time: a broad message aimed at the general public and a specific communication targeted at a narrower audience. In the case of the ISIS attacks in Paris, for instance, one of the purposes of the assaults was to prove to movement members that the leadership was still strong enough to engender the life-and-death dedication of their commandos. In other cases, the point was to intimidate followers of the movement and to force them to follow a hard-line position rather than a conciliatory one. In the case of Anders Breivik, his manifesto was aimed at an imagined community of supporters who shared his vision of violently defending Christendom against the forces of multiculturalism.

Motives such as these help to explain one of the most puzzling forms of contemporary violence: silent terror. These intriguing acts of terrorism are ones in which the audience is not immediately apparent. The public is often mystified by an explosion accompanied only by an eerie silence, with no group claiming responsibility or explaining the purpose of its act. Even in the cases in which the accused have been brought to trial and convicted, the guilty have still denied their complicity. Mahmud Abouhalima, even after being convicted of participation in the World Trade Center bombing, told me that he was "nowhere near" the building at the time of the blast and that he had no relationship with Sheik Omar Abdul Rahman, the spiritual leader of the group convicted of the terrorist act.[14] Assuming for the moment that the government case against him was strong and that he was in fact involved in the crime for which he was convicted, why would he or any other activist involved in a violent incident deny it?

In a world in which information is a form of power, public demonstrations of violence have conveyed potent messages indeed. When groups are able to demonstrate their capacity for destruction simultaneously in different parts of the world, as in the case of the US embassy bombings in 1998, this is a display even more impressive than single-target events. It is no less so if the only audiences that know who did it, that can appreciate the perpetrators' accomplishments, and that can admire their command over life and death are within the group itself. The act demonstrates their ability to perform a powerful event with virtually global impact. Since terrorism is theater, the catastrophes at the World Trade Center, the Oklahoma City federal building, and the US embassies in Africa broadcast that message to the world. From the point of view of the perpetrators, this was enough; the message was successfully sent, and they did not need to brag about their ability to convey it.

The forms of religious terrorism that emerged in the last decade of the twentieth century were global in at least two senses. Both the choices of their targets and the character of their conspiratorial networks were often transnational. The very name of the World Trade Center indicates its role in transnational global commerce, and citizens of eighty-six different countries were among its victims. The members of the al-Qaeda network of perpetrators of these and other attacks were multinational, as were the ISIS attackers in Paris, Brussels, Istanbul, and Bangladesh. These incidents were also global in their impact, in large part because of the worldwide, instantaneous coverage by transnational news media.

Increasingly, terrorism has been performed for Internet and television audiences around the world. This means that a single individual—a "lone-wolf" terrorist—can make as much of a public spectacle as an organized cadre. Thus Omar Mateen, Anders Breivik, Timothy McVeigh, and the Tsarnaev brothers were able to have an impact on public life that few organized movements have been able to achieve. Yet their actions were intended for a hidden audience of their imagined admirers as much as they were for the supporters of the status quo. In this peculiar way, therefore, lone acts of terrorism have been collective events, events that have drawn people together by the power of performance.

This global dimension of terrorism's audience, and the transnational responses to it, gives special significance to the understanding of terrorism as a public performance of violence—as a social event with both real and symbolic aspects. As Bourdieu has observed, our public life is shaped as much by symbols as by institutions. For this reason, symbolic acts—the "rites of institution"—help to demarcate public space and indicate what is meaningful in the social world.[15] In a striking imitation of such rites, terrorism has provided its own dramatic events—whether by organized movements or by lone individuals who imagine themselves as part of a larger group. These rites of violence have brought an alternative view of public reality—not just a single society in transition, but a world challenged by global war and strident visions of transforming change.

## NOTES

Research support for this project has come from the Resolving Jihadist Conflicts Project of the Department of Peace and Conflict Resolution Research at Uppsala University in Sweden.

1. I explore the distinction between "inspired" and "branded" in my essay "ISIS Inspired—or Branded?" posted in *Huffington Post*, June 20, 2016.

2. Anders Behring Breivik, "2083: A European Declaration of Independence," posted online by Public Intelligence, July 28, 2011, https://publicintelligence.net/anders-behring-breiviks-complete-manifesto-2083-a-european-declaration-of-independence/.

3. Andrew Macdonald, *The Turner Diaries* (Hillsboro, WV: National Vanguard Books, 1978).

4. Mark Juergensmeyer, *Terror in the Mind of God* (Berkeley: University of California Press, 2003).

5. Walter Laqueur, *The Age of Terrorism* (Boston: Little, Brown, 1987), 73.

6. Abdul Aziz Rantisi, interview with the author, Khan Yunis, Gaza, March 1, 1998.

7. Mahmud Abouhalima, interview with the author, Lompoc Federal Penitentiary, September 30, 1997.

8. Martha Crenshaw, "The Logic of Terrorism: Terrorist Behavior as Strategic Choice," in Walter Reich, ed., *Origins of Terrorism: Psychologies, Ideologies, Theologies, States of Mind* (Washington, DC: Woodrow Wilson International Center for Scholars; Cambridge: Cambridge University Press, 1990).

9. J.L. Austin, *How to Do Things with Words* (Oxford: Clarendon Press, 1962).

10. Pierre Bourdieu, *Language and Symbolic Power* (Cambridge, MA: Harvard University Press, 1991), 117.

11. David Rapoport, "Introduction" to David Rapoport and Yonah Alexander, eds., *The Morality of Terrorism* (New York: Pergamon Press, 1982), xiii.

12. Don DeLillo, *Mao II* (New York: Penguin, 1991), 157.

13. Jean Baudrillard, *The Transparency of Evil* (London: Verso, 1993), 75.

14. Abouhalima, interview with the author.

15. Bourdieu, *Language and Symbolic Power*, 117.

# 6. Constructing Terrorism

## From Fear and Coercion to Anger and Jujitsu Politics

Clark McCauley

In this chapter I begin by reviewing common definitions of terrorism to show the popularity of assuming that terrorists intend to coerce governments and their citizens through fear. Then I draw out some of the costs of this assumption for both analysts of terrorism and practitioners of counterterrorism. In particular I argue that the predominant reaction to terrorism is not fear but anger, and that terrorists aim to elicit anger and overreaction in order to gain support for their cause, a strategy Sophia Moskalenko and I have called *jujitsu politics*.

## DEFINING TERRORISM AS INTENT TO COERCE BY FEAR

It is no secret that there has been grave difficulty in finding agreement on a definition of terrorism. It is perhaps more surprising to note the degree to which Western definitions share the idea that terrorists aim to create fear in order to coerce a government or its citizens. In other words, terrorists are those who aim to terrorize. Some salient definitions of terrorism are represented in this section to show the popularity of defining terrorism by intent; the relevant part of each definition is represented in bold.

### Proposed United Nations Comprehensive Convention on International Terrorism

1. Any person commits an offence within the meaning of this Convention if that person, by any means, unlawfully and intentionally, causes:

   (a) Death or serious bodily injury to any person; or

   (b) Serious damage to public or private property, including a place of public use, a State or government facility, a public transportation system, an infrastructure facility or the environment; or

(c) Damage to property, places, facilities, or systems referred to in paragraph 1 (b) of this article, resulting or likely to result in major economic loss, **when the purpose of the conduct, by its nature or context, is to intimidate a population, or to compel a Government or an international organization to do or abstain from doing any act.**[1]

Because of disagreement about whether this definition would apply to government forces and government leaders, this definition has been under discussion at the United Nations since 2002.[2]

## United Kingdom

The United Kingdom's Terrorism Act 2000 defined terrorism as follows:

"(1) In this Act "terrorism" means the use or threat of action where:

(a) the action falls within subsection (2),

(b) **the use or threat is designed to influence the government or to intimidate the public or a section of the public** and

(c) the use or threat is made for the purpose of advancing a political, religious or ideological cause.

(2) Action falls within this subsection if it:

(a) involves serious violence against a person,

(b) involves serious damage to property,

(c) endangers a person's life, other than that of the person committing the action,

(d) creates a serious risk to the health or safety of the public or a section of the public or

(e) is designed seriously to interfere with or seriously to disrupt an electronic system."[3]

## US Definitions

Title 22 of the US Code of Federal Regulations, Section 2656f(d), defines terrorism as "premeditated, politically motivated violence perpetrated against noncombatant targets by subnational groups or clandestine agents, usually intended to influence an audience."[4] The US State Department uses this definition for its yearly reports on terrorist activity, and the CIA likewise uses this definition.

The US Federal Bureau of Investigation (FBI) defines terrorism as "**the unlawful use of force or violence against persons or property to**

**intimidate or coerce a government, the civilian population, or any segment thereof,** in furtherance of political or social objectives."[5]

The US Department of Defense defines terrorism as **"the unlawful use of violence or threat of violence to instill fear and coerce governments or societies.** Terrorism is often motivated by religious, political, or other ideological beliefs and committed in the pursuit of goals that are usually political."[6]

The US Federal Emergency Management Agency (FEMA) also has a definition of terrorism:

> . . . the use of force or violence against persons or property in violation of the criminal laws of the United States **for purposes of intimidation, coercion, or ransom.** Terrorists often use threats to:
>
> - Create fear among the public.
> - Try to convince citizens that their government is powerless to prevent terrorism.
> - Get immediate publicity for their causes.[7]

The USA PATRIOT Act of 2001 defines domestic terrorism as "activities that (A) involve acts dangerous to human life that are a violation of the criminal laws of the United States or of any state; (B) **appear to be intended (i) to intimidate or coerce a civilian population; (ii) to influence the policy of a government by intimidation or coercion;** or (iii) to affect the conduct of a government by mass destruction, assassination, or kidnapping; and (C) occur primarily within the territorial jurisdiction of the U.S."[8]

The Department of Homeland Security, in the law creating DHS, defines terrorism as "any activity that—(A) involves an act that—(i) is dangerous to human life or potentially destructive of critical infrastructure or key resources; and (ii) is a violation of the criminal laws of the United States or of any State or other subdivision of the United States; and (B) **appears to be intended—(i) to intimidate or coerce a civilian population; (ii) to influence the policy of a government by intimidation or coercion; or (iii) to affect the conduct of a government by mass destruction, assassination, or kidnapping**."[9]

Of these eight definitions of terrorism, seven include terrorist motivation to intimidate, coerce, or compel. Two of the US definitions, from the US Department of Defense and the US Federal Emergency Management Agency, refer explicitly to coercion by fear. Only one definition, in the US

Code of Federal Regulations (CFR), does not refer to intimidation and coercion: "premeditated, politically motivated violence perpetrated against noncombatant targets by subnational groups or clandestine agents, usually intended to influence an audience."

The US CFR definition is notably close to Martha Crenshaw's 1995 definition: "Terrorism is a conspiratorial style of violence calculated to alter the attitudes and behavior of multitude audiences. It targets the few in a way that claims the attention of the many. Terrorism is not mass or collective violence but rather the direct activity of small groups."[10]

## WHAT DO TERRORISTS WANT?

Terror as a tactic of political conflict and political control goes far back in history, notably in the actions of states seeking to control citizens or subjects. Thus the Romans lined roads with crosses bringing agonizing death to "bandits" who today might be called terrorists. Naming this tactic *terrorism* goes back only to the French Revolution, in which the new government embraced killing of aristocrats, clerics, and even peasants loyal to the old regime. "Kill one man, frighten a thousand" may be the shortest description of terror as a political tactic.

As states through history have used terror to coerce, compel, and intimidate, states facing nonstate violence find it an obvious assumption that coercion based on fear is what the terrorist threat is about. This easy projection of state motives to terrorist motives must be resisted, however, because it has several unhelpful consequences.

*The first consequence* is to make terrorist motivations difficult to analyze. When one among many possible motives for a terrorist attack is included in the definition of terrorism, all other possibilities tend to vanish. For this reason, no social scientist would put a hypothetical explanation of a phenomenon in the definition of the phenomenon of interest.

For instance, if we were interested in why people give to charity, it would not be helpful to define giving to charity as a behavior based on intent to help others. Such a definition would make other possible intentions disappear. What if some people give to charity to gain the admiration of others or to avoid being seen as stingy and selfish? Similarly, terrorists may have many motives other than coercion, including such individualist motives as revenge, thrill-seeking, and status. It is perhaps an indicator of the status of social science in government offices that so many government definitions of terrorism enshrine one possible motive for terrorism in the very definition of terrorism.

*A second consequence* of identifying terrorism with coercion is that the competition between terrorist groups becomes invisible. When groups advancing the same political cause are in competition for the same base of sympathizers and supporters, these groups are likely to escalate gradually to more extreme tactics. Mia Bloom has called this kind of competition *outbidding*. If one group begins using suicide bombers, for instance, competing groups are likely to follow.

Outbidding violence can often be identified in the locations and timing of attacks. This is the case for attacks in Paris attributed to al-Qaeda and the Islamic State. On January 7, 2015, Saïd and Chérif Kouachi killed eleven people in the Paris offices of the French satirical magazine *Charlie Hebdo*. They credited their training and support to al-Qaeda in Yemen. At almost the same time, between January 7 and 9, 2015, Amedy Coulibaly killed a policeman and four people in a Jewish kosher grocery store in Paris. He credited the Islamic State for his inspiration.[11] The rivalry between al-Qaeda and the Islamic State has been seen also in attacks in Yemen and Mali.[12]

Violence motivated by competition among militant groups is invisible when our view of terrorism begins and ends in coercion of those attacked. For outbidding violence, the intended audience is not the government or citizens attacked, but those who already sympathize with the terrorist cause.

*A third consequence* of identifying terrorism with coercion is that fear becomes the key emotion for understanding and resisting terrorism. Terrorists want to terrorize! If the target of terrorist attacks, both the government and its citizens, can resist fear and intimidation, the terrorists cannot succeed. And how better to demonstrate the conquest of fear than to strike back against the terrorists, to mobilize new resources to fight terrorism, to strengthen government power to fight terrorism—in short, to declare war on terrorism. Unfortunately for this simple view, terrorists count on anger and outrage at least as much as they count on fear, as will be discussed in the following section.

*A fourth consequence* of including fear and coercion in government definitions is that citizens are misled about the danger that terrorism poses. This is a mass psychology problem, not a problem for specialists and analysts. Many who study terrorism, inside government as well as outside, understand that fear and coercion are not the only goals of terrorist attacks. But the citizens who read and hear government definitions of terrorism, especially as these are embodied in the opinions of politicians and pundits, believe that, if they do not give in to fear and if they support war against terrorists, they have done their best. The next section shows the costs of this misplaced confidence.

## BEYOND COERCION: JUJITSU POLITICS

Decades of research with small face-to-face groups have shown that out-group threat leads to increased group cohesion, increased respect for ingroup leaders, increased sanctions for ingroup deviates, and idealization of ingroup norms. In larger groups, reference to cohesion is often replaced with references to ingroup identification, patriotism, or nationalism, but the pattern in response to outgroup threat is similar to that seen in small groups.

Consider the changes brought to US politics after the terrorist attacks of September 2001: increased patriotism visible in rallies, flags, banners, and bumper stickers; polls showing increased support for the president and for every agent and agency of government; increased sanctions for Americans challenging the consensus (Bill Maher sacked for suggesting the 9/11 attackers were not cowards); and reification of American values ("They hate us for our values").

Consider also the emotions associated with the 9/11 attacks. An innovative study by Back, Kufner, and Egloff examined emotion words in millions of words of texts sent in the United States on September 11, 2001.[13] Anger-related words increased throughout the day, their incidence ending six times higher than that of fear- and sadness-related words.

Anger and fear have different action tendencies. Experiments described by Wetherell and colleagues show that individuals responding with anger to images of the 9/11 attacks are more likely to favor aggressive reactions to terrorism, whereas reactions of fear and sadness are related to support for more defensive reactions.[14] Across several studies Wetherell et al. found that anger reactions are related to support for attacking terrorist leaders in foreign countries, support for war against countries harboring terrorists, and outgroup derogation of Arab Americans and Palestinians. In other studies fear reactions were associated with increased support for government surveillance and restriction of civil liberties.

In short, the predominant US reaction to the 9/11 attacks was not fear, but anger. Anger is associated with aggression and outgroup derogation; fear is associated with defensive strategies of surveillance and curtailed civil rights. Anger is the emotion sought by terrorists aiming to elicit overreaction to their attacks—using the enemy's strength against him in a strategy of *jujitsu politics*.[15] The power of this strategy, and the importance of anger reactions in making the strategy successful, is hidden by definitions of terrorism that focus only on fear and coercion.

Al-Qaeda had good reason to be hopeful that jujitsu politics would work for them on 9/11.

In 1986, the United States attempted to reply to Libyan-supported terrorism by bombing Libya's leader, Muammar al-Qaddafi. The bombs missed Qaddafi but a bomb or two did hit an apartment building and killed a number of civilians. This mistake was downplayed in the United States, but it was a public-relations success for anti-US groups across North Africa.

In 1998 the United States attempted to reply to al-Qaeda attacks on US embassies in Africa by sending cruise missiles against a weapons factory in Sudan and against al-Qaeda training camps in Afghanistan. It turned out that the weapons factory was making medical supplies—more fuel for anti-US feelings. Worse yet, the cruise missiles landing in Afghanistan blew off the table a deal in which Afghanistan's Taliban would turn over Osama bin Laden and other of his troublesome Arab colleagues to Saudi Arabia—where the Saudi royals were still smarting from bin Laden's criticism.

Dr. Ayman al-Zawahiri enunciated the strategy of jujitsu politics in his memoir *Knights under the Prophet's Banner*.

> The masters in Washington and Tel Aviv are using the apostate Muslim regimes to protect their interests and to fight the battle against the Muslims on their behalf. If the shrapnel from the battle reach their homes and bodies, they will trade accusations with their agents about who is responsible for this. In that case, they will face one of two bitter choices: either personally wage the battle against the Muslims, which means that the battle will turn into clear-cut jihad against infidels, or they reconsider their plans after acknowledging the failure of the brute and violent confrontation against Muslims.[16]

Al-Zawahiri argues that if the shrapnel of war reaches American homes, Americans must either give up their control of Muslim countries or come out from behind their Muslim stooges to fight for control. But if American troops move into Muslim countries, these troops would become a magnet for jihad of the kind the Russians faced in Afghanistan. Although the US war against the Taliban was faster and cleaner of collateral damage to civilians than al-Qaeda had expected, the US move into Iraq did indeed bring out more terrorists, both in Muslim and in Western countries.

More recently, jujitsu politics is part of the motivation behind the ISIS-sponsored attacks in Paris on November 13, 2015, which killed 130 and wounded 367, as well as the Brussels attacks on March 22, 2016, which killed 32 and injured more than 300. These attacks left a big question: Why would a group aiming for a Sunni state in Syria and Iraq, a group already under attack by the government forces of Syria, the United States, the United Kingdom, France, and Russia, mount a terrorist attack in Paris or Brussels?

Every terrorist attack and every counterterrorist response is a communication to multiple audiences. We need to look at these audiences separately to see the logic of the Paris attacks.

For Sunni Muslims chafing under Shi'a power in Iraq and Syria, the message is power. ISIS can best defend Sunnis because ISIS has the power. For young Sunni men in the Middle East, the message is "Don't think about joining 'moderate' Sunni rebels; don't think about joining a local tribal militia; join the winning team—join ISIS."

For Muslims in Europe there is also a message of power, but more important, there is jujitsu politics—ISIS trying to use Western strength against the West. A response to terrorism that creates collateral damage, that harms individuals previously unsympathetic to the terrorists, can bring new status and new volunteers for the terrorists.

This is the result ISIS sought from the Paris and Brussels attacks. In France and in other European countries, ISIS aimed for a government response that would target Muslims with new restrictions and new surveillance. ISIS hoped also for a public reaction against Muslims and the strengthening of anti-immigrant political parties, not only in France but in other European countries as well. It wanted increased discrimination and hostility aimed at European Muslims.

In short, ISIS looked and is still looking for European reactions to push European Muslims toward joining in the construction of a new caliphate. There are more than 20 million Muslims living in the European Union. So far perhaps 2,000 have traveled to Syria to join ISIS. Jujitsu politics can bring more volunteers, more home-grown terrorists, and more security costs for European countries.

Will it work? Political speeches and newspapers are full of war talk. French forces have joined with US forces in dropping more bombs on the areas of Syria and Iraq controlled by the Islamic State. As Islamic State fighters try to blend in with civilians, the escalation of bombing means escalation of collateral damage.

In France new powers of investigation and detention have been advanced for use by police and security forces. These will be felt more in Muslim immigrant neighborhoods than elsewhere. The French parliament in May 2016 approved another two-month extension of the state of emergency that curtails civil liberties. "The state of emergency," the *New York Times* reported, "had enabled the authorities to put people under house arrest and to carry out police raids without the prior authorization of a judge. Sixty-nine people are currently under house arrest . . . and more than 3,500 raids have been carried out since Nov. 14."[17]

Perhaps the most dangerous force for hostility and discrimination is the definition of the enemy as "fundamentalist Muslims." Marine Le Pen, leader of an anti-immigrant party in France, offered this target in an interview with NPR's Robert Siegel: "And we must eradicate Islamic fundamentalism from our soil."[18] Siegel did not challenge Le Pen's definition of the problem. But the fact is that the great majority of Islamic fundamentalists are devout, rather than political. Defining religious ideas and religious practice as the enemy will attack ninety-nine peaceful Muslims for every jihadist reached. Jujitsu politics will be winning.

Even better for ISIS than training and supporting people to attack in Western countries is inspiring homegrown attackers to claim allegiance to ISIS. Syed Rizwan Farook and Tashfeen Malik began preparing for their December 2015 attack in San Bernardino before ISIS hit the news in summer 2014, but their last-minute invocation of "Islamic State" was enough to raise the brand name in American eyes. Similarly, Omar Mateen claimed allegiance to the Islamic State in a 911 call made during his June 2016 attacks in Orlando; most news media accounted him an Islamic terrorist despite his history of mental health problems and despite his having chosen a target—Latino gays—that undermined the political significance of his attack.[19]

Despite the fuzzy motivations of the attackers, these two attacks have been credited to Muslim extremism in general and to the Islamic State in particular. We need to ask why it is so easy to turn the actions of a few individuals into calls for excluding Muslims from the United States, profiling Muslims already living in the United States, and increasing public hostility toward Muslims.[20] When and why is it easy to project onto the many the actions of a few? Research in this direction is urgently needed, but it is already clear that an important part of the power of jujitsu politics is our easy projection from the actions of a few terrorists to suspicion of the whole group the terrorists claim they represent.

## COUNTERTERRORISM: A DYNAMIC PERSPECTIVE

Jujitsu politics points to the importance of action and reaction in the conflict between terrorists and their targets. Overreaction to a terrorist attack produces its own reaction in escalated sympathy and support for the terrorists. In turn, terrorists escalate their attacks or broaden their targets. Action and reaction produce a trajectory of escalating violence over time.

To understand terrorism is to understand this trajectory. It is not possible to understand or anticipate terrorist actions without understanding how terrorists see and respond to government actions. Studying the terrorists "out there" is a mirage: they do not exist out there; they exist in a dynamic relation with us, their targets. This is a difficult perspective for officials and officers charged with fighting terrorism to take. To get into the mind of a terrorist can make it more difficult to shoot one. To get into the mind of a terrorist can raise doubts about what we, the terrorists' targets, may have done to instigate terrorist attack.

Returning now to the popularity of definitions of terrorism that assume that terrorists aim to terrorize, it becomes clear how these definitions can blind analysts, officials, and citizens alike to the danger of overreaction. If terrorists want to coerce us with fear, then we will be safe so long as we are not intimidated and fight back. But if we do not see the power in the dynamics of interaction, we cede this power to the terrorists, who are pleased that we do not understand their best weapon.

Why are we so easily blinded? Defining terrorism as an attempt to coerce with fear is part of the answer, but the definition itself requires explanation. What is the attraction of a definition that appears ignorant or bizarre to any social scientist? It is possible that our blindness arises from some cognitive deficit associated with asymmetric conflict or from some form of cognitive bias in attributions about intergroup violence. But, as already suggested in relation to getting into the mind of the terrorist, there is a simpler possibility.

Perhaps ours is a motivated blindness. Not seeing terrorism as interaction saves our self-image as blameless victims and eases our way to violence as retribution for terrorist violence. Our retribution can include not just boots on the ground but assassination from the air and torture in a prison. Seeing conflict as an interaction humanizes the enemy; heroic resistance to fear and coercion makes the enemy into monsters.

Here it is useful to note the strong parallel between counterterrorism and counterinsurgency. The *US Army/Marine Corps Counterinsurgency Field Manual* pays close attention to the insurgent strategy that aims to mobilize new support by eliciting government overreaction to insurgent attacks.[21] The need to counter this strategy of jujitsu politics comes through in the first five "Paradoxes of Counterinsurgency Operations":

1. Sometimes, the more you protect your force, the less secure you may be.

2. Sometimes, the more force is used, the less effective it is.

3. The more successful the counterinsurgency is, the less force can be used and the more risk must be accepted.

4. Sometimes doing nothing is the best reaction.

5. Some of the best weapons for counterinsurgents do not shoot.[22]

Insurgency and terrorism are forms of political conflict. Counterinsurgency and counterterrorism are thus also forms of political conflict. Mao Zedong's slogan is perhaps the shortest summary of the road to success for both counterinsurgency and counterterrorism: *Politics takes command!* For analysts of terrorism and practitioners of counterterrorism, a more political and interactive perspective requires going beyond definitions of terrorism that focus only on fear and coercion. For citizens of a democratic state, increased resistance to jujitsu politics similarly requires getting beyond the idea that we have nothing to fear but fear.

## NOTES

1. Draft Comprehensive Convention against International Terrorism, UN Doc. A/59/894, App. II (12 August 2005).

2. On the developments leading toward the Draft Comprehensive Convention, see A. Rohan Perera, "Reviewing the U.N. Conventions on Terrorism: Towards a Comprehensive Terrorism Convention," in C. Fijnaut, J. Wouters, and F. Naert (eds.), *Legal Instruments in the Fight against International Terrorism* (Leiden, Netherlands: Martinus Nijhoff, 2005), 567.

3. The Terrorism Act 2000 (ch. 11), http://www.legislation.gov.uk/ukpga /2000/11.

4. Available at Office of Justice Programs, National Institute of Justice, "Terrorism," http://www.nij.gov/topics/crime/terrorism/pages/welcome.aspx #note1.

5. Ibid.

6. Department of Defense Dictionary of Military and Associated Terms, Joint Publication 1–02, 8 November 2002 (as amended through 31 January 2011), http:// www.people.mil/Portals/56/Documents/rtm/jp1_02.pdf.

7. Federal Emergency Management Agency, "Terrorism," https://www.fema .gov/media-library-data/20130726–1549–20490–0802/terrorism.pdf.

8. H.R. 3126 (USA PATRIOT Act, Sec. 802, "Definition of Domestic Terrorism," *ratville times*, http://www.ratical.org/ratville/CAH/Section802.html#802.

9. Public Law 107–296, 25 November 2002, 107th Congress, Department of Homeland Security, https://www.dhs.gov/xlibrary/assets/hr_5005_enr.pdf.

10. M. Crenshaw (ed.), *Terrorism in Context* (University Park: Penn State University Press, 1995), 4.

11. E. Karmon, "Islamic State and al-Qaeda Competing for Hearts and Minds," *Perspectives on Terrorism* 9:2 (2015), http://www.terrorismanalysts.com/pt/index .php/pot/article/view/420/html.

12. J. Malsin, "What to Know about the Deadly ISIS vs. al-Qaeda Rivalry," *Time*, 24 November 2015, http://time.com/4124810/isis-al-qaeda-rivalry-terror-attacks-mali-paris/.

13. M.D. Back, A.C.P. Kufner, and B. Egloff, "The Emotional Timeline of September 11, 2001," *Psychological Science* 21:10 (2010): 1417–19.

14. G. Wetherell, B.M. Weisz, R.M. Stolier, A.J. Beavers, and M.S. Sadler, "Policy Preference in Response to Terrorism: The Role of Emotions, Attributions, and Appraisals," in S.J. Sinclair and D. Antonius (eds.), *The Political Psychology of Terrorism Fears* (New York: Oxford University Press, 2013).

15. C. McCauley and S. Moskalenko, *Friction: How Radicalization Happens to Them and Us* (New York: Oxford University Press, 2011). Essentially the same argument about terrorists seeking overreaction to their attacks is made by Antony Pemberton in "Al Qaeda and Vicarious Victims: Victimological Insights into Globalized Terrorism," in R.M. Letschert and J.J.M. Van Dijk (eds.), *The New Faces of Victimhood: Globalisation, Global Justice, and Victim Empowerment* (Dordrecht, Netherlands: Springer, 2011).

16. G. Kepel, J.P. Milelli, and P. Ghazaleh (eds.), *Al Qaeda in Its Own Words* (Cambridge, MA: Harvard University Press, 2008), 202.

17. A. Breeden, "French Parliament Votes to Extend State of Emergency," *New York Times*, May 19, 2016, http://www.nytimes.com/2016/05/20/world/europe/french-parliament-votes-to-extend-state-of-emergency.html.

18. National Public Radio, "France's National Front Leader Criticizes Hollande's Response to Paris Attacks," *All Things Considered*, 16 November 2015, http://www.npr.org/2015/11/16/456254001/frances-national-front-leader-criticizes-hollandes-response-to-paris-attacks.

19. J. Meyer, "Al Qaeda: Orlando Shooter Should Have Targeted Whites," *NBC News*, 24 June 2016, http://www.nbcnews.com/storyline/orlando-nightclub-massacre/al-qaeda-orlando-shooter-should-have-targeted-whites-n598576.

20. J. Bosman, "A Chill Grips a U.S. Haven for Syrian Families," *New York Times* (24 November 2015), 1.

21. U.S. Department of the Army, *U.S. Army/Marine Corps Counterinsurgency Field Manual* (Chicago: University of Chicago Press, 2006).

22. Ibid., 47–51.

# 7. Framing Terrorism

## The Communicative Constitution of the Terrorist Actor

Benjamin K. Smith, Scott Englund,
Andrea Figueroa-Caballero, Elena Salcido,
and Michael Stohl

In the aftermath of the attacks on September 11, 2001, al-Qaeda emerged not only as the specific perpetrator of the act but also as the focus of the "war on terror." Until 2014 or so, and during the almost decade and a half following 9/11, al-Qaeda did not recede from its perceived position as a primary (if not *the* primary) international terrorist threat and enemy of the United States. Despite al-Qaeda's having attained such a strong foothold on how the media and government portrays, and how the American public understands and responds to, the international terrorist threat, several new players have surfaced as potentially problematic enemies (e.g., Boko Haram, al-Shabaab, and most important, Daesh), especially during the past two years. Media coverage of these groups often connects them, either implicitly or explicitly, to al-Qaeda, using al-Qaeda to explain their form and function. As such, it is important to take a critical look at the way al-Qaeda and its actions have been depicted in the media during this ascendant period for other terrorist threats, and to explore the effects and consequences of these portrayals.

## THE DISCURSIVE CONSTRUCTION OF THE TERRORIST ACTOR

The field of terrorism studies has long been dominated by questions of what terrorism is, what causes it, who are the terrorists, and how we can counter their actions.[1] Much of the research focuses on understanding and combating the terrorist actor, to unearth the origins, structures, and operations of terrorists and terrorist organizations. These questions have been explored from a variety of academic disciplines, with psychologists and social psychologists exploring the terrorist mind,[2] criminologists and economists using information about the financial and social networks of terrorists to better understand

and predict their actions,[3] and sociologists and political scientists exploring the role of social, political, and economic power as drivers of terrorism.[4]

Studying the terrorist actor has been a useful venture, providing greater insight into the motives, functions, and structures of terrorist organizations, thereby allowing for better counterterrorism strategies. However, as Hülsse and Spencer argue, "the focus on the terrorist actor in terrorism research is misleading. It is based on the assumption that knowledge about the terrorist means knowledge about terrorism."[5] Thus, much of existing terrorism research is based on the assumption that there is an objective reality of terrorism, rather than the far more tenable assumption that terrorism is only "an interpretation of events and their presumed causes."[6] If terrorism is not only constituted by the violence of its action but is also a social construction, as many have argued,[7] and furthermore if the reaction to this social construction is more important than the act itself in understanding terrorism,[8] then it is incumbent upon researchers to explore not only the "objective" realities of terrorist organizations but also how these organizations and actors are discursively constructed.

This approach to studying terrorism has been widely embraced by media scholars, especially as it concerns media framing of terrorism writ large. Scholars have explored the Bush administration's framing of the 9/11 attacks and the "war on terror,"[9] the framing of Muslim Americans and Islam in relation to the broader terrorism discourse,[10] and even the rhetorical usage of the word *terrorist*.[11] However, there has been little research looking at the framing of specific terrorist actors and organizations.

It is our contention that framing theory can serve as a useful lens for understanding the communicative constitution of the terrorist actor, providing deeper insight into the core questions of terrorism studies while answering the call of Hülsse and Spencer for a new kind of terrorism studies—one that "analyses the making of terrorism in academic, political and popular discourse."[12] By using framing theory to closely explore media constructions of the terrorist actor, we believe it is possible to gain a better understanding of how the American public interprets and responds to terrorism in general, and how the public perceives the origins, structures, and operations of terrorists and terrorist organizations.

## DEFINING FRAMES FROM A CONSTRUCTIONIST PERSPECTIVE

### Framing

In the process of crafting news stories, journalists are confronted with choices regarding how they construct meaningful narratives about the issues, events, and actors being depicted, simplifying often complex topics and explaining their importance in order to make them more accessible to lay publics.[13] *Framing* is the process wherein journalists (and others) provide an interpretive structure for understanding the provided information and, in so doing, prioritize some facts, images, or developments over others.[14] This process of selection and interpretation serves to ensure that the complexities of reality are reduced to a graspable, plausible whole[15] and, whether intentional or not, functions to promote a particular problem definition, causal interpretation, moral evaluation, and/or treatment recommendation of the events, issues, or actors being portrayed.[16]

## Frames

The framing process inherently relies on the selection of one or more *frames*, which can be viewed as socially shared and persistent sets of organizing principles that "media and individuals rely on to convey, interpret, and evaluate information"[17] and "that work symbolically to meaningfully structure the social world."[18] An important distinction arising from this conceptualization is that frames and media content must be viewed as distinct entities. From a cultural constructivist perspective, frames exist solely within the collective memory of a group or society and serve simply as *conceptual tools* for condensing the dense complexity of life into easily digestible narratives;[19] they are distinct from their symbolic manifestation.[20] In other words, frames "live" in the public consciousness; they become embedded and manifest only in discourse products (e.g., news texts) through the framing process.

## THE CURRENT STUDY

This chapter combines the results of three lines of research in an effort to better understand the communicative constitution of the terrorist actor. First, using semantic network analysis methods, we examine the landscape of media terrorism discourse and find that al-Qaeda is the primary referent for understanding global terrorism. Next, we provide a brief explication of the attribute frames that journalists use when constructing a meaningful understanding of al-Qaeda and its actions. We conclude by exploring the application of these attribute frames to other organizations and discuss the implications.

## DATA COLLECTION AND SAMPLING METHODS

### Body of Texts

As part of an ongoing research project we developed a database of newspaper articles from the *New York Times* and *Wall Street Journal* that discuss terrorism, terrorist organizations, and/or terrorist actors. The database includes all print articles published in either paper between January 1, 1996, and December 31, 2014. We obtained articles using the ProQuest News & Newspapers databases. Stories included in our database were located using a highly inclusive search command (available to readers upon request).

## Article Sampling

The studies reported on in this chapter can be split into two major sections. In the first, we focus on the differential coverage of terrorist actors, with the second section focused on the actual content of that coverage. Each section utilizes a different part of the database discussed above. In the first section, we look specifically at articles that the newspapers themselves identified as covering terrorism, using the "subject" meta-tag. We also limited the sample to actual "news" articles (in contrast to editorials, commentary, and the like) that mentioned at least one of the organizations designated as a terrorist organization by the US State Department between 1996 and 2014. This resulted in a total sample of 22,006 articles—16,740 from the *New York Times* and 5,266 from the *Wall Street Journal*.[21]

Most of this study (i.e., the parts centered on the framing of al-Qaeda and the use of al-Qaeda as a framing device) focuses specifically on articles printed between January 1, 2013, and December 31, 2014, that explicitly mention al-Qaeda. The goal in selecting this specific time period was to sufficiently limit the influence of the 2012 US presidential election while allowing us to investigate the impact of the emergence of Daesh. To be as inclusive as possible, articles were included in our sample if the words *Qaeda, Qaida,* or *Qa'ida* were mentioned anywhere in the article's file (the title, body text, photo caption, etc.).[22] This resulted in a sample of 2,734 unique newspaper articles—1,498 from the *New York Times* and 1,236 from the *Wall Street Journal*. To create a set of coding units, each article was searched to identify instances of the term *al-Qaeda*, using the same procedure we used to identify relevant articles. Each time al-Qaeda was mentioned, the paragraph containing the reference was recorded in a separate database for use in our analysis, resulting in a collection of 6,332 coding units. The actual coding was conducted on randomly selected units from the database.

## DOMINANT ACTORS IN THE MEDIA'S TERRORISM DISCOURSE

The first part of this investigation aimed simply at understanding the landscape of media terrorism discourse. Using the 22,006 articles published between January 1, 1996, and December 31, 2014, in the *New York Times* and *Wall Street Journal* that were tagged by the respective newspapers as covering "terrorism," we attempted to determine the number of articles mentioning each of the different organizations designated as "terrorist" by the US State Department. The results were somewhat surprising. We began the research expecting to observe a predominant amount of coverage about al-Qaeda (due to the events of 9/11), but beyond that we expected to observe a rather uniform distribution of articles, dependent upon the region where the organization was located and the frequency of attacks or other newsworthy events conducted or threatened by the organization. What we found instead was a nearly perfect example of Zipf's Law, a special case of a power-law probability distribution.

A power law can be defined colloquially as a functional relationship between two quantities in which one quantity varies as a power of another. Power-law relationships generally imply that small-magnitude occurrences are extremely common, whereas large-magnitude instances are extremely rare. Notable examples include incomes, city populations, and the size of wildfires. More formally, a power-law probability distribution "specifies that the probability of observing an item of size k is proportional to $k^{-\alpha}$."[23] Zipf's Law is a special case applied to the frequency of words in which it has been empirically demonstrated that the frequency with which a word is used in natural language is inversely proportional to its rank of usage. In other words, the most commonly used word will be used roughly twice as much as the next most commonly used word, which is used roughly twice as much as the next most commonly used word, and so forth. We see this exact relationship when looking at the frequency of articles mentioning terrorist organizations, as shown in figure 1. Al-Qaeda is mentioned in 5,459 articles, followed by Hamas with 1,063 case occurrences, Gama'a al-Islamiyya with 697, and Daesh with 349. What makes this interesting is the generally agreed-upon psychological and evolutionary explanation for why natural language use follows Zipf's Law: the principle of least effort.[24]

Complex language has evolved to be as efficient as possible, and Zipf's Law is the natural "outcome of the nontrivial arrangement of word-concept associations adopted for complying with hearer and speaker needs."[25] In other words, language has evolved to follow a Zipfian distribution because all other configurations take more effort: it is cognitively easier to use highly symbolic words frequently, using less symbolic (and less universally meaningful) words only when absolutely necessary for sharing meaning. Thus when we see the frequency of articles mentioning each terrorist organization falling into a Zipfian distribution (rather than, for example, a normal or

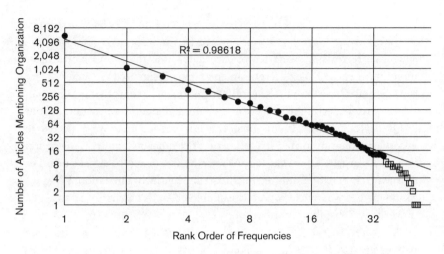

FIGURE 7.1.    Case Occurrence Frequency of Organization Mentions by Rank Order. This graph shows the case occurrence frequency (i.e., the number of articles mentioning each State Department–designated terrorist organization) by frequency rank. The straight line is the expected distribution if case occurrence frequency follows a power-law distribution (e.g., Zipf's Law) and has a coefficient of determination of .986, meaning that expected distribution explains 98 percent of the variance in the observed distribution. As is typical with a Zipfian distribution (and with all power-law distributions), the power-law distribution tends to break down at small quantities. For this reason, we have excluded those organizations from the calculation of the trend line (they are included in the graph, displayed as squares). The $R^2$ for all organizations = .925.

uniform distribution), we are left to assume that the organizations discussed most frequently must carry the most symbolic meaning, and are therefore used to characterize the less frequently mentioned organizations.

We confirm this assumption—specifically in reference to the distribution anchor, al-Qaeda—by looking at the co-occurrence of organizations within news articles and using a simple inclusion index measure. This coefficient measures the conditional probability that an article mentioning organization X (e.g., al-Qaeda in the Arabian Peninsula [AQAP]) also mentions organization Y (e.g., Core al-Qaeda). It takes the maximum value of 1 when one of these organizations always appears when the second one appears, and a minimum value of 0 when the organizations never co-occur.

Confirming the assumptions derivative of Zipf's Law, al-Qaeda frequently has very high inclusion index coefficients, with a co-occurrence rate over 30 percent for 33 of the 53 other State Department–designated terrorist organizations.[26] The inclusion index coefficient can be considered

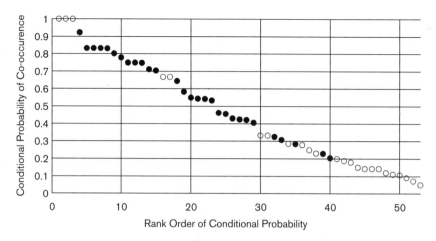

FIGURE 7.2. Conditional Probability of Co-occurrence between al-Qaeda and Organization X. This graph shows the probability that al-Qaeda is mentioned in an article when organization X is mentioned, by rank order of the inclusion index coefficient. Significance is determined by the association strength coefficient (> 0), which measures the co-occurrence of items, taking into consideration the possibility that two items will occasionally co-occur by chance. By this method, 29 of the 53 inclusion index co-occurrence coefficients (indicated by black circles) cannot be attributed to chance alone, and as such should be considered statistically significant.

significant in 29 of 53 cases, as shown in figure 2. No other organization has comparable rates of co-occurrence. This demonstrates the central role that al-Qaeda has played over the past two decades. Further, given what we know about the principle of least effort discussed above, we can conclude that al-Qaeda is a symbolically meaningful organization used to characterize lesser-known threats.

## FRAMING AND AL-QAEDA

Having demonstrated the central role held by al-Qaeda within the broader media discourse of terrorism, our attention now turns to understanding the discourse itself. Using a constant comparative method, we first identify the attributes of al-Qaeda most commonly referenced (e.g., their organizational structure and motivations) and the "values" these attributes most commonly take. Because of the length restrictions of this chapter, we do not provide a full explication of each attribute value, but instead offer a general overview of our findings. We then shift from identifying the framing of al-Qaeda to looking at the utilization of al-Qaeda as a framing device.

## Coder Assumptions

Three basic assumptions underlie the dual investigation of al-Qaeda as a framing device and the framing of al-Qaeda. It was assumed, first, that communication through language is based on the idea that words have a shared meaning within a set context; second, that the process of encoding information into language requires choosing from among the options available in grammar; and finally, that the choices made while encoding information into language, though not always conscious, are deliberate. Based on these assumptions, we can state that our primary concern was to identify the repertoire of signs employed by journalists when writing about al-Qaeda or when using al-Qaeda as a symbolic reference. In addition, our interest was to identify how the use of particular signs in context served to communicate wider ideas, identities, and attitudes. Finally, we sought to make interpretative judgments as to why certain choices were made to shape meaning instead of others, and the implications of those choices.

### ATTRIBUTE FRAMING AND THE DISCURSIVE CONSTRUCTION OF AL-QAEDA

In this section we identify and explicate the repertoire of attributes and attribute frames that journalists use when writing about al-Qaeda and its actions. Our analysis of news articles published in the *New York Times* and the *Wall Street Journal* that reference al-Qaeda revealed four distinct attribute classes and a total of nineteen different attribute frames (see table 7.1):[27] inter- or intra-organizational structure (network, hierarchical-type corporation, franchise-type corporation), functional identity (paramilitary, government/corporation, nefarious/shadowy, movement), motivation (idealistic/ideological, Islamic/religious, anti-American/anti-Western, confrontational/reaction seeking), and evaluative judgment (destabilizing entity, evil/bad, radical/extreme, terrorist, criminal, extraordinary threat, enemy). The manifestation of these attribute classes and frames are explicated in full in a separate research report.[28] What follows is an abridged discussion of the findings that compares and contrasts the frames with a focus on their application within texts.

Initially one of the differences among the attribute classes is how they were manifest within the text. Whereas the inter/intra-organizational structure and functional identity classes were most often identified through the use of allusions or metaphors (e.g., network or relational metaphors such as "hubs" and "cells"), the motivation attribute class was often stated explicitly (e.g., al-Qaeda has an overtly ideological motivation). Further, a

TABLE 7.1  Attributes and Attribute Frames Used in the
Communicative Construction of al-Qaeda

| Al-Qaeda Attributes | Attribute Frames |
| --- | --- |
| **Inter/Intra-organizational Structure** | Network |
| | Corporate (hierarchical) |
| | Corporate (franchise) |
| **Functional Identity** | Paramilitary |
| | Government/Corporate-like |
| | Nefarious/Shadowy |
| | Movement |
| **Motivation** | Idealistic/Ideological |
| | Islamic/Religious |
| | Anti-American/Anti-Western |
| | Confrontational/Seeking Reaction |
| **Evaluative Judgment** | Destabilizing |
| | Evil/Bad |
| | Radical/Extremist |
| | Terrorist |
| | Criminal |
| | Extraordinary Threat |
| | Enemy |

review of these attributes and frames reveals several areas of contradiction, overlap, and mutual exclusivity.

Our analysis showed that although some of the attribute frames seem to contradict one another (e.g., hierarchical-type corporation versus franchise-type corporation), this is not the case overall. In fact, most of the attribute frames share the underlying connotation of al-Qaeda as an adversarial force (e.g., al-Qaeda as evil/bad, anti-American/anti-Western, paramilitary, or nefarious/shadowy). Although these results are not entirely surprising, a review of previous work on attribute framing suggests that the application of such attribute frames to al-Qaeda and its actions influences how the group is fundamentally understood by the American public.[29] In this case, the attribute frames contribute to the overarching conception of al-Qaeda as a hostile enemy, and as such, they both shape and limit our understanding of the group in that regard. Echoing Hülsse and Spencer,[30] our intent is not to argue that al-Qaeda is not a hostile enemy or that its actions do not constitute terrorism, but rather to assert that how the group is discussed at large has implications for how we understand the group and interpret its actions.

Further, our results indicate that most of the attribute classes are composed of mutually exclusive frames. For example, the inter-/intra-organizational structure attribute class is composed of three wholly distinct structure-related attribute frames used to refer to al-Qaeda within the text: network, hierarchical-type corporation, and franchise-type corporation. Importantly, these attribute frames were not used in conjunction with one another. That is to say, al-Qaeda was not referenced as having both a network and a hierarchical-type corporation infrastructure within the same coding unit. Likewise, within the functional identity attribute class, al-Qaeda is labeled as having a paramilitary, government-like/corporate-like, nefarious/shadowy, or movement function; it was not portrayed as having more than one of these at a time.

Although in most instances attribute frames within a class are mutually exclusive, the attribute classes themselves are not. Thus, it was not uncommon to find attribute frames embedded in the coding unit that are drawn from, for example, both the functional identity and motivation classes. In the same vein, there exists a stronger connection between some classes than between others, such that some attributes were identified together more often than others. For instance, evaluative judgments characterizing the organization and its actions as terrorists or as terroristic are often accompanied with language establishing the functional identity of al-Qaeda as a network. Alternatively, the criminal evaluative judgment is rarely associated with mentions of al-Qaeda as a paramilitary group; rather, it is associated with al-Qaeda as a network whose functional identity is characterized as nefarious or shadowy and whose motivation is confrontational or reaction seeking.

One instance in which attribute frames are not wholly separate, but in fact additive, is within the evaluative judgments attribute class. Attribute frames in this class were often used in conjunction with one another; for example, it was not unusual to find al-Qaeda referred to as both "radical and extreme" and as "a destabilizing entity" within the same coding unit. Indeed, as noted above, evaluative judgment attribute frames often appear in groups of two or three, and, although our analysis revealed a level of interconnection among all of the attribute classes, the evaluative judgment attribute class was rarely found alone in the text. Instead, its primary role was to serve as an amplifier for the other attributes.

The use of framing theory to identify how al-Qaeda is communicatively constituted led to the identification of these four attribute classes and their eighteen distinct attributes frames. By pinpointing the manner in which al-Qaeda is constructed in American discourse, we can begin to look at some of the questions that have long been the focus of terrorism studies more generally: what causes terrorism, who are the terrorists, and how do they work to carry out their terrorist actions?[31] The overarching manifestation of al-Qaeda as an adversarial force throughout the attribute frames is the one clear and consistent theme that can be derived from our study, and it necessarily colors how al-Qaeda and its actions are evaluated.

Beyond this, the remaining characteristics needed to address the above questions appear to have a fluidity that make answering them a difficult task for communication and terrorism studies scholars alike. Perhaps the best example of this fluidity is how the organizational structure of al-Qaeda is left untenably amorphous in the popular press. This lack of cohesion in conceptualizing the structure of al-Qaeda is echoed in academic work. As a consequence it reflects how the public understands al-Qaeda and, thus, how it responds to the terrorist threat. However, it is worth taking a closer look at two specific attribute frames related to the theme of al-Qaeda as an adversarial force, as they appear to be the predominant frames for understanding al-Qaeda and its actions: al-Qaeda as having a paramilitary function and al-Qaeda as being motivated by ideology.

## Function: Al-Qaeda as a Paramilitary

The most common function attributed to al-Qaeda was that of a paramilitary. Members of al-Qaeda were often referred to as "militants," "commandos," "insurgents," "rebels," "fighters," or the like. Al-Qaeda members were also described as taking "orders." In turn, al-Qaeda was frequently described as "attacking" or engaging in "offensives," often with the organization's "allies." The organization was described as acquiring "footholds" or setting up "beach heads," "training camps," "staging areas," or "command centers." The use of military metaphors and descriptions painted al-Qaeda as a "foreign invading force," and in turn implied a particular solution to a problem, namely, "military intervention."

## Motivations: Al-Qaeda as Idealistic or Ideological

More than any other motivational attribute frame, al-Qaeda was described in this sample of texts as motivated by ideology. Importantly, this attribute frame does not concern religious ideology, which we conceptualize as a separate motivational attribute. Instead, this attribute frame connoted al-Qaeda's primary motivation as driven by a set of rules, both explicit and implicit, that bind what al-Qaeda will do in any given situation. The implication throughout the texts was that actions against al-Qaeda would be responded to, and that an attack against one al-Qaeda "branch" was an attack against all al-Qaeda branches. Moreover, the ideology of al-Qaeda was manifest primarily in descriptions of what al-Qaeda would not do because of the organization's ideological motives. This was especially true when contrasting the organization against other groups, like Daesh. Several texts noted that al-Qaeda was bound by its ideals and that, in fact, it was its ideological motivations that forced al-Qaeda to break with Daesh.

## PROJECTING THE KNOWN ONTO THE UNKNOWN: THE FRAMING OF NONDOMINANT ACTORS

Identification of the available repertoire of attribute classes and frames used by journalists when discussing al-Qaeda (especially the organization's function and motive) have allowed us to start thinking beyond the terrorist actor and its actions as wholly objective phenomena based on a knowable reality, and shift to an examination of how they are interpreted and are thus socially constructed. In doing so, the data show that the manner in which al-Qaeda was discussed has implications not only for how the organization itself is understood but also for how its framing shapes the broader terrorism discourse and how emerging terrorist threats are attended to.

Our preliminary analysis revealed a recurring theme: the use of al-Qaeda as a cultural frame of reference in media discussions of other terrorist groups. Indeed, the organizational metaphors present in texts were often used to paint other groups and actors as having an association (whether real or not) with al-Qaeda. For instance, the phrase "al-Qaeda-like" was frequently used in lieu of naming less familiar terrorist organizations. As we demonstrate earlier in this chapter, al-Qaeda is clearly the predominate focus of terrorism coverage, serving as the anchor for the Zipfian distribution of articles mentioning different terrorist organizations. In turn, we demonstrate that the implications of this finding, as summarized in the principle of least effort, were realized in the frequent inclusion of al-Qaeda in articles ostensibly discussing lesser-known organizations with no known relationship to al-Qaeda.

The implications of this discursive practice are twofold: first, it binds the cultural understanding of international terrorism to a particular actor and, in doing so, limits our understanding of the causes of terrorism to the particular set of framing attributes associated with al-Qaeda's motivations. This, in turn, constricts our ability to conceive of a solution to the problem, because we employ only al-Qaeda–centric solutions. Hülsse and Spencer echo this point in their discussion of counterterrorism policies as inherently limited by a discursively derived understanding of al-Qaeda. As they explain, "By mapping a source domain onto a target domain, a metaphor puts the target domain in a new light. By projecting the known onto the unknown, metaphors create reality; they constitute the object they signify."[32] Similarly, when using al-Qaeda as a framing device, the framed organization, or organizational actor, takes on (to some extent) the attributes associated with al-Qaeda. However, we extend this line of thought by noting not only that other terrorist groups are also implicated in this discourse but also that this particular facet constrains how we understand and tackle emerging terrorist threats—the second implication of using al-Qaeda as a cultural frame of reference. Thus, it is our contention that although not every terrorist group falls neatly within the heretofore-outlined attribute classes and attribute frames used to communicatively constitute al-Qaeda, they are most often treated as if they do. Further, the power of al-Qaeda as a framing device is such that it imposes important limitations on the understanding of terrorism more generally and hence the development of potential responses.

It should be noted that the use of al-Qaeda as a framing device is not an inherently bad practice: by employing a familiar and culturally shared frame of reference, journalists are able to more clearly get information across to a wide audience. However, Entman notes that "most frames are defined by what they omit as well as include, and the omissions . . . may be as critical as the inclusions in guiding the audience."[33] To treat the unfamiliar groups within the framework used to understand al-Qaeda necessarily masks the ways in which the organizations differ, limiting the public's understanding of terrorism and terrorist organizations.

Table 7.2 provides an extremely abridged version of our findings as they pertain to the identification of framing packages that utilize al-Qaeda framing device. As with our investigation of how al-Qaeda is framed, it is not within the scope of this chapter to fully explicate the different framing packages, but instead to simply provide an abridged discussion of the findings. The results are explicated in full in a separate research report.[34]

Looking specifically at articles mentioning al-Qaeda published between 2013 and 2014 in the *New York Times* and the *Wall Street Journal*, we identified eleven distinct framing packages that utilize al-Qaeda as a framing device: (a) devil you know, (b) to be or not to be, (c) excuse, (d) team awesome, (e) descriptor/exemplar, (f) bad guy, (g) bad group, (h) enhancer, (i) something wicked this way comes, (j) good guy, and (k) axis of evil.

TABLE 7.2  Framing Packages Utilizing al-Qaeda as a
Framing Device

| Framing Package | Description of Package and Connotations |
| --- | --- |
| **Devil you know** | Gives a frame of reference to unknown or little-known entities; generally uses organizational metaphors to make connection between entities |
| **To be or not to be** | Similar to "devil you know" in manifestation, but expressed with caveats; framed entity is explicitly not part of the organization, or its link to the organization is explicitly in doubt |
| **Excuse** | Excusing or justifying action or (more commonly) inaction because . . . al Qaeda |
| **Team awesome** | Saying how "awesome" a country group or individual is because of actions taken against al-Qaeda (e.g., glorification) |
| **Descriptor/exemplar** | Al-Qaeda as simile; used to identify the typology under consideration ("al-Qaeda-style"; something similar to what al-Qaeda does) |
| **Bad guy** | Individual linked to group; therefore individual is bad (explicit individual, explicit connection, generally implicit connotation) |
| **Bad group** | A group or country that is not the threat, but actively "supports" or previously "supported" (loosely defined) the threat, therefore bad; manifests differently than and implies different conclusions than the "bad guy" frame |
| **Enhancer** | Al-Qaeda multiplies an existing threat (e.g., fighters, radicals); "radicals" = bad, "al-Qaeda radicals" = worse |
| **Something wicked this way comes** | Shadowy actions/vague fears used to highlight the specter of the evil; fears are approaching but not present (generally) |
| **Good guy** | Individual linked to actions against al-Qaeda (past— also present?); therefore individual is good (explicit individual, explicit connection, generally implicit connotation) |
| **Axis of evil** | Using al-Qaeda as a baseline to describe something else (generally direct comparison between al-Qaeda and another group; better than/worse than/same as) |

One of the most surprising elements of this investigation was the realization that framing packages utilizing al-Qaeda as a framing device rarely draw direct links to al-Qaeda, but rather make implicit connections to the organization. The primary exception to this rule being the "devil you know" framing package, which utilizes organizational metaphors to directly associate different organizations to al-Qaeda, whether a real link exists or not.[35] Similar to the framing of "Islamic terrorism" proposed by Jackson, using al-Qaeda as a framing device appears to provide for "a series of oppositional binaries" that create "particular kinds of subjects within the overall discourse and enforce highly constricting subject positions upon them vis-à-vis other subjects."[36] Therefore, using al-Qaeda as a frame is significant not only in transferring attributes to unfamiliar object references, but also in terms of this "oppositional binary." For example, if al-Qaeda is used in a claim such as "French troops routed a militant group associated with al-Qaeda," the attributes associated with al-Qaeda are applied to the unfamiliar and ill-defined "militant group" (an example of the "devil you know" frame package). However, opposite attributes are applied to the "French troops" merely by the troops' being placed in opposition to al-Qaeda (an example of a relatively mild "team awesome" frame package). These oppositional binaries serve a critical role as reasoning devices throughout the corpus of texts.

## CONCLUSION

We argue that the media play a significant role in the transmission and construction of the understanding of terrorism and consequently how the public (and public officials) think about the construction of counterterrorism choices and policies. We examine how al-Qaeda has dominated the construction of the terrorist threat through their emergence as the primary referent for understanding terrorism and the organizations that employ it. We found four attribute classes and eighteen distinct attribute frames that have been used to describe al-Qaeda and its behaviors. In addition to the importance that these frames have had for shaping the public's understanding of terrorism, perhaps the more important impact has been the use of these al-Qaeda frames and attributes to frame Daesh and other emerging threats, masking the ways in which the organizations and their threats differ, harming the public's understanding and quite possibly policy makers' understanding as well. The power of frames to structure not only what we think about when we think about threats and the organizations that employ them, but also how these frames eliminate choices most vividly illustrates the importance of identifying the frames that structure our understanding of terrorism.

## NOTES

1. R. Hülsse and A. Spencer, "The Metaphor of Terror: Terrorism Studies and the Constructivist Turn," *Security Dialogue* 39, no. 6 (2008).

2. J. Victoroff, "The Mind of the Terrorist: A Review and Critique of Psychological Approaches," *Journal of Conflict Resolution* 49, no. 1 (2005).

3. D. Gambetta, *The Sicilian Mafia: The Business of Private Protection* (Cambridge, MA: Harvard University Press, 1993); A.B. Krueger, *What Makes a Terrorist? Economics and the Roots of Terrorism*, Lionel Robbins Lectures (Princeton, NJ: Princeton University Press, 2007).

4. P. Joosse, S.M. Bucerius, and S.K. Thompson, "Narratives and Counternarratives: Somali-Canadians on Recruitment as Foreign Fighters to Al-Shabaab," *British Journal of Criminology* 55, no. 4 (2015).

5. Hülsse and Spencer, "The Metaphor of Terror," 571.

6. A.T. Turk, "Sociology of Terrorism," *Annual Review of Sociology* 30 (2004): 271. As Hülsse and Spencer stress, "To avoid any misunderstanding, let us clarify that such a constructivist perspective does not deny terrorism, Islamic or other. There are real people who purport real actions, but what these people and their deeds mean is a matter of interpretation." Hülsse and Spencer, "The Metaphor of Terror," 575.

7. See, for example, Hülsse and Spencer, "The Metaphor of Terror"; Aditi Bhatia, "Discursive Illusions in the American National Strategy for Combating Terrorism," *Journal of Language and Politics* 7, no. 2 (2008).

8. E.V. Walter, *Terror and Resistance: A Study of Political Violence, with Case Studies of Primitive African Communities* (New York: Oxford University Press, 1969); Michael Stohl, "Demystifying Terrorism: The Myths and Realities of Contemporary Political Terrorism," in *The Politics of Terrorism*, 3rd ed., ed. Michael Stohl (New York: Marcel Dekker, 1988), 1–28.

9. R.M. Entman, "Cascading Activation: Contesting the White House's Frame after 9/11," *Political Communication* 20, no. 4 (2003); S.D. Reese and S.C. Lewis, "Framing the War on Terror: The Internalization of Policy in the US Press," *Journalism* 10, no. 6 (2009).

10. Brigitte L. Nacos and Oscar Torres-Reyna, "Framing Muslim-Americans before and after 9/11," in *Framing Terrorism: The News Media, the Government, and the Public*, ed. Pippa Norris, Montague Kern, and Marion Just (New York: Routledge, 2003).

11. Christopher J. Finlay, "How to Do Things with the Word 'Terrorist,'" *Review of International Studies* 35, no. 4 (2009).

12. Hülsse and Spencer, "The Metaphor of Terror," 588.

13. D.V. Shah, D. Domke, and D.B. Wackman, "'To Thine Own Self Be True': Values, Framing, and Voter Decision-Making Strategies," *Communication Research* 23, no. 5 (1996).

14. P. Norris, M. Kern, and M. Just, *Framing Terrorism: The News Media, the Government, and the Public* (New York: Routledge, 2003).

15. See B. Van Gorp, "The Constructionist Approach to Framing: Bringing Culture Back In," *Journal of Communication* 57, no. 1 (2007): 65.

16. R.M. Entman, "Framing—Toward Clarification of a Fractured Paradigm," *Journal of Communication* 43, no. 4 (1993); Entman, *Projections of Power: Framing News, Public Opinion, and U.S. Foreign Policy* (Chicago: University of Chicago Press, 2004).

17. W.R. Neuman, M.R. Just, and A.N. Crigler, *Common Knowledge: News and the Construction of Political Meaning*, American Politics and Political Economy Series (Chicago: University of Chicago Press, 1992), 60.

18. S. D. Reese, "Framing Public Life: A Bridging Model for Media Research," in *Framing Public Life: Perspectives on Media and Our Understanding of the Social World*, ed. Stephan D. Reese, Oscar H. Gandy Jr., and August E. Grant (Mahwah, NJ: Lawrence Erlbaum Associates, 2001), 11.

19. M. C. Nisbet, "Knowledge into Action: Framing the Debates over Climate Change and Poverty," in *Doing News Framing Analysis: Empirical and Theoretical Perspectives*, ed. P. D'Angelo and Jim A. Kuypers (New York: Routledge, 2010).

20. Reese, "Framing Public Life."

21. The disparity in the number of articles between the *New York Times* and the *Wall Street Journal* can be attributed to the newspapers' differing foci. Most *Wall Street Journal* articles discussing terrorism are found in the paper's editorial section.

22. To be as inclusive and complete as possible, we used wildcard search terms, which allow us to find articles with any version of these three spellings; for example, Qaeda, Qaeda's, al Qaeda.

23. Lada Adamic, "Complex Systems: Unzipping Zipf's Law," *Nature* 474 (2011): 164.

24. Ibid.; Ramon Ferrer i Cancho and Ricard V. Solé, "Least Effort and the Origins of Scaling in Human Language," *Proceedings of the National Academy of Sciences of the United States of America* 100, no. 3 (2002).

25. Ferrer i Cancho and Solé, "Least Effort and the Origins of Scaling in Human Language," 790.

26. This total excludes terrorist organizations with no mentions in our data set.

27. All articles were published between January 1, 2013, and December 31, 2014; we did not limit the sample solely to news articles, opting for maximum inclusion for this analysis.

28. See B. K. Smith, A. Figueroa-Caballero, and M. Stohl, "Al Qaeda in the American Consciousness: Communicative Construction of the Terrorist Actor through Attribute Framing," paper presented at the International Communication Association conference, Fukuoka, Japan, 2016.

29. I. P. Levin, S. L. Schneider, and G. J. Gaeth, "All Frames Are Not Created Equal: A Typology and Critical Analysis of Framing Effects," *Organizational Behavior and Human Decision Processes* 76, no. 2 (1998).

30. Hülsse and Spencer, "The Metaphor of Terror."

31. That is to say, the terrorists' structure and operations. Ibid.; Harmonie Toros, "Terrorists, Scholars and Ordinary People: Confronting Terrorism Studies with Field Experiences," *Critical Studies on Terrorism* 1, no. 2 (August 2008): 279–92 (doi:10.1080/17539150802184652).

32. Hülsse and Spencer, "The Metaphor of Terror," 578.

33. Entman, "Framing—Toward Clarification of a Fractured Paradigm," 54.

34. See B. K. Smith, E. Salcido, and M. Stohl, "Al Qaeda in the American Consciousness: The Role of Al Qaeda in Framing the Global Terrorist Threat," paper presented at the Western States Communication Association conference, San Diego, CA, 2016.

35. In some cases, direct "links" may indeed exist, but in all cases this was unclear from the text itself, especially as many of the texts did not actually name the organization being framed, instead referring to its members as "militants" or "rebels."

36. Richard Jackson, "Constructing Enemies: 'Islamic Terrorism' in Political and Acadmic Discourse," *Government and Opposition* 42, no. 3 (2007): 401.

# 8. Some Thoughts on Constructions of Terrorism and the Framing of the Terrorist Threat in the United Kingdom

Anthony Richards

One of the objectives of the "Constructions of Terrorism" conference on December 3–4, 2015, was to investigate "how states and societies construct understandings and categories of terrorism and extremism," and how an appreciation of this "construction" can "contribute to the development of more effective strategies for countering the extremist ideas that lead to the acts labelled as terrorism."[1]

This chapter is divided into two parts. The first offers some thoughts and potential avenues for research prompted by discussions at the conference. These reflections are a response to what seemed to the author a recurring theme at the conference (and in this volume) and a source of some frustration—that counterterrorism strategies so often seem to be counterproductive. It is in this context that it might be useful to try to generate a *deeper* appreciation as to why states respond to terrorism the way they do, even if, at a more superficial level (i.e., the ultimate manifestation of "counterterrorism"), some responses might be difficult to comprehend. What are the factors, perhaps even *systemic* ones, that condition states—and democratic states in particular—to respond to terrorism in certain ways (factors that may have very little concern with reducing the terrorist threat, or indeed that might even exacerbate it)? And what impact do such factors have on the construction of the "terrorist threat"? Richard Falk further suggests, in the context of his view of the distinctiveness of American "political consciousness," that a comparative study of how other major countries view and respond to "megaterrorist" events might be very useful.[2]

The second part of this chapter assesses how the contemporary terrorist threat has been constructed in the United Kingdom and what the implications of this construction are. Since the emergence of the United Kingdom's Contest strategy in the mid-2000s, one can reasonably argue that the parameters of British counterterrorism have widened. This expansion has been due largely to the way that the terrorist threat has been framed, with an increasing counterterrorism concern with the way people *think* as well as the way they *act*, and it is the Prevent strand of Contest that has been the most controversial in this regard.[3]

The chapter will, by briefly outlining the evolution of Prevent, describe how the terrorist threat has been characterized in the past decade in the United Kingdom and how this has impacted the remit of counterterrorism. It will then compare this contemporary understanding and "construction" of the terrorist threat with traditional conceptions of terrorism within the academic literature of the past five decades. For example, to most terrorism studies scholars the idea of a *nonviolent* ideology that is "conducive" to terrorism is something of a paradox,[4] because terrorism has been understood as ineluctably about violence or the threat of violence. The chapter goes on to argue that this anomaly is a symptom of, and indeed part of, what has been the increasing convergence of the discourses of terrorism, radicalization, and extremism in the United Kingdom.

## WHY STATES RESPOND TO TERRORISM THE WAY THEY DO

One of the recurring themes in the contributions to this volume is the view that responses to terrorism are very often counterproductive. Military responses, in particular, most notably through declarations of war, rather than reducing terrorism, often seem to actually serve both to sustain the narrative of terrorist adversaries and to perpetuate the terrorist threat. Richard Falk argues in chapter 9 of this volume that the "war template" of counterterrorism "locks the response into an extreme mode that appears to exclude compromise, accommodation, self-scrutiny, and even clarifying political enquiry. . . . By treating the conflict as absolute, it removes from view an assessment of both legitimate grievances and root causes, and thus unwittingly fuels a continuation of this vicious cycle" and its "seemingly indefinite prolongation." In chapter 6 Clark McCauley argues that "anger is the emotion sought by terrorists aiming to elicit overreaction to their attacks." Drawing on a number of examples, he suggests that the United States has duly obliged in fulfilling the adversary's strategy of jujitsu politics, which "points to the importance of action and reaction in the conflict between terrorists and their targets" and a "trajectory of escalating violence over time." Laura Dugan and Erica Chenoweth, in chapter 14, also question the utility of "retributive counterterrorism" in relation to deterring terrorism and point out that empirical evidence shows that "despite the political appeal of relying on harsh retaliation to deter terrorism, such efforts could fuel more conflict." And in chapter 5 Mark Juergensmeyer suggests that the declaration of war plays into the hands of ISIS and its own depiction of a "global war." These sentiments correspond with existing research that has shown that military retaliations either have no deterrent value or actually lead to greater levels of terrorism.[5]

It is not without a little frustration, then, that at times states, almost willfully it seems, employ strategies that are counterproductive and that lessons from the past, or from research findings such as those above, often appear to go unheeded. Why does this happen? One of the reflections that occurred to this author arising from the December conference, and prompted by Richard Falk's remarks in particular, was that it would perhaps be useful to try and generate a *deeper* appreciation as to why states respond to terrorism the way they do. Thus, while we ponder the counterproductive nature of some counterterrorism responses, we should appreciate that *there are underlying drivers for counterterrorism that may have very little to do with reducing the terrorist threat.* Assessing such drivers as potential explanations for, first, the way that the "terrorist threat" is constructed and, second, how "counterterrorism" is ultimately manifested might be a useful avenue of research.

Perhaps, when considering such research avenues, it would be useful to adapt some theoretical approaches from international relations that endeavor to explain state behavior and decision making. A good example might be the "levels of analysis" theories that seek to understand and explain foreign policy decision making (i.e., at the system level, state level, bureaucratic or organizational level, and the individual level), theories that can perhaps be applied to counterterrorism decision making.

First, then, to what extent, if at all, are there factors that condition how democratic states respond to terrorism? In other words, to what extent, if at all, is our response in some way structurally predetermined, regardless of whether or not the ultimate counterterrorism outcome actually reduces the threat from terrorism? Second—and this question resonates with remarks made by Richard Falk—at the state level, what are the political cultural factors that come into play that underpin predispositions toward particular counterterrorism responses and that might help us to understand why different states respond to terrorism in different ways? Falk proposes a comparative study of the way different states perceive "megaterrorist" incidents. He suggests that there is, for example, "something very distinctive about American political consciousness that bears on the way in which these large-scale incidents are perceived and on the response pattern that is generated by these events."[6]

What, for instance, prompted Norway to respond to the Breivik attacks with "more democracy"? What has led Denmark to liaise with "extremists" to prevent those with similar belief systems from engaging in acts of terrorism, but has prompted the United Kingdom to exclude such nonviolent extremists as potential collaborators against violence? And, further, what are the cultural and institutional constraints and facilitators that may favor one counterterrorist approach over another? A telling example in a different context might be President Barack Obama's self-confessed frustration over his inability to introduce more stringent gun control measures in the United States.

Exploring the potential impact of systemic and political cultural factors might, then, engender a deeper appreciation of (1) the roots of counterterrorism; (2) how, in this context, the "terrorist threat" is subsequently constructed; (3) how this appreciation might be beneficial when trying to understand and explain the ultimate manifestations of "counterterrorism."

## DEMOCRACY AND COUNTERTERRORISM

Democratic states are, by definition, answerable to their populations. In chapter 6 of this volume Clark McCauley convincingly argues that, in the case of the United States, anger rather than fear is the overriding emotive response to terrorism, and that the tendency is for this anger to favor more aggressive reactions. Andrew Silke, using case studies to argue that military reprisals for acts of terrorism are often counterproductive (he focuses on the examples of the United States and Israel in the 1980s and 1990s), notes that there nevertheless appears to be a human psychological desire for revenge and retribution: "Human psychology is inclined to support and tolerate such hard-line approaches even if the policies only exacerbate and prolong the conflict."[7] From McCauley's and Silke's research, it seems, then, that a popular response is a military one. It is not surprising, therefore, that, at times and in particular states, politicians and leaders present themselves as "tough on terrorism" and employ strategies accordingly, even if they turn out to be counterproductive. An *effective* response in reducing the terrorist threat might look very different.

Democratic governments are inherently sensitive to public opinion when contemplating counterterrorism approaches. In general, governments must demonstrate to their populations that "they are doing something" about terrorism, even if that something has little bearing on, or indeed may even exacerbate, the level of terrorist threat. Yet, quite apart from military retaliations, there is often an inexorable compulsion to act in other ways that more broadly "do the terrorists' job for them." The core essence of terrorism, in this author's view, lies in the intent to generate a wider psychological impact beyond the immediate victims.[8] Yet, it is difficult to see how governments, when faced with terrorist events, can avoid facilitating this objective. It is in many ways inevitable that the response to acts of terrorism from democratic governments, their societies, and their free media helps to ensure that such attacks do indeed generate maximum psychological impact—that, in fact, our own responses largely provide the attention and impact that terrorists crave.

From this "psychological impact" perspective, the perpetrators of the January 2015 *Charlie Hebdo* attack in Paris, for example, would have seen it as an unqualified success. They had, after all, managed to provoke the deployment of 80,000 French security personnel in the hunt for them, while the attacks prompted more than 3 million French citizens and more than forty world leaders to march in protest against them. In what way other than through their acts of terrorism could such a small number of people have hoped to galvanize the attention of such an enormous domestic and global audience?

The intended psychological impact of terrorism is to breed wider uncertainty and insecurity, and the truth is that states often oblige—through hastily convened government "crisis" meetings and security briefings, through the ratcheting up of armed security to unprecedented levels nationwide, and through responding to the need "to do something" in the face of political and public expectation, perhaps in the form of promised security reviews and overhauls and fresh legislative appraisals to cope with the evolving terrorist threat. There appears, then, to be an inexorable impulse to provide the terrorists with the very attention and impact they seek. This pattern was also evident after the London Woolwich attack in May 2013, and after the Boston Marathon attack in April 2013. This is not a criticism, for such responses are in many ways inherent to democratic societies. States are, after all, obliged to show that they are treating such threats with the utmost seriousness. One of the long-standing dilemmas of counterterrorism has therefore been how democratic societies and governments should respond to those who carry out acts of terrorism without playing into their hands.

There are certainly understandable reasons why, in these ways, democratic states are bound to "do the terrorists' job for them." Research shows that terrorism generates public fear disproportionate to its actual threat and that governments need to address this imbalance and reassure their populations.[9] Yet the political traction of "counterterrorism," and its exploitation, can serve the purposes of those who employ terrorism in ways where governments and leaders arguably *do* have greater liberty to exercise choice. Constructing the terrorist threat as an existential one, for example, lends itself to expansive and draconian "counterterrorism" measures, as leaders may seek to reap political capital by portraying themselves as the true protectors of the public in the face of such peril. Donald Trump, in the aftermath of the Orlando shooting attack, left few people in doubt as to his avowed perception of the terrorist threat: "If we do not get tough and smart real fast, we are not going to have a country anymore."[10]

John Mueller and Mark Stewart, in chapter 2 of this volume, describe at some length how the threat of terrorism in the United States has been grossly exaggerated. It is perhaps paradoxical, then, that the construction of the threat in this way actually helps to sustain the very narrative that terrorists seek to project. One can imagine that the terrorist adversary would take some satisfaction from Trump's apparent fear, and the projection of that fear, that Americans would not "have a country anymore." Mueller and Stewart agree (in chapter 2) that "the persistent exaggeration of the capacities of terrorists has the perverse effect of glorifying the terrorist enterprise in the minds of many of its practitioners," and, as Juergensmeyer observes in chapter 5, the war model serves to sustain the ISIS depiction of a global war. Further back, in the years immediately after 9/11, the Bush administration framed the campaign against terrorism in precisely the same way that al-Qaeda had depicted it: using the parallel rhetoric of "you are either with us or against us," the administration helped to elevate al-Qaeda to the status of global adversary in a bipolar struggle, when it was nothing of this kind. (This elevation was perhaps no more evident than when both main party leaders in the 2004 US presidential election obliged Osama bin Laden's attempt to intervene in the poll by responding to his taped message.)

The author surveyed numerous polls carried out in the United Kingdom in the decade after 9/11 with the aim of determining the attitudes toward counterterrorism of the British public in general and the Muslim population in particular.[11] One theme was constant: there was a general public desire for much harsher counterterrorism measures at home, while polls of British Muslims showed an increasing fear of being targeted by such measures. Yet there is potential danger in the relationship between the majority of the general public believing that more draconian measures are necessary and a government that presents itself as the solution to such concerns. Hence, as this author has argued elsewhere, "the very community that the government needs to engage with could feel further marginalized. Reassuring the majority at the expense of further alienating a minority is not a recipe for reducing terrorism."[12]

There are, then, factors that may not necessarily be concerned with the reduction of the terrorist threat or with preparation for its consequences, but that nevertheless contribute to the ultimate "counterterrorism" position, even if elements of it are counterproductive. Some factors may be on the "systemic" end of the spectrum, where democracies are duty-bound to reassure their populations. Others may be more opportunistic in nature, where "terrorism" may be exploited, exaggerated, and constructed for political gain. "Counterterrorism" is thus constructed accordingly, and it may entail the pursuit of broader strategic objectives that might not only have little to do with responding to terrorism but that may actually exacerbate its threat or serve to sustain more broadly the narratives of those employing terrorism.

Related to this is perhaps a further factor that potentially underpins counterproductive terrorism responses: the innate and natural desire of states and their governments to preserve the status quo against any perceived threats, terrorist or otherwise. It is in this context that the concept of terrorism, and its pejorative connotation in practice, may provide a useful means through which to discredit adversaries, and the "terrorist threat" may then be constructed accordingly. Michael Blain, for example, has argued that "the emergence of terrorism as a concept and political problem was associated with the development of modern liberal democracies" and, drawing on Michel Foucault's concept of subjection, that "the invention of a discourse of terrorism was a strategic response to danger, and could be deployed through basic regulatory practices of subjection."[13]

The contested meaning of "terrorism" facilitates enormous elasticity in the construction of the terrorist threat, which in turn can determine the (sometimes dangerous) scope of "counterterrorism." The Policy Working Group on the United Nations and Terrorism has cautioned:

> The rubric of counter-terrorism can be used to justify acts in support of political agendas, such as the consolidation of political power, elimination of political opponents, inhibition of legitimate dissent and/ or suppression of resistance to military occupation. Labelling opponents or adversaries as terrorists offers a time-tested technique to de-legitimize and demonize them. The United Nations should beware of offering, or being perceived to be offering, a blanket or automatic endorsement of all measures taken in the name of counter-terrorism.[14]

The word *terrorism,* then, particularly since 9/11, has been and can be deployed to discredit opposition movements, and draconian measures can be invoked accordingly.[15] Because of its contested meaning and its pejorative use in practice, the term is often constructed according to where one's interests lie. Conversely, perhaps just as important are processes of *deconstruction* for activity that one would prefer not to call terrorism. Donald Rumsfeld, for example, stressed the importance of assisting the "anti-terrorist, anti-Taliban effort,"[16] yet the Northern Alliance (part of the "anti-terrorist" effort) had itself been noted for committing many acts that might themselves be interpreted as acts of "terrorism" or "terror" (depending on how one conceptualizes these terms).[17]

Counterterrorism can, of course, be effectively and plausibly merged with other policy goals that may also help to counter terrorism or at least that do not exacerbate the terrorist threat. In the United Kingdom the overhaul of Civil Contingencies legislation in 2004, for example, is designed to be applicable for responses to natural disasters as well as other threats such as terrorism, while prophylactic measures, or indeed simply good governance, may be carried out in order to preserve general peace and stability against a number of potential threats, terrorism being but one of them.

"Terrorism," and therefore "counterterrorism," however, can be exploited to pursue agendas that may have little to do with reducing the threat of terrorism or preparing for its consequences, but instead may have everything to do with the pursuit of broader national and strategic objectives (under the rubric of "counterterrorism"), which can at times lead to new terrorist threats or exacerbate existing ones. Richard Falk argues that the American response to 9/11 was intertwined with US grand strategy in relation to reconfiguring the Middle East, and that the post-9/11 environment provided the international and political climate through which these grandiose designs could potentially be realized.[18] Such an interpretation might help to explain the Bush administration's persistent attempts to link Saddam Hussein's Iraq with al-Qaeda. Iraq was constructed as part of the global terror threat and was therefore a focus of the "war on terror," a focus that paradoxically (but not altogether unexpectedly) had a counterproductive effect on the terrorist threat (both internationally and in postinvasion Iraq).

In summary, then, perhaps a useful avenue of research would be to explore the factors that underpin democratic responses to terrorism, but that may have little bearing or intended effect on the terrorist threat. The above embryonic thoughts have touched on four potential areas of inquiry: (1) the impulse for democratic states to respond to the perceived demands of their populations; (2) the temptation to exploit "terrorism" and to exaggerate its threat for political purposes; (3) states' innate general desire to preserve the status quo in dealing with threats (terrorist or otherwise) and the impact this has on constructions of terrorism; and (4) the pursuit of national, international, and strategic macro-objectives and the potential exploitation of "terrorism" and "counterterrorism" to achieve these goals. Of course, different states respond to terrorism in different ways, and, as Falk suggests, it would also be useful to engage in a comparative study of the relationship between political culture or "political consciousness" and counterterrorism. All of these factors potentially underpin how the "terrorist threat" is constructed and therefore what the ultimate "counterterrorism" response might be.

## CONSTRUCTING THE TERRORIST THREAT IN THE UNITED KINGDOM

### Terrorism and Counterterrorism

Terrorism has, of course, not been a new challenge for the United Kingdom. The "Troubles" of Northern Ireland that emerged in the late 1960s spawned a number of violent republican and loyalist groups. Despite the endurance of the conflict over more than two decades, and at a cost of more than thirty-five hundred lives, a peace process was set in motion in the 1990s that culminated in the Good Friday Agreement in 1998. While the new political dispensation was fragile to begin with (it was suspended on several occasions in the initial years after 1998), Northern Ireland has emerged from its dark past into a period of relative peace.

While the terrorism related to Northern Ireland dissipated (notwithstanding the persistence of the dissident republican threat), a very different type of terrorist threat was emerging in the 1990s, culminating in the devastating attacks on September 11, 2001. (Al-Qaeda had already carried out the US embassy attacks in Kenya and Tanzania in August 1998, which killed more than 200 people, as well as the audacious maritime attack on the USS *Cole* in October 2000, which killed 17 American sailors.) The attacks of 9/11 prompted the United Kingdom to add a new chapter to its Strategic Defence Review of 1998. While the original review had already pointed to the need for rapidly deployable forces, this was further emphasized in the "New Chapter" and underpinned by the view that "it is much better to engage our enemies in their backyard than in ours, at a time and place of our choosing and not theirs."[19] In March 2004 al-Qaeda carried out simultaneous bomb attacks on the Madrid train system, killing 192 people. It was, as far as the United Kingdom was concerned, and in the opinion of senior police officers at that time, merely a case of when, rather than if, the United Kingdom would be attacked, and on July 7, 2007, the country suffered its first multiple-suicide terrorist attack with the loss of 52 lives.

The United Kingdom set about revamping its response to the emergence of the contemporary terrorist threat. It developed what is known as the Contest strategy, first published in July 2006 and revised in 2009 and 2011. Within this model are four broad and distinct areas of response, known as the Four Ps:

*Pursue.*   The Contest strategy states that "the purpose of Pursue is to stop terrorist attacks in this country and against our interests overseas."[20] This entails early detection and disruption of terrorist plots, and effective prosecution.[21] The United Kingdom's intelligence effort has been fundamental to this strand of Contest (indeed MI5, the Secret Service, has doubled in size since 9/11).

*Prevent.*   This strand of Contest is chiefly concerned with preventing people from becoming terrorists or supporting terrorism. It aims to prevent people being "drawn into" terrorism and advocates a multisectoral approach toward radicalization.[22] Prevent has, at times, changed its focus (see below), with the 2011 version stating that the strategy would also respond to the "ideological challenge of terrorism."[23]

*Protect.*   The strategy states that "the purpose of Protect is to strengthen our protection against a terrorist attack in the UK or against our interests overseas and so reduce our vulnerability."[24] In particular Protect aims to enhance border security, to better protect the transport network (including aviation security), to increase the resilience of the United Kingdom's critical national infrastructure, and to better protect crowded places.[25]

*Prepare.*   This strand entails being as prepared as possible whenever a terrorist attack takes place.[26] At the heart of Prepare is an effective emergency response along with the preparation for new and evolving terrorist modes of attack (including mass shooting attacks, such as that in Paris in November 2015). In the early 2000s the United Kingdom overhauled its civil contingencies legislation. While this was initially due to the need to revamp civil contingencies arrangements in the face of fuel protests, the outbreak of foot-and-mouth disease, and flooding in 2000, the attacks on September 11, 2001, gave it a whole new impetus.

## PREVENT AND ITS SHIFTING FOCUS

Perhaps the most controversial of the Four Ps, and the most relevant to the construction of the contemporary terrorist threat in the United Kingdom, has been the Prevent strand. In its original form (2006) Contest stated that Prevent aimed "to tackle the radicalization of individuals," and since the mid-2000s there has emerged a discourse of radicalization (both in policy making and academia). Yet there has been some confusion over what is meant by "radicalization" and who "the radicalized" are. Related to this, it is fair to suggest that there was some confusion as to what the remit of Prevent should be, and more particularly, the extent to which it should be concerned with the way people *think ideologically*, not just the way they *act* (i.e., "preventing" acts of terrorism). The revised version of Prevent (2011), however, addressed this and was unequivocal: its focus was not just on those who were violent or who engaged in acts of terrorism, or those who appeared to be on a trajectory toward violence, but also those who held certain "extremist" but *nonviolent* views. The strategy was henceforth also to be focused on extremist but nonviolent ideology that Contest describes, rather paradoxically, as "conducive" to terrorism.[27]

## CONCEPTUALIZING TERRORISM

Any discussion of what constitutes the "terrorist threat" should logically hinge on what one means by *terrorism* in the first place. How, then, has terrorism been traditionally understood in the academic literature? *Terrorism* is, of course, like any other social science concept, a *social construction*, and so one cannot, by definition, speak "truth" or be definitive as to what it means. Indeed, those who claim that the term *terrorism* has been abused are therefore themselves culpable of making some kind of knowledge claim as to what terrorism is and is not.

This does not mean to say, however, that one should not strive for an agreed conceptualization of terrorism at a given time in a contemporary context, even if the outcome can never amount to the truth. Indeed, the lack of such endeavors can have profound real-life consequences. Taking the concept of crime as an example, it would be folly not to identify the parameters of what we mean by crime; otherwise, appropriate laws cannot be drafted and implemented to counter what are deemed criminal behaviors. This is notwithstanding that crime, the laws enacted to counter it, and indeed the states that introduce the laws are all social constructs. Similarly, to use another example, in order to develop norms regarding the protection and advancement of human rights, there has to be some agreed-upon notion as to what constitutes human rights, even though this concept is again socially constructed.

If we accept that it is still a worthwhile endeavor to conceptualize the phenomenon of terrorism, then what is it that is analytically distinctive about it compared with other forms of political violence? In any such conceptual endeavor the challenge is to carefully consider the criteria that need to be satisfied for an act of violence to be deemed an act of terrorism—and one should not seek out more "positive" labels if that act of terrorism is carried out for a cause that one sympathizes with, just as one should not be more inclined to use the concept if one disagrees with the cause. Such tendencies simply entrench *terrorism* as a pejorative label at the expense of a more neutral and analytical approach.

Notwithstanding its social construction, a general consensus as to what the core essence of terrorism is does appear to have developed in the terrorism literature of the past five decades. This consensus revolves around its psychological dimension: that terrorism entails the intent to generate a psychological impact beyond the immediate victims, that terrorism is a form of violent communication for a political motive, that victims are not the intended targets—rather it is the wider audience(s) that are the intended recipients of the "terrorist message."

Two further points are worth drawing from the conceptual literature of terrorism, points that are pertinent when scrutinizing contemporary constructions of the phenomenon. The first is that terrorism is best understood as a *method* of political violence, rather than as something that should be conceptualized according to who the perpetrator is or what the cause is. Thus, if an act of violence satisfies one's criteria in order to be labeled terrorism, then an act of terrorism it remains, regardless of the cause. Of course, there are ideologies and belief systems that may justify, endorse, or advocate the use of terrorism, but such belief systems cannot take ownership of the phenomenon. This is because terrorism has also been carried out in the name of ideologies that are not in and of themselves violent—including many nationalist ideologies and single-issue causes (such as animal rights and abortion). Terrorism is therefore best conceptualized as a *method* that can be carried out in the cause of a wide variety of belief systems, whether or not these doctrines are themselves intrinsically violent or "terroristic."

The second point to draw from the conceptual literature of terrorism is that it is ineluctably about *the use of violence or the threat of violence*. If an ideology is nonviolent, it cannot itself be responsible for terrorism—rather it is those who adopt the method of terrorism who are culpable. If an ideology *is* itself responsible for terrorism in some way, *then it is not nonviolent*—hence the paradox in the 2011 Prevent strategy of an extremist but *nonviolent* ideology that is deemed "conducive" to terrorism. The terrorism threat in the United Kingdom has therefore been constructed as including nonviolent but "extremist" thought *as well as* violence or the threat of violence in pursuit of that thought.

## THE STRUCTURE OF TERRORISM

The concern with any nonviolent ideology said to be "conducive" to terrorism has arisen in the context of a structural shift in the nature of the terrorist threat. The forms of terrorism that confronted the United Kingdom from the late 1960s and throughout the "Troubles" of Northern Ireland emanated from terrorist organizations that were primarily centralized or hierarchical in structure. Accordingly, the threshold for the remit of counterterrorism was arguably more straightforward than it is today. In other words, the existence of such groups meant that there was in the main an organizational threshold between those who would resort to political violence and those who would not.

While it would be a mistake to conclude that this type of relatively centralized structure no longer exists, it is the case that the terrorism of most concern to the United Kingdom over the past fifteen years has been that perpetrated by those claiming to be acting on behalf of Islam, and one of the features of this international terrorist threat has been its decentralized nature. This has manifested itself in the form of al-Qaeda and also, more recently, through the threat presented by ISIS and those inspired by them. There is a particular concern over the threat from "self-starter," "lone-wolf" or "small-group" terrorism, consisting of inspired individuals with no obvious organizational affiliation.[28] Part of this threat includes the impact of the Internet and social media that serve as "horizontal platforms" well-suited to the grassroots mobilization and recruitment of would-be perpetrators of violence.

It is in this context that the British government has been concerned with intervening in the trajectory of terrorism at the *earliest* possible stage and with identifying all those it deems "vulnerable" to terrorism. Indeed, the Institute for Policy Research and Development has argued that, if it is believed that there is no "typical pathway to violent extremism," the "scope of risk-assessment is rendered potentially unlimited" for British Muslims.[29]

Thus the construction of the terrorist threat in the United Kingdom has led to the expansion of "counterterrorism" in two ways. First, as argued above, there is an increased *wider* concern with the way citizens think ideologically—a broader view that if they believe in certain *nonviolent* dogmas said to be "conducive" to terrorism, they are part of the "terrorist problem," even if they deplore the violent methods of al-Qaeda and ISIS. This represents an unhelpful counterterrorism conundrum, manifested in the policy of excluding such people as potential collaborators and dissuaders against those who resort to terrorism.[30] Second, beyond this wider concern and the broadening of the potential "terrorism problem," there is also a *linear* concern where, in the context of the contemporary "low-level" and decentralized threat, there is the impetus for intervention at the earliest possible stage of any pathway or trajectory toward the use of violence.

## THE MERGING OF THE DISCOURSES OF TERRORISM, RADICALIZATION, AND EXTREMISM

The widening of the remit of counterterrorism has been facilitated by the merging of the discourses of, initially, terrorism and radicalization and, more recently, of terrorism, radicalization, and extremism in the United Kingdom.[31] It is in this context that the construction of "terrorism" or the "terrorist threat" has evolved. This convergence, however, has blurred the important distinction between extremism of thought and extremism of method.

This is not to suggest that the ideologies in general of those who carry out acts of terrorism are not relevant for counterterrorism. They certainly are. First, ideologies that are themselves violent or "terroristic" are, of course, of concern to counterterrorism; and second, whether violent or not, the doctrines of those who carry out acts of terrorism are important to scrutinize because they can give some indication as to the likely parameters of terrorist targeting. But the idea of a *nonviolent ideology* that is somehow intrinsically linked to the method of terrorism does not square well with conventional academic understandings of terrorism.

## THE CONSTRUCTION OF "EXTREMISM"

In this context it is also worth drawing attention to British government understandings of "extremism." As argued above, extremist activity (in this case terrorism) has been carried out for non-extremist ideologies (such as nationalism and single-issue causes). It is also possible, conversely, that non-extremist activity can be carried out in pursuit of "extremist" doctrines. These distinctions between method and belief system appear to be over-looked in the UK definition of extremism: "vocal or active opposition to fundamental British values, including democracy, the rule of law, individual liberty and mutual respect and tolerance of different faiths and beliefs."[32] Thus peaceful activity itself becomes extremist if it supports an extremist ideology, while, conversely, the definition *excludes* extremist activity (such as terrorism and violence) if it is carried out in the cause of a non-extremist doctrine. Saul, for example, notes that the international community might regard "some terrorist-type violence as 'illegal but justifiable' . . . where it was committed in the 'collective defence of human rights'"; this would surely be a case of extremist activity undertaken in the cause of what would be considered a non-extremist doctrine (defense of human rights).[33]

As this author has noted elsewhere,[34] the Prevent definition, then, appears to extrematize *activity* (whatever activity that might be) if it is carried out for an extremist cause at the same time that it excludes the possibility of extremist activity carried out in the name of a non-extremist doctrine. Yet *it makes no analytical sense to extrematize the method just because of antipathy toward the goal, nor to dilute the extremity of the method just because one has greater sympathy with the cause.*[35] Adopting such positions would have clear parallels with the subjective application of the term *terrorism* at the expense of a more objective analytical approach.[36]

## CONCLUSION

This chapter begins by offering some thoughts prompted by the December conference in Santa Barbara, California. In particular, while there is frustration at the apparent propensity of governments to at times adopt counterterrorism responses that seem counterproductive, the suggestion here is that we should strive for a deeper appreciation of why democratic states respond to terrorism the way they do. This chapter proposes that we should strive to appreciate and explore underlying factors behind counterterrorism, factors that may contribute to our understanding of how the "terrorist threat" is constructed and how counterterrorism is then ultimately manifested. Such factors may have little intended impact on the terrorist threat, and, indeed, may even exacerbate it. This deeper appreciation might help us to explain some counterterrorism responses that at a more superficial level may seem perplexing, and it calls for a self-reflexive approach. As Richard Falk aptly puts it in chapter 9 of this volume, "The potential relevance of critical self-scrutiny cannot be exaggerated in shaping an effective counterterrorist approach."

Turning to the case of the United Kingdom, the chapter argues that we have in recent years seen the merging of the discourses of terrorism, radicalization, and extremism in public, political, and academic discourse. This has helped to blur the important distinction between *extremism of method* and *extremism of thought*. If we are to engage with the concept of extremism, particularly in a counterterrorism context, there needs to be a clearer distinction made between the two, because it is surely violence and the threat of violence (integral to terrorism) that should be of primary concern to counterterrorism. Through the way the "terrorist threat" has been constructed in the United Kingdom, it seems, counterterrorism has become increasingly counterideology over and above its remit of countering terrorism.

## NOTES

1. See Constructions of Terrorism Conference, TRENDS Research and Advisory, http://trendsinstitution.org/?p=1379 (last accessed July 1, 2016).

2. Richard Falk, in "Richard Falk & Richard Burchill at the Constructions of Terrorism Conference" (video), December 3, 2015, http://trendsinstitution.org/constructions-of-terrorism-conference/ (last accessed March 23, 2017).

3. Contest consists of the four strands known as the Four Ps: Pursue, Protect, Prevent, and Prepare.

4. Secretary of State for the Home Department, "Contest: The United Kingdom's Strategy for Countering Terrorism" (July 2011), 12, http://www.homeoffice.gov.uk/publications/counter-terrorism/counter-terrorism-strategy/strategy-contest?view=Binary (last accessed July 1, 2016).

5. See, for example, W. Enders and T. Sandler, "The Effectiveness of Antiterrorism Policies: A Vector-Autoregression-Intervention Analysis," *American Political Science Review*, 87:4 (December 1993); A. Silke, "Retaliating against Terrorism," in A. Silke (ed.), *Terrorists, Victims and Society* (New York: Wiley, 2003); B. Hoffman, *Inside Terrorism* (New York: Columbia University Press, 1998), 191–93.

6. Falk, in "Richard Falk & Richard Burchill at the Constructions of Terrorism Conference."

7. Silke, "Retaliating against Terrorism," 231.

8. A. Richards, *Conceptualizing Terrorism* (London: Oxford University Press, 2015).

9. See the subsection "Measuring Public Anxiety" in A. Richards, "Countering the Psychological Impact of Terrorism: Challenges for UK Homeland Security," in A. Silke (ed.), *The Psychology of Counter-terrorism* (London: Routledge, 2011). See also Hoffman, *Inside Terrorism*, 148–50.

10. For transcript, see "Donald J. Trump Statement Regarding Tragic Terrorist Attack in Orlando, Florida," donaldjtrump.com, June 12, 2016, https://www.donaldjtrump.com/press-releases/donald-j-trump-statement-regarding-tragic-terrorist-attacks (accessed February 27, 2017).

11. Richards, "Countering the Psychological Impact of Terrorism."

12. Ibid., 197.

13. M. Blain, "On the Genealogy of Terrorism," in D. Staines (ed.), *Interrogating the War on Terror: Interdisciplinary Perspectives* (Newcastle, UK: Cambridge Scholars, 2007), 50–51.

14. Policy Working Group on the United Nations and Terrorism, quoted in A. Schmid (ed.), *The Routledge Handbook of Terrorism Research* (London: Routledge, 2011), 56.

15. For examples of this, see B. Saul, "Defining Terrorism to Protect Human Rights," in Staines, *Interrogating the War on Terror*, 201–2.

16. Rumsfeld, quoted in "A Nation Challenged: The Rebels; Bush Approves Covert Aid for Taliban Foes," *New York Times*, October 1, 2001, http://www.nytimes.com/2001/10/01/world/a-nation-challenged-the-rebels-bush-approves-covert-aid-for-taliban-foes.html (last accessed July 1, 2016).

17. See "Military Assistance to the Afghan Opposition," Human Rights Watch (October 5, 2001), 3–4, http://www.hrw.org/legacy/backgrounder/asia/afghan-bck1005.pdf (last accessed July 1, 2016).

18. Falk, in "Richard Falk & Richard Burchill at the Constructions of Terrorism Conference."

19. Geoffrey Hoon, "The Strategic Defence Review: A New Chapter," Ministry of Defence, p. 5, http://archives.livreblancdefenseetsecurite.gouv.fr/2008/IMG/pdf/sdr_a_new_chapter_cm5566_vol1.pdf (last accessed September 11, 2016).

20. Secretary of State for the Home Department, "Contest," 10.

21. Ibid.

22. Ibid., 12.

23. Ibid.

24. Ibid., 12–13.

25. Ibid., 13.

26. Ibid., 13–14.

27. Ibid., 12.

28. After the Paris attacks of November 2015 there was some debate over the extent to which acts of terrorism would become increasingly prepared and organized from within the territory that ISIS controlled. Through ISIS's encouragement of "homegrown" attacks in European countries, however, and through the return of so-called foreign fighters (some of whom may wish to carry out attacks in their home countries), at this writing, ISIS-inspired terrorism still represents a formidable decentralized threat.

29. Institute for Policy Research and Development, cited in Communities and Local Government Select Committee, House of Commons, "Preventing Violent Extremism: Sixth Report of Session 2009–10" (March 30, 2010), 9, http://www.publications.parliament.uk/pa/cm200910/cmselect/cmcomloc/65/65.pdf (last accessed July 1, 2016).

30. For example, "intervention providers" tasked with preventing individuals from becoming terrorists are not permitted to share the same ideological outlook as them: "intervention providers must not have extremist beliefs," but "they must have credibility" and be "able to reach and relate to" them (Secretary of State for the Home Department, "Contest," 65).

31. For a fuller discussion, see A. Richards, "From Terrorism to 'Radicalization' to 'Extremism': Counterterrorism Imperative or Loss of Focus?" *International Affairs* 91:2 (March 2015).

32. Secretary of State for the Home Department, "Prevent Strategy" (June 2011), 107, https://www.gov.uk/government/uploads/system/uploads/attachment_data/file/97976/prevent-strategy-review.pdf (last accessed July 1, 2016).

33. Saul, "Defining Terrorism to Protect Human Rights," 208.

34. Richards, "From Terrorism to 'Radicalization' to 'Extremism,'" 376.

35. Ibid.

36. For example, the more one refrains from using the word *terrorism* because of sympathy with the cause, or the more one is inclined to use it because of antipathy toward the goal, the further away one is from enhancing terrorism as an analytical (and more neutral) concept. See A. Richards, "Conceptualizing Terrorism," *Studies in Conflict and Terrorism* 37:3 (2014).

# 9. Contradictions in the Terrorist Discourse and Constraints on the Political Imagination of Violence

Richard Falk

The horrific Paris (2015) and Brussels (2016) terrorist incidents both recall the September 11, 2001, attacks on the World Trade Center and the Pentagon, but also contain new and diverse elements that make it timely and conceptually relevant to rethink the terrorism and counterterrorism discourses.[1] Particular attention should be given to how transnational political violence and terrorist labels are being used by a variety of political actors to demonize their adversaries while validating their own violent behavior. Perhaps the most innovative feature of this recent cycle of transnational political violence by both terrorist and counterterrorist actors is to delimit a combat zone that potentially encompasses the entire planet and that is media oriented to the extent of pursuing visually spectacular events (whether it be the execution of Osama bin Laden or exploding bombs in airports, music halls, and soccer pitches).

## COMPETING CONSTRUCTIONS OF TERRORISM AND THE TERRORIST CHALLENGE

The ensuing conflict between these antagonists is unfolding on this borderless global battlefield, especially in relation to the tactics and doctrinal formulations relied upon as much by the United States as by its principal nonstate adversaries.[2] Even after Paris and Brussels, not to mention such earlier events as the London and Madrid attacks, there remains a greater European reluctance to expand the combat zone, and a greater tendency to respond to disruptive attacks mainly within the traditional law enforcement paradigm coupled with major enhancements of internal security arrangements. In this respect there is a comparison to be drawn between the maximal approach adopted by the United States since 9/11 and the more moderate approach pursued so far by European states, especially those on the Continent.[3] There is a further distinction to be made between the drastic rhetoric used by the presidency of George W. Bush in the immediate aftermath of 9/11 and the far less histrionic language relied upon during the Obama administration that governed the United States from 2009 to the beginning of 2017, though the policies pursued exhibit more continuity than discontinuity.

The most innovative and consequential aspect of the post-9/11 discourse and approach was to break the earlier connection between terrorism and "crime," and insist on treating the counterterrorist undertaking as a type of "war" rather than as a form of law enforcement undertaken in relation to a particularly disruptive form of criminality.[4] Such a reclassification of non-state political violence has its own distinctive implications, above all the apparent exclusion of diplomacy and the claim that such violence is a form of "unprivileged belligerency" not regulated by international humanitarian law, at least as far as the treatment of enemy combatants and restraints on the use of force are concerned. The American torture debate that challenged what the Bush presidency called "enhanced interrogation" and the controversy concerning the applicability of either international humanitarian law or American constitutional law to the detention of suspects at Guantánamo are conceptual and behavioral effects of the merging of counterterrorism with war after 9/11.[5]

Controversy also surrounds the identification of terrorist actors. Of particular relevance is the sensitivity associated with linking the religion of Islam to the perpetration of such acts, and the polemical reaction of the American right wing to President Barack Obama's reluctance to denounce certain acts of political extremism as motivated or caused by the jihadist worldview of the perpetrator. The issue is complicated by the indistinct character of such incidents as San Bernardino and Orlando, which are predominantly perceived as "lone-wolf" events, while possessing a seemingly superficial link to ISIS that is exaggerated by the media and opportunistic politicians.[6] Serious political consequences are produced by deciding to speak of such acts as generic expressions of "political extremism," rather than relying on the more inflammatory terminology of "radical Islam" or "*jihadi* extremism."

The justification for this momentous shift in consciousness and behavior arises, above all, from the magnitude, originality, and severe shock caused by these attacks, especially 9/11, which did have societal effects that were in crucial respects certainly comparable to, or even greater than, past initiations of war. The 9/11 events were in many respects more threatening and harmful to the American homeland than was the Japanese attack on Pearl Harbor in 1941, and also more consequential. Al-Qaeda and ISIS attacks in Europe and the lone-wolf attacks in the United States carried out by Muslims with explicit connections to ISIS, while less spectacular, are also being perceived as part of an ongoing warlike struggle.[7] All of these events to varying degrees exposed the vulnerabilities of modern societies to political extremists who are prepared to engage in suicidal missions either out of conviction or as expressions of acute alienation.[8] From a psycho-political perspective it can be argued that any response less than the heightened atmosphere of war would trivialize the events and encourage domestic demagogues to seize the occasion to mock the political leadership as weak by proposing far bolder action to intimidate and eventually eliminate a terrorist enemy.[9] In effect, choosing the terminology of war was a way of signaling the scale of the challenge confronting and confounding governments after 9/11. Political leaders in the United States seemed generally gripped by panic after 9/11, fearing disastrous follow-up attacks.[10]

Yet for several reasons this fundamental shift in approach to transnational nonstate political extremism is more problematic than it might seem at first glance. It locks the response into an extreme mode that appears to exclude compromise, accommodation, self-scrutiny, or even clarifying political inquiry. By partially suspending the applicability of international humanitarian law and the Geneva Conventions, it loses some of the moral and legal high ground and invites a breakdown of humanitarian limits in the conduct of warfare. By treating the conflict as absolute, it removes from view an assessment of both legitimate grievances and root causes, and thus unwittingly fuels a continuation of this vicious cycle that seems to be morphing into a condition of permanent war.

Of course, frequently in the past other nonstate actors have made a transition from "terrorist" outlaw to negotiating partner with political grievances to assert. The Palestinian Liberation Organization (PLO) and Irish Republican Army (IRA) are two examples, but there are many others. There are recurrent reports of ongoing negotiations with the Taliban in efforts, so far without success, to end active combat operations in Afghanistan by reaching political compromise of the sort achieved in the Good Friday Agreement, which brought "a cold peace" to Northern Ireland in 1998.

In "wars" resulting from major *transnational* terrorist provocations, there has so far been no end game evident except the seemingly indefinite prolongation of conflict, a condition called "the long war" by Pentagon analysts in the aftermath of 9/11, and the hope that the terrorist adversary would disappear from the face of the earth or be eliminated.[11] As has been the subject of criticism, to declare a "war on terror" is to embark upon an unprecedented struggle against a type of behavior, rather than a discrete enemy, and given the degree of alienation and the depth and range of grievances felt around the world, there is no prospect of closure as in the ending of a traditional war by either diplomacy or military defeat. Perhaps the closest analogy to terrorism is piracy, which has never been dignified by being treated as a war, nor were pirates regarded as combatants or prisoners of war.[12]

Another question has generally been sidestepped in the media and in the language of political leaders: Does the term *terrorism* signify the identity of the actor or the nature of the violence? I published a book in 1988 with the title *Revolutionaries and Functionaries: The Dual Face of International Terrorism*.[13] Its thesis was that the only morally coherent use of *terrorism* is to reference violence that deliberately targets "the innocent" and seeks to induce widespread societal fear and passivity. Such a definitional perspective means that states as well as nonstate actors can be properly identified as perpetrators of terrorism.

Adopting this approach to the nature of terrorism makes it problematic to deny that during World War II the indiscriminate bombing of German and Japanese cities and the use of atomic bombs against Hiroshima and Nagasaki were examples of "state terror." More recently, as in the Israeli attacks on Gaza and the debates surrounding drone warfare, more controversial questions of categorizing political violence are posed. Concern about fixing the legally and morally proper limits of state violence has been discussed in the Israeli case by reference to the Dahiya Doctrine and associated practices that occurred in the course of the Lebanon War of 2006 and the Gaza attacks of 2008–9, 2012, and 2014.[14] The issue is also raised by military interventions that deliberately target civilian areas, inflicting "collateral damage" grossly disproportionate to any anticipated legitimate military result. The widespread use of "barrel bombs" in the Syrian civil war by the Damascus regime against residential communities supposedly sympathetic to anti-Assad rebel forces provides a chilling illustration of state terrorism.

There are also manipulative goals promoted by the selective use of *terrorism* to demonize adversaries while using friendlier language to describe similar tactics relied on by those whose political goals one supports. Ronald Reagan notoriously described the Contras in Nicaragua as "freedom fighters" despite their widespread reliance on civilian assassinations and torture. Currently the West speaks favorably of those "saboteurs" who severely damaged the power grid in eastern Ukraine, where the population leans toward Russia, while Moscow castigates the attackers as "terrorists." Turkey and Israel treat attacks on their soldiers and police as terrorism even though such targets seem to involve lethal violence against individuals whom the Kurdish and Palestinian resistance perceive as combatants, a view reinforced, especially in the Kurdish case, by confining political violence mainly to ways that minimize harm to civilians.

The question raised is whether such a politicized use of *terrorism*, combined with the related issue of the definition's inclusiveness (that is, whether limited to nonstate violence or extended to all acts of political violence that do not respect civilian innocence), makes the term hopelessly ambiguous and vague. With this in mind, a case could be made that it would clarify the analysis of political violence to abandon *terrorism* altogether, or at least avoid the term in academic settings. Tempting as it is to avoid the word, it seems impractical to do so.

This issue of terminology is complex for several reasons even if the argument to avoid the word *terrorism* is persuasive. Above all, it is difficult to ignore the widespread use of *terrorism* to describe nonstate political violence. Furthermore, society needs a widely shared mode of communication that expresses moral outrage in the aftermath of such spectacular events as the Paris and Brussels attacks. There is something socially compelling about regarding some forms of political violence or warfare as horrifying beyond what the law declares as impermissible. Denouncing the violence as "terrorism" is one means of achieving this result. Politically, the governing authorities use such a denunciation to unify the populace and justify a response that has some likelihood of restoring security. To avoid the escalation of intercivilizational hatred, *terrorism* seems more internationally "normal" than castigating the enemy as "barbaric," the only readily familiar linguistic alternative. Furthermore, "terrorism" is a crime according to the duly enacted domestic criminal law of most modern states; thus, in legal settings, the language of terrorism is associated with domestic and international criminality even if recently proclaimed to be a species of "war" from the perspective of US governmental policy.

Explaining retention of *terrorism* as a term of art for nonstate political violence does not address the arguments for and against extending the coverage of *terrorism* to encompass political violence undertaken by the state. Here the question relates, above all, to discerning the core reality of those forms of political violence described as terrorism. In brief, is it appropriate to identify the core of terrorism with the nature of the violence and its goals, or is it more useful and in keeping with mainstream usage to restrict the proper usage of *terrorism* to antistate violence? In some respects, the perpetrator of antistate political violence is more understandably identified as a "terrorist" than are political and military leaders responsible for indiscriminate violence.

## A CRITIQUE OF THE COUNTERTERRORIST IMAGINARY

There is a discernible tendency among those who rely most stridently on the language of *terrorism* to advocate a militarist orientation toward what is labeled *counterterrorism*. Such an outlook has several disadvantages. It confines the "political imagination," magnifies underlying conflicts, and discourages political approaches to the containment and elimination of threats to homeland security. Such threats derive from alienated individuals living within targeted societies, from radicalized movements operating internationally, and from various mixtures of these internal and external sources of extreme political violence.[15]

The main terrorist and counterterrorist discourse as carried on within the United States has been weakened by a militarist approach to perceived security threats. A few years ago I attended a meeting addressed by former British prime minister John Major, who indicated that he began to make progress toward a resolution of the conflict in Northern Ireland only when he began to treat the IRA as a political actor rather than a terrorist organization. He explicitly contrasted his approach with that of George W. Bush after 9/11. The same phenomenon in a more dramatic manner occurred in South Africa when the apartheid government decided to release Nelson Mandela from prison after confining him for twenty-seven years as a dangerous terrorist. Such an electrifying act was a signal that the Afrikaner leadership was ready for a political solution in which the apartheid structure of the South African state would be dismantled.[16]

Part of my questioning of the war template in response to these horrific attacks by political extremist movements is that it tends to gloss over the distinctiveness of the violence and suppress the political dimensions of the challenge, as well as confuse the nature of what is being challenged. I would argue that the Islamic Revolution in Iran, al-Qaeda, and even more so ISIS are new kinds of political actors that do not subscribe to Western assumptions about the state-centric nature of world order. Especially in the Middle East, and also in central Africa, the earlier willingness of nationalist leaders to accept the colonially imposed borders is rapidly dissipating in the face of current conflicts.

Even individuals on the American right are supporting new conceptions of political community. For instance, neocon John Bolton's put forward a proposal to eliminate ISIS from the territory it was holding but replace it with a new Sunni state carved out from what had been Iraq and Syria.[17] Bolton, for his own reasons, supports an approach that resembles what ISIS was doing, to the limited extent of redrawing Middle East boundaries—a deferred acknowledgment that the territorial delimitations imposed by World War I diplomacy (the Sykes-Picot Agreement of 1916) may not be viable given present realities.

In effect, Bolton is endorsing a post-Westphalian conception of political community more congruent with the self-determination of the people on the ground. Such an endorsement is indirectly sensitive to the fact that the ISIS occupation was initially welcomed by much of the resident population because it was viewed as overcoming the severe and genuine sectarian grievances of Sunni populations living in regions of Iraq and Syria victimized by abusive Shiite governance. Bolton's proposal amounts to an opportunistic revival of Woodrow Wilson's compromised vision of the post-Ottoman Middle East after World War I, a vision undermined by Anglo-French colonial ambitions, though in a vastly different sociopolitical context than currently exists. In essence, then, the political extremism that has surfaced in the Middle East is partially seeking redefinitions of political community along post-Westphalian lines that emphasize religion, culture, and ethnicity, and this quest resonates with significant segments of the resident populations. Such attitudes are reinforced by postcolonial antagonisms toward remnants of the colonial era in forms of intervention and economic exploitation, and by corrupting ties between national elites and neoliberal globalization.[18]

Another parallel consideration that complicates simplistic and moralizing counterterrorist constructions of conflict arises from recent research into the motivations of those engaging in suicide missions. In Marzio Barbagli's carefully researched *Farewell to the World* the most important finding is that Islamic suicide bombers are not primarily motivated by visions of martyrdom or even by aimless alienation, but rather by intense feelings of abuse that seek redemption via vengeance in any form, whether or not rational.[19] What policymakers' militarist-terrorist blinders do is to remove these findings from any role in fashioning a response that is sensitive to the root causes of terrorism and will be effective in diminishing the threat at its source. We need to ask questions about what the West has been doing in the Middle East over the past hundred years or so that has provoked extremist reactions that shock the conscience with horrific outbursts of violence directed at those who are perceived in the West to be innocent.

The potential relevance of critical self-scrutiny cannot be exaggerated in shaping an effective counterterrorist approach. On one level, we know that defense of the homeland against those viewed as intruders constitutes the foundation of an ethos of resistance with strong ties to history and tradition. The area of the Holy Land surrounding Jerusalem continues to be affected, as well, by the ancient memories associated with the Crusades.

Confronting such aspects of current transnational violence does not by itself lead to obvious policy adjustments in counterterrorist tactics and strategy, but it may help produce a better understanding of why militarist approaches have led to such disappointing results.

Robert Pape and James K. Feldman have conducted the most systematic and comprehensive research on suicide terrorism, which has accompanied all the spectacular terrorist incidents in the post-9/11 era. "The principal cause of suicide terrorism," they write, "is resistance to foreign occupation, not Islamic fundamentalism. Even when religion matters, moreover, it functions mainly as a recruiting tool in the context of national resistance."[20] I think such assessments cast doubt on the militarist reflex of coping with enhanced expressions of the transnational terrorist threat, as after the Paris bombing, by making widespread calls for "doing more," which is understood as meaning more air attacks and an increased willingness to intervene with force. An extreme instance is the so-called Dissent Memo by fifty-one State Department diplomats calling for air strikes targeting Assad's Damascus regime.[21] Such advocacy seems oblivious to the reality that militarist tactics have the primary effect of pouring oil on the flames of vengeance. This interpretation of the dysfunction of the militarist impulse also seems to be strengthened by the expressed desire of ISIS operatives to confront American "boots on the ground" as a means to unify resistance in Islamic countries and to demonstrate the greater readiness to sacrifice lives on behalf of the struggle against infidel forces.

Officially classifying the adversary as "terrorist," through listing it as such by the US government, forecloses inquiry into the merits of its political motivations and grievances, overlooking the psychological insight associated with accurately assessing motivations. With this insight it may become possible to find a political solution for the conflict that saves lives and restores normalcy. In the context of the Middle East, with such intrusions associated with Sykes-Picot, military interventions associated with favorable access to oil and strategic ambition, support for Israel's dispossession of Palestinians and control over Jerusalem, and interferences with domestic politics, there are many reasons for the West to critically reconsider its relationship to the region, and take this review into account in shaping present policies.

I find useful in this regard a line from W.H. Auden's celebrated poem "September 1, 1939": "Those to whom evil is done do evil in return." Breaking this cycle of violence in the Middle East, which all sides view as justifiable, requires the West to take far better account of "the other." It is such reliance on reconstructive reason that is being discouraged, if not precluded, by this insistence on describing adversaries as terrorists and determining policies by options delimited by the counterterrorist discourse. The Western political imagination finds itself trapped within this militarist box.

It may be helpful to contrast the approach taken toward the Assad regime in Syria with that used to deal with ISIS. With Assad, acts of "terror" are dealt with as "crimes against humanity," diplomatic channels are kept open, and despite the sustained magnitude of the violence unleashed by the Damascus government against its own civilian population, the political door to accommodation is kept ajar. In contrast, ISIS's comparable despicable acts of terror are described as "barbaric acts," "atrocities," or even genocide. The idea of establishing some kind of agreed-upon cease-fire through negotiation is considered inappropriate even to contemplate as a means to end the violence. Yet as a recent CNN documentary of life in ISIS-controlled Mosul showed, despite the harshness of its enforcement of *sharia* law, there was a kind of normalcy that most residents interviewed seemed to believe was preferable to the oppression experienced when the city was under Baghdad's control and sectarian persecution prevailed.[22]

## BEYOND WAR AND MILITARISM: CONCLUDING OBSERVATIONS

In some respects, neither the war nor the crime paradigm is adequate to encompass the specific character of the security challenge posed by the 9/11 attacks on US targets or the Paris massacre of November 13, 2015, or any of the other kindred happenings since the year 2000. Reconfiguring a security paradigm that captures the distinctiveness of such events is needed to avoid policies that kill and devastate without contributing to improved security and that, often via unintended consequences, have the opposite effect of causing additional insecurity. It is this pattern of failure and frustration that has ensued from an exaggerated reliance on military force as a policy instrument and the corresponding disregard of nonmilitary approaches to security.

There is, to begin with, the need to agree on the originality of this challenging conflict configuration, which cannot be effectively addressed as either a species of war or of crime. Several of its distinguishing features can be described:

1. The salience of blowback phenomena and unintended consequences. It is unlikely, for instance, that the United States would have been targeted by al-Qaeda after the Afghanistan war if large numbers of American troops had not been deployed near the sacred sites of Islam in Saudi Arabia in the aftermath of the Iraqi annexation of

Kuwait in 1991. Similarly, ISIS would not exist had the United States not embarked in 2003 on a regime-changing intervention in Iraq that included an occupation for over a decade that deliberately displaced Sunnis from their positions in government and the armed forces and thereby incubated a sectarian dimension of conflict within Iraq and in the region.

2. The pattern of terrorist attacks such that terrorists generally design their violent plans to strike at soft and symbolically resonant targets in a Western civil society through the orchestration of spectacular events that spread fear and arouse anger, leaving modern societies with limited and often ineffectual means of response, especially if the attackers themselves are killed. Retaliation against the presumed sponsors of the attack is quite likely to give rise to resentment without weakening the nonstate adversary, thereby strengthening the stature of the terrorist actor. There is no obvious way to end such a struggle, which has the effect of militarizing state-society relations and leads to the reproduction of extremist nonstate actors.

3. The dispersion of such nonstate actors, the absence of a conventional military encounter, and the suicidal motivation of the extremist combat personnel put a premium on advance knowledge so as to enable a preventive approach. This need for intelligence in turn creates an "information war" that prompts maximal surveillance and torture as an instrument of coercive interrogation. The entire world, including the homeland, is a potential battlefield for *both sides*, which subverts territorial sovereignty by creating covert bases and recruits combatants to plan and launch attacks in foreign countries that may or may not give consent, and which also creates counterterrorist incentives to strike blows against those planning and directing such operations.

4. The continuing uncertainty as to whether to acknowledge or suppress the ideological claims of "radical Islam," or even whether the Islamic religion is responsible for inflaming anti-Western passions, supposedly justifying high levels of surveillance, monitoring, and even deportation and detention. Such dispositions are controversial because of the tendency to make counterterrorism into "a clash of civilizations," and hence more difficult and dangerous.

5. Important innovations in weaponry and doctrine seek to find and destroy the "enemy" even if situated in the midst of civil society, illustrated by the use of attack drones and special ops task forces, giving rise to counterterrorist approaches subject to ethical and legal charges of "state terrorism."[23]

6. Against the background described above, strong pressures are exerted against the rule of law and human rights, and even international humanitarian law, threatening to produce a disposition toward authoritarian politics and a more coercive relationship between state and society throughout the West, generating vicious cycles of persisting conflict and structures of governance that are anti-democratic.[24]

In the end, the new wave of terrorism and counterterrorism poses both security and normative challenges of a profound character. On the security side, the basic question posed is whether society can be protected against such threats without undue encroachment on liberties, and this seems to depend on weakening the preoccupation with the military defeat of the enemy and on strengthening political approaches that include diminishing hostile motivations and addressing legitimate grievances. On the normative side, the basic questions posed concern what limitations on freedom and privacy are prudent and reasonable in light of the reality that the threat can be generated from within the homeland as well as from remote places anywhere in the world, and what protective means can be developed that reject state terrorist options. Also relevant is the realization that in a globalizing world different religious and civilizational orientations must coexist and cooperate for the sake of an overriding human interest in the collective well-being of the human species, and this suggests that Islamophobic explanations of conflict and related policies toward refugees and immigrants should be minimized, if not outright rejected.

NOTES

1. Use of the terminology of counterterrorism is itself an acceptance of self-serving governmental descriptive language that implies a reactive recourse to violence that is against terrorism rather than itself being a species of terrorism. An alternative term more in accord with the effects of such reactive violence on the civilian population would be *state terrorism*.

2. Recently, ISIS has been by far the most salient among such adversaries, and its political identity is blurred, claiming to be a state on the basis of governing a considerable expanse of territory and people in Syria and Iraq, but without establishing international recognized boundaries and failing to receive diplomatic

recognition from any state or the United Nations. ISIS also endorses lone-wolf terrorism if the perpetrator claims affinity with its mission, as in the San Bernardino and Orlando incidents.

3. Britain has been an outlier, not only geographically but also strategically, seeming to join in controversial American counterterrorism undertakings, as in the Iraq intervention and occupation, but more constrained in responding to terrorism in its homeland. The British response to the London attacks of 2005 was constrained, but possibly because the link to external actors was weak or non-existent.

4. Richard Falk, *The Great Terror War* (Northampton, MA: Olive Branch Press, 2002).

5. Two aspects of the legal dimensions of this counterterrorist approach should be distinguished: on the one side, the treatment of the violence as international rather than intranational; on the other side, the stigmatization of the violence as "terrorism" was connected with systematic efforts to evade the constraints on treatment standards applicable to captured "enemy" personnel as embodied in international humanitarian law, including the Geneva Convention on Prisoners of War (1949) and the International Convention on the Prohibition of Torture (1984).

6. Omar Mateen, the American-born gunman who carried out the 2016 massacre in Orlando, swore allegiance to ISIS at the time of the killings, and ISIS reciprocated by acknowledging Mateen as an ISIS warrior. As more information about Mateen became available, it seems that his lethal motivations were predominantly homophobic and only peripherally political. The mystery surrounding Mateen was further magnified when it was learned that he was previously investigated by the FBI, which reportedly may have tried to recruit him for counterterrorist activity.

7. As broadly depicted in Samuel P. Huntington, *The Clash of Civilizations and the Remaking of World Order* (New York: Touchstone, 1996).

8. Robert Pape, *Dying to Win: The Strategic Logic of Suicide Bombing* (New York: Random House, 2005).

9. It is widely believed that the rise of Donald Trump in American politics, though primarily driven by domestic nativist and populist attitudes, also reflects dissatisfaction with the governmental approach taken by Washington and criticized as insufficient. This more militant viewpoint gained a wider resonance in the United States after the San Bernardino and Orlando incidents, creating the impression that such terrorist attacks in the country are pushing public opinion, as well as aspiring and elected leaders, toward recourse to suppressive policies at home and reckless militarism overseas. It should be observed, as well, that the core motivation at the Orlando nightclub seems to have been homophobic, with the invocation of ISIS as an afterthought, perhaps connected to a dream of martyrdom.

10. Jack Goldsmith, *The Terror Presidency: Law and Judgment inside the Bush Administration* (New York: W.W. Norton, 2007).

11. President Obama, in a major speech on drone warfare delivered at the National Defense University, indicated the importance of finding ways to avoid the posture of permanent war, but he did not give any insight as to how the ongoing struggle against al-Qaeda and ISIS, as well as their affiliates, would end, nor did he offer any forthcoming policy modifications. See Barack Obama, "Remarks of the President at the National Defense University," May 23, 2013, https://www.whitehouse.gov/the-press-office/2013/09/24/remarks.

12. Again, as with international terrorism, there is some ambiguity as to classification. The United States waged the Barbary Wars (1804) against pirates operating off the coast of North Africa, but in contrast to the terrorist challenge, there was a distinct group of pirates associated with a particular region, providing a clear combat zone and end point.

13. Richard Falk, *Revolutionaries and Functionaries: The Dual Face of International Terrorism* (New York: E. P. Dutton, 1988).

14. See Adam Horowitz, Lizzy Ratner, and Philip Weiss, eds., *The Goldstone Report: The Legacy of the Landmark Investigation of the Gaza Conflict* (New York: Nation Books, 2011).

15. The Orlando massacre offers an instance in which it is impossible to clearly categorize the violent event. See note 6, this chapter. Omar Mateen was an alienated American-born security guard who combined complex attitudes toward the gay community with signs of alignment with ISIS, which returned the favor, without any evidence as yet of direct ties. The Orlando shooting is neither purely domestic nor purely international, neither purely political nor purely apolitical.

16. Such a shift in perspective amounted to a radical break with the presuppositions of the South African political imagination, which ruled out accommodation and was convinced that the options were effective suppression of African discontent or civil war. The choice of the leadership in Pretoria to pursue a political option was not a result of a moral shift with respect to the apartheid regime, but reflected the views that the suppression, even if effective, was accompanied by too high costs in terms of international opprobrium and sanctions and that the likely prospect of an eventual civil war would be calamitous for the interests of the ruling class. This precedent is important to keep in mind, despite the great differences posed by the emergence of various anti-Western forms of political extremism, as it illustrates the beneficial possibility of a radical shift in the approach taken by political leaders to uphold societal interests. Such a shift could not have occurred without its prior presence in the political imaginary of those entrusted with leadership roles. As far as we can tell, there is no such presence in the political imaginary of the West with respect to ISIS.

17. John Bolton, "To Defeat ISIS, Create a Sunni State," *New York Times*, November 24, 2015.

18. Attitudes and conditions vary country by country. One form of encounter is associated with the establishment of Israel in historic Palestine, accompanied by the dispossession and displacement of a large majority of the native population.

19. Marzio Barbagli, *Farewell to the World: A History of Suicide* (Cambridge: Polity, 2015).

20. Robert Pape and James K. Feldman, *The Explosion of Global Suicide Terrorism and How to Stop It* (Chicago: University of Chicago Press, 2010); "State Department Draft Dissent Memo on Syria Strikes," *New York Times*, June 17, 2016.

21. The oppressiveness of ISIS governance was not worse than what is practiced by the government of Saudi Arabia, which is rarely questioned when it happens. In other words, the demonization of ISIS as compared to the withholding of judgment when it comes to Saudi Arabia or other friends of the West suggests that it is not the severity of the behavior that explains the difference in treatment, but matters of geopolitical alignment.

22. See Jeff Halper, *War against the People: Israel, the Palestinians, and Global Pacification* (London: Pluto Press, 2015); see also Alexander J. George, *Western State Terrorism* (Cambridge: Polity, 1991); Mark Selden and Alvin So, eds., *War and State Terrorism: The United States, Japan, and the Asia-Pacific in the Long American Century* (Lanham, MD: Rowman & Littlefield, 2004).

23. Such developments are reinforced by populist reactions against waves of foreign migration threatening the stability and moderation of several European countries, as well as the rising levels of economic inequality and chronic unemployment generated by neoliberal globalization.

24. See, generally, Scott Poynting and David Whyte, eds., *Counter-terrorism and State Political Violence* (Milton Park, Abingdon, Oxford, UK: Routledge, 2012).

# 10. Legal Constructions of Terrorism

Richard Burchill

In 1934, following the high-profile political assassinations of King Alexander I of Yugoslavia and French foreign minister Louis Barthou, France proposed to the League of Nations the idea of creating an international treaty for the prevention and punishment of terrorism, along with an international court to prosecute those accused under this treaty. In the resolution starting the process of adopting the treaty, the Council of the League of Nations declared that "the rules of international law concerning the repression of terrorist activity are not at present sufficiently precise to guarantee efficiently international co-operation with this matter."[1] The 1937 Convention on the Prevention and Punishment of Terrorism was drafted for the purpose of "making more effective the prevention and punishment of terrorism of an international character."[2] Fast-forwarding almost eighty years, the combination of international and domestic developments has created a substantial legal regime addressing terrorism.[3] Nevertheless, at the end of 2015, the secretary general of the United Nations set out that "there is a growing international consensus that . . . counter-terrorism measures have not been sufficient to prevent the spread of violent extremism."[4] There now appears to be a continual process calling for more laws and more effective legal cooperation among states to address the threat of terrorism, even though such measures do not appear to be working. This process of constructing more and more legal instruments in response to terrorism raises questions as to how effective these legal regimes are, domestically and globally.[5]

The call for enhancing the legal regimes for dealing with terrorism are premised on the belief that the existing system is not effective and more is needed. Following the March 2016 attack in Brussels, a number of European states announced the introduction of further legislation to address the threat of terrorism. Hungarian officials stated, "The events in Paris and Brussels have settled the debate, the terrorism threat has grown," and in response there is the perceived need for more and more law.[6] There is no doubt that states are required, and expected, to provide security for their citizens and others, but we have to ask if the legal regimes constructed for addressing terrorism are effectively achieving the objective of creating more security. Despite the fact that governments have been addressing the threat to security caused by terrorism for a considerable period of time, calls continue for more laws as the solution to improve security.[7]

The continual construction of legal regimes to address the threat of terrorism can be described as an overreaction, as terrorist activities are criminal in nature and every state has a legal system for dealing with the crime: so why is more law addressing terrorism needed? This chapter asserts that the continual legal constructions to deal with terrorism are an overreaction as they make more actions criminal, allow for the government to interfere in personal lives with minimal evidence, and increase the force that can be used in responding to acts. As Clark McCauley explains in chapter 6 of this volume: "Overreaction to a terrorist attack produces its own reaction in escalated sympathy and support for the terrorists. In turn, terrorists escalate their attacks or broaden their targets. Action and reaction produce a trajectory of escalating violence over time." More law is an immediate response to terrorist events, but it is not bringing about better efforts to prevent, counter, or even prosecute and punish terrorism, or deliver on a more secure world.

## LAW AND SECURITY

Governments have a responsibility to ensure the state has a degree of security; otherwise legitimacy to rule, regardless of the form of government, will be lost. The purpose of counterterrorism law is to bring about more security in states and societies. It does this by constructing legal regimes that empower government authorities to prevent acts of terrorism or, when the acts are committed, to apply the full force of the law for punishment and deterrence. Laws exist to establish boundaries for behavior, to condemn particular acts, to ensure that those who commit such acts are prosecuted and punished. Law is the primary tool for organizing and ordering social groups. Law is not the only tool in social organization, but it is seen as having greater importance and authority than other tools for organization and control.[8] As a higher-order system that supports the exercise of power for the purpose of social organization, law is seen as a key instrument for dealing with matters that upset security and social organization. In the wake of the insecurity and emotion brought about by a terrorist attack, no government official is going to reinforce the need for more social programs to address root causes or for the furtherance of education to better understand divergent worldviews. Governments will call for more laws to ensure they can deal with the problem, more power to (we hope) prevent violence from occurring, more authority to stop sources of funding or the supply of material, and better regulations for ensuring cooperation with other governments. Any government that is "soft" on terror will lose respect and perhaps legitimacy. It has to be recognized, however, that in calling for more laws in response to terrorism, governments are putting security in jeopardy. Seeing police with automatic weapons, or even the military patrolling the streets, or knowing that security services can interfere in our personal lives with ease does not give a clear impression of security as a result of more law. Governments view the need for more law as necessary in dealing with current threats; at the same time, governments are not "convey[ing] a sense of calm and determination when communicating with the public."[9]

The effectiveness of law in delivering social objectives relies on its greater precision and predictability as compared to other social conventions or practices that determine behavior. For law to be effective, there needs to be a clear sense of where the line between acceptable and unacceptable behavior exists. There also needs to be clarity and precision in relation to procedures and processes for upholding the law or for any actions taken thereunder. Of course no legal system is ever perfect, but in looking at the construction of legal regimes dealing with terrorism, we are seeing a wide range of flaws. There is the absence of any agreed-upon global definition of what constitutes terrorism, which is leading to definitions in national law that, in many cases, criminalize any behavior that the government determines as being a threat, no matter how innocuous the actions may appear. Brazil's new anti-terrorism law includes as an offense—exposing society to danger—without defining what constitutes danger.[10] Egypt's 2015 anti-terrorism law criminalizes acts of violence normally associated with terrorism along with other acts such as endangering the interests of the community, upsetting social peace, and damaging the environment, antiquities, food, or water supplies. The law also criminalizes any intention to carry out any of the acts mentioned in the legislation, even though there is no clear definition of what these actions may entail.[11] It is laws of this nature that criminalize widely so as to include a range of ancillary or inchoate offenses that may or may not be related to terrorism, which in turn permits government authorities to investigate, detain, or interfere pervasively in the lives of suspected individuals. Such laws threaten the idea that legal regimes should be constructing more secure environments in response to terrorism.

The current process of ongoing legal constructions to address terrorism is occurring at both the domestic and international levels, and these are closely intertwined. It is clear that following the events of 9/11, the construction of additional law escalated dramatically and continues today. Yet the seemingly continual adoption of new laws around the globe raises a variety of questions: Why are more new laws needed? Does the continual adoption of more law signify that governments are getting it wrong in the construction of legal regimes? Or is the threat from terrorism extremely dynamic and evolving, requiring more and different responses?

Terrorists rely on "symbolic acts of extra-normal violence whose purpose is the creation of fear."[12] State responses through legal constructions are both symbolic acts and substantive assertions of power. Symbolically, states make extensive use of legal constructions to demonstrate their efforts to provide substantive measures to ensure security. The scene is common: A violent event occurs and is labeled terrorism. The government expresses outrage at the event and its methods, usually condemning the perpetrators as having no respect for existing systems of social organization. This is followed by calls for more law to make the security services more powerful and allow for more force in preventing and punishing. During this process officials may engage in public displays and announcements to convince the public that more security will follow. This leads to action directed at increasing security—more police on the street, greater security screenings in nontraditional places, more programs for greater awareness and reporting suspicious behavior, and more interventions in relation to suspect behavior. Central to these acts is showing that there is more security as a result of more law—a cycle of action and reaction being repeated globally and nationally.

INTERNATIONAL LEGAL CONSTRUCTIONS

International law is a system in which states collectively agree to create normative and legal frameworks for what is acceptable in the international system and then construct legal regimes to address the unacceptable behavior. In relation to counterterrorism, international law has, as discussed in this chapter's introduction, been cognizant of the threat for a considerable period of time. More recently, international law has provided a justification for states to increasingly construct more law as a response to terrorist attacks, giving it a strong influencing role.[13] Following the 1937 League of

Nations Conventions, little action was taken in constructing international legal regimes regarding terrorism.[14] This is not to say that terrorism was not occurring, but rather that the focus was on much larger issues of global security, such as World War II and its aftermath. In the decolonization period following the war, the extensive use of terrorist tactics by all sides did not raise any particular concern of terrorism, as the focus was on the character of the wars being fought (see chapter 2 of this volume).

We can chart the development, beginning in the 1960s, of the international legal regime addressing terrorism. To begin with, however, this legal regime did not specifically target terrorism per se. The action then taken addressed "sectoral" matters, with the focus on certain acts in a particular context. The first of these treaties came in 1963 and dealt with offenses committed aboard aircraft,[15] and the first three of the international counterterrorism treaties all dealt with aircraft and airports.[16] The treaties were reactive in that international air travel was a relatively new phenomenon and various extremists were using this mode of transport as part of their methods. This period also witnessed the growth of mass media providing terrorists a much greater set of outlets in which to portray their activities for a global audience. Criminal activity involving aircraft and international air travel presented a range of issues that could be managed only through transnational cooperation. The original intention of the legal system, then, was to help states cooperate in an area of complexity. This cooperation continued, and the 1970s brought about further treaties as a response to terrorist activity, conventions that addressed new methods, such as hijacking and taking hostages—in particular, internationally protected persons.[17] These treaties still did not use the term *terrorism* or speak of the need to ensure more effective international cooperation to prevent terrorism specifically. The scope of the international legal regime expanded to include the use of nuclear materials and plastic explosives, along with addressing further methods such as maritime navigation.[18]

The primary purpose of these treaties was to ensure cooperation among states in addressing a criminal act prioritized as a major threat to international security. The treaties permitted states to take jurisdiction over the act covered. This is an important element—allowing states to change their domestic law. Furthermore, the treaties attempted to ensure that accused persons were brought to trial. States agreed to either prosecute in their own jurisdiction or, if not, there was an expectation and obligation to extradite the suspected individual(s) to a state that would prosecute. Furthermore, the treaties spoke of the need of states to cooperate and share information as necessary to deal with the matter covered. The treaties also called on states to change domestic law so as to impose "severe penalties,"[19] thus sending the message that these acts are not just unacceptable but are more severe than similar acts of violence. These early treaties never used the term *terrorism* in relation to the acts in question.

The international legal treaties began to use *terrorism* beginning with the 1997 International Convention for the Suppression of Terrorist Bombing. In this treaty we see the legal construction addressing an act that is presumably illegal—setting off explosives in a public place—but adding the term *terrorism* to describe the act in order to demonstrate its severity. This shift to speaking directly about terrorism continued with the 1999 International Convention for the Financing of Terrorism. This treaty addresses a key part of transnational terrorism and shows how slow states can be in recognizing issues related more to the causes of terrorism and not just the outcomes. The treaty also includes a definition of terrorism in order to indicate what activities could not be funded, but "terrorism" as a crime under international law still did not exist due to disagreement over its definition and application.[20]

There are now nineteen international legal instruments dealing with terrorism. It is worth noting that this number is far from certain as some of the instruments are supplements to primary treaties or updates of previous treaties. What is still missing from the international legal regime is a clear agreement on what constitutes terrorism as an illegal act. The struggle over a globally acceptable definition is strange given that every state has a definition for its domestic system. This then points to the lack of agreement as to what constitutes terrorism as a crime. If there is no agreement on what constitutes terrorism, attention is then given to acts commonly associated with terrorism, and states then just add the adjective *terrorist* to these acts or declare certain acts more "severe," requiring further construction of legal cooperation.

Prior to the events of September 11, 2001, the international treaties enumerated above had minimal uptake from states as measured by the number of signatures and ratifications (the necessary step to make the treaty part of domestic law). Things changed dramatically across the system when, after September 2001, member states accomplished more than seven hundred ratifications, representing 40 percent of the total number of ratifications across this international legal regime. Following 9/11 the UN Security Council adopted Resolution 1373, which has become the foundation for increased legal constructions of counterterrorism legislation.[21] Resolution 1373 called on all states to sign and ratify the suppression treaties and to exchange more information and cooperate more effectively in the suppression of terrorism.

Adopted under Chapter VII of the UN Charter, the terms of Resolution 1373 are mandatory for all member states. In line with this, the Security Council also established a monitoring committee to oversee the resolution's implementation by the member states of the United Nations, a process that has supported states in enacting more domestic laws to address terrorism.

## DOMESTIC LEGAL CONSTRUCTIONS: THE POWER OF EMOTION

Resolution 1373 directed all UN member states to strengthen their legal systems, sign on to the international treaties, and cooperate further in dealing with terrorism—essentially setting the agenda for the construction of counterterrorism law.[22] From this imperative has emerged a massive growth of counterterrorism laws around the world criminalizing more activities, increasing punishments when persons are convicted, and giving more power to police and security services to gather intelligence and detain and question suspects. While it is not possible to provide a comprehensive review of the growth in the law, it is possible to identify broad trends in legal constructions from the Security Council's reviews of the implementation of Resolution 1373. Reviews were published in 2008, 2009, 2011, and 2016.[23] The thematic areas guiding the review process are taken directly from Resolution 1373, with attention directed to legislation, counterfinancing of terrorism, border control, law enforcement, international cooperation, and human rights. The recommendations offered in the course of the reviews point overwhelmingly to the need for additional laws to further criminalize terrorism specifically, or the acts normally associated with terrorists, more regulation to control movement of people and goods across borders, greater attention to legislation to monitor and control financing, more training for judges and prosecutors, and institutional capacity for courts and police. Each review is considerably larger in scope and content than its predecessor. This progression means either that more law is being developed domestically or that the Security Council is recommending more law be adopted, or a combination of the two. It is this final observation that best explains the current trends.

The most recent survey of the implementation of Resolution 1373 was issued in January 2016, and this review added to the abovementioned thematic areas a new focus of attention: "national comprehensive and integrated strategies." The 2016 review declares, "Most national counterterrorism strategies developed by Member States thus far tend to focus too narrowly on law enforcement measures." The review further finds these strategies insufficient to address the causes of terrorism, as terrorists are able to bypass law enforcement by using legal methods, such as social media. The review calls for national strategies that "seek to strengthen the resilience of the population through a balanced, multidisciplinary approach that integrates law enforcement measures and measures to address the socioeconomic, political, educational, developmental, human rights and rule of law dimensions."[24] It is worth noting that the review does not call for distinct social, political, or educational efforts, but rather recommends these be part of law enforcement measures—a further indication of the reliance on the law in constructing counterterrorism regimes.

The reviews of Resolution 1373 demonstrate that states have utilized the resolution's authority to define terrorism to suit their own political purposes and to broaden what constitutes "terrorism" to excessively broad limits. States will, of course, be quick to justify each and every addition to the legal regime, but concerns exist over governments' motivations in adopting extensive, if not excessive, laws under the guise of protecting society from terrorism. The extensive growth of domestic law may be a direct result of the absence of agreement on what constitutes a stand-alone "crime of terrorism." The attention given to the wide range of acts potentially linked to terrorism may be of some value in focusing on the particular acts committed, rather than trying to identify who is likely to carry out such acts or why they are engaging in these acts.[25]

As indicated above, one of the reasons driving the creation of more and more law to address terrorism is the emotion that terrorism produces. This has fed a tendency by governments to see all opposition, violence, or potentially divergent behavior as terror. This perspective overlooks the fact that even with changing methods, those engaging in terrorist activities are participating in illegal activity, even without the adjective *terrorist* added. Many cite Brian Jenkins's statement that "terrorists blow up things, kill people, or seize hostages. Every terrorist attack is merely a variation on these three activities."[26] In any jurisdiction these actions would constitute illegal activity, as would the preparation and direct support of the activity. However, the United Nations and individual states have felt the need to construct further offenses related to inchoate actions, such as "causing terror" or disturbing public order, constructions capable of encompassing any action the government finds to be a threat. There is no doubt that terrorists have continued to develop their methods, so that violence is unpredictable and indiscriminate, different weapons are being used, and extremist groups are competing to see who can have the most violent impact.[27] But does this mean more and more law is needed? Apparently so, for even though the events of 9/11 and subsequent attacks have been seen as changing the game, states could have responded to these events through existing law, yet the emotive response persists of enacting more and new laws.[28]

As a result, the continual construction of counterterrorism laws allows governments to criminalize as "terrorism" a wide range of actions deemed inappropriate, as evidenced by developments in Egypt and Turkey. Russia, in order to make a more effective response to terrorism, has recently brought changes to its counterterrorism law that include extending criminal liability for specific offenses to accused persons as young as fourteen, requiring communications companies to monitor phone calls and messaging, and allowing the Russian security services access to all messaging applications.[29] Such approaches allow the government to target individuals and groups for actions that might be questionable, such as antagonizing the government or attempting to undermine the national narrative, but fall far short of terrorism. It is through expansive legal constructions, Nicholas Onuf has observed, that states are making terrorism what they say it is.[30]

These extensions of the law to cover just about any activity a government believes to threaten security appear difficult to justify, but governments maintain they are essential for fighting terrorism. Even states that have a history of dealing with terrorism and enacting counterterrorism legislation have been continually adding and modifying their laws. The United Kingdom stands out as an example as it has had counterterrorism legislation in place since the 1970s to address the threats from transnational terrorist organizations. However, in the wake of 9/11 and Resolution 1373 the British government adopted extensive new measures in the Anti-Terrorism Crime and Security Act of 2001, which declared all existing laws (including the Terrorism Act of 2000) insufficient and granted the government more extensive powers. Six major pieces of legislation (not including orders) followed in the next fifteen years. In introducing the 2015 legislation, the government said that further powers were needed to deal with the increased threat posed by terrorism.[31] It appears that the creation of new laws to counter terrorism have been wrong or misdirected each time, or that more and more symbolic acts are necessary in response to each newly discovered terrorist act, even if those acts are very similar to past events.

As the increase in power granted the security services is a common theme in the construction of more law, it is worth underscoring that this increase has not brought about more security, and one can even raise the question of whether more law has impeded the security services. In the United Kingdom the inquiry into the death of Lee Rigby found multiple mistakes and oversights by the security services, leading to calls for more powers of surveillance.[32] The attacks in Belgium and Paris have highlighted substantial problems in national coordination and international cooperation in the sharing of information and intelligence.[33] The lack of coordination between states impacts intelligence sharing, investigation cooperation, and extradition, where action is prevented due to the lack of harmony across the domestic laws and the overly restrictive approaches taken by domestic legal constructions.[34]

## WHAT NEXT?

We have criminalized or are criminalizing more and more elements of human behavior in the name of making our societies more secure from terror. Each time a terrorist attack occurs, and even when a terrorist attack is thwarted, there are calls for more legislation either to give the security forces more authority or to sweep more behavior into the category of terrorist criminal action. It is tempting to say that the increase in law is creating more terrorism, but that is a causal argument impossible to prove. At the same time, actions taken by governments through the expansive constructions of counterterrorism do serve to further radicalized views.[35] Of greater concern is how governments are drafting counterterrorism laws that are in turn being used for other purposes to control behavior that may be disruptive but does not amount to terrorism. In one stand-out case, the United Kingdom detained the partner of a journalist working on a story about national security in the United States. Invoking the Terrorism Act of 2000, authorities detained the individual without charge, explanation, or access to a lawyer; questioned him; and searched his electronic devices.[36] If a state like the United Kingdom uses its counterterrorism law in this way, we can raise legitimate concerns about how legal constructions are threatening security in other jurisdictions.

The extensive growth of law in relation to terrorism since 2001 might suggest that we have reached a peak and the legal constructions of a counterterrorism regime are subsiding. But the trends appear to be toward more law to deal with the changing methods of terrorism, to ensure more and more acts can be scrutinized. The focus of the law is on addressing the sense of fear in society, a fear that governments have no difficulty in supporting, it appears. A commentator on the situation in France explains: "Measured responses to terrorist outrages are alas rare. In times of national trauma, politicians will not even dare utter words of restraint lest they be swept up in the righteous anger gripping the populace."[37] By engaging in the emotive side of terrorism, governments are in many ways providing support and structure for the cause of the terrorist. In the process of erecting new legal constructions in response to terrorism, we are mixing emotion with systems and structures that should be based on precision and certainty. As a result the legal constructions are reinforcing insecurity.

As McCauley suggests (in chapter 6 of this volume), there is much to learn from the "Paradoxes of Counterinsurgency Operations" of the *U.S. Army/Marine Corps Counterinsurgency Field Manual:* sometimes the more you protect, the less secure you may be; the more force that is used, the less effective it may be; sometimes doing nothing is the best reaction. We are not calling for states to do nothing; they are expected and required to provide security for society. Equally, it appears the construction of legal regimes to address terrorism and provide further cooperation has failed to deliver in the form of substantive impacts. But the legal constructions do provide a forum for expressing emotions and showing, on the face of it, powerful responses. It is likely we will continue to construct more and more laws in response to terrorism in the hope it provides better and more effective responses, but we are unlikely to feel any more secure as a result.

NOTES

I wish to thank Sydney Bender, a student of New York University–Shanghai for research assistance on this chapter.

1. League of Nations, *Official Journal,* 15th Year, No. II (Part I), at 1760.
2. League of Nations Doc. C.546.M.383.1937. The idea of an international criminal court to enforce the treaty was not adopted.
3. Ben Saul, "Old and New Terrorist Threats: What Form Will They Take and How Will States Respond?" *Sydney Law School Legal Studies Research Paper,* No. 15/82 (September 2015), 1.
4. United Nations General Assembly, "Report of the Secretary General—Plan of Action to Prevent Violent Extremism," UN Doc. A/70/674, 24 December 2015, para. 4.
5. John Hudson, "Is the International Community Out of Ideas to Combat Terrorism?" *Foreign Policy,* 30 March 2016, http://foreignpolicy.com/2016/03/30/is-the-international-community-out-of-ideas-to-combat-terrorism/.
6. "Poland Joins Hungary in Planning Stringent Anti-terrorism Laws in Wake of Brussels Attacks," *Deutsche Welle,* 24 March 2016, http://www.dw.com/en/poland-joins-hungary-in-planning-stringent-anti-terrorism-laws-in-wake-of-brussels-attacks/a-19141781.
7. Sandra Walklate and Gabe Mythen, *Contradictions of Terrorism: Security, Risk, and Resilience* (Abingdon, UK: Routledge, 2015), 4.
8. H.L.A. Hart, *The Concept of Law* (Oxford: Clarendon Press, 1961).
9. Peter R. Neumann, *Old and New Terrorism: Late Modernity, Globalization, and the Transformation of Political Violence* (Cambridge: Polity, 2011), 153.
10. Brazil Law No. 13,260, 16 March 2016, Article 2. See also Human Rights Watch, "Brazil: Veto Overboard Counterterrorism Bill," 14 March 2016, https://www.hrw.org/news/2016/03/14/brazil-veto-overbroad-counterterrorism-bill.

11. Egypt Anti-terrorism Law, *Official Gazette*, No. 33 (15 August 2015).

12. Neumann, *Old and New Terrorism*, 16.

13. Elena Pokalova, "Legislative Responses to Terrorism: What Drives States to Adopt New Counterterrorism Legislation?" *Terrorism and Political Violence* 27:3 (2015): 475.

14. One exception is the 1938 Hague Academy of International Law lectures, in which the Italian jurist Antoine Sottile observed, "The intensification of terrorist activity in the past few years has made terrorism one of today's most pressing problems." Antoine Sottile, "Le Terrorisme International," 65 *Recueil des Cours* 89 (1938), at 91.

15. Convention on Offences and Certain Other Acts Committed on Board Aircraft (1963), United Nations Office on Drugs and Crime, https://www.unodc.org/tldb /en/1963_Convention_on%20Board%20Aircraft.html (accessed 6 March 2017).

16. Along with the 1963 convention, there is the Convention for the Suppression of Unlawful Seizure of Aircraft (1970) and the Convention for the Suppression of Unlawful Acts against the Safety of Civil Aviation (1971).

17. The treaties adopted in the 1970s include the Convention on the Prevention and Punishment of Crimes against Internationally Protected Persons (1973) and the International Convention against the Taking of Hostages (1979).

18. Convention on the Physical Protection of Nuclear Material (1980); Convention for the Suppression of Unlawful Acts against the Safety of Maritime Navigation (1980); Convention on the Marking of Plastic Explosives for the Purpose of Detection (1991).

19. Article 3, Convention for the Suppression of Unlawful Acts against the Safety of Civil Aviation (1971).

20. Sudha Setty, "What's in a Name? How Nations Define Terrorism Ten Years after 9/11," *University of Pennsylvania Journal of International Law* 33:1 (2011): 6–17.

21. United Nations Security Council Resolution 1373 (2001), UN Doc. S/RES /1373, 28 September 2001.

22. Victor RamRaj, Michael Hor, Kent Roach, and George Williams, eds., *Global Anti-Terrorism Law and Policy*, 2nd ed. (Cambridge: Cambridge University Press, 2012), 4.

23. The reviews of Resolution 1373 are available from the UN Security Council Counter Terrorism Committee, http://www.un.org/en/sc/ctc/resources/.

24. UN Security Council, "Global Survey of the Implementation by Member States of Security Council Resolution 1373 (2001)," UN Doc. S/2016/49 (20 January 2016), 392.

25. Ronald Crelinsten, *Counterterrorism* (Cambridge: Polity Press, 2009).

26. Cited in Neumann, *Old and New Terrorism*, 25.

27. Ibid., 3.

28. S. Payne, "Britain's New Anti-terrorist Legal Framework," *RUSI Journal* 147:3 (2002): 44.

29. Anna Borshchevskaya, "'Brave New World': Russia's New Anti-terrorism Legislation," *Forbes Online*, 8 July 2016, http://www.forbes.com/sites/annaborsh-chevskaya/2016/07/08/brave-new-world-russias-new-anti-terrorism-legislation /#4f554a3c60fo.

30. Nicholas Onuf, "Making Terror/ism," *International Relations* 23:1 (2009): 54.

31. Theresa May, "Home Secretary: International Action Needed to Tackle Terrorism," GOV.UK, 16 February 2016, https://www.gov.uk/government /speeches/home-secretary-international-action-needed-to-tackle-terrorism.

32. Intelligence and Security Committee of Parliament (UK), "Report on the Intelligence Relating to the Murder of Lee Rigby," HC 795, 25 November 2014.

33. Edoardo Camilli, "The Paris Attacks: A Case of Intelligence Failures?" *NATO Review,* 2015, http://www.nato.int/docu/review/2015/ISIL/Paris-attacks-terrorism-intelligence-ISIS/EN/index.htm.

34. Ben Saul, "Old and New Terrorist Threats: What Form Will They Take and How Will States Respond?" Sydney Law School Legal Studies Research Paper, 15/82, September 2015.

35. Ibid., 2.

36. "Glenn Greenwald's Partner Detained at Heathrow Airport for Nine Hours," *The Guardian,* 19 August 2013, https://www.theguardian.com/world/2013/aug/18/glenn-greenwald-guardian-partner-detained-heathrow.

37. Jeremy Shapiro, "How Not to Overreact to ISIS," Brookings Institution, 17 November, 2015, https://www.brookings.edu/blog/order-from-chaos/2015/11/17/how-not-to-overreact-to-isis/.

# 11. Do Different Definitions of Terrorism Alter Its Causal Story?

Rachel Levin and Victor Asal

*Terrorism* often means different things to different people. There are many definitions of nonstate terrorism,[1] but what the term actually means is strongly debated among scholars and policy makers,[2] and this divide has affected research and theorizing about the topic. How one defines terrorism impacts how researchers measure and model the theoretical basis of terrorism.[3] While existing literature has examined the causes of terrorism, there is a gap in the research in which scholars have neglected to examine if the way we construct the definition of terrorism actually impacts the term's explanatory factors.

The categorical guidelines that different researchers have developed for defining terrorism vary widely. Some describe terrorism as any attack by nonstate actors, while others specify that the attacks must be against civilians, and still others argue that attacking security personnel outside warfare is also terrorism.[4] This divergence raises the question of how different definitions of terrorism may create variation in the causal factors that explain terrorism. In this chapter we discuss the arguments over how terrorism is defined, and model occurrences and severity of terrorism to analyze if causes change when the construction of the term *terrorism* changes. We discuss results of the statistical analysis used to model counts of incidents and fatalities collected from the Global Terrorism Database (GTD).[5] To examine the effects of differing terrorism definitions, we aggregate the data into three different subsets: attacks against civilians only, attacks against civilians and government employees, and indiscriminate attacks (civilians, government employees, and security personnel). Our results reveal that the definitional debate surrounding the term may be a waste of time, as different constructions of terrorism do not appear to have different causal factors.

## DEFINING TERRORISM

The definition of terrorism can be quite contentious. Some define terrorism as an act perpetrated by those whom they do not like,[6] but this classification creates bias. As Merari argues, "As long as the term 'terrorism' simply denotes a violent behavior which is deplorable in the eyes of the user of the term, its utility is in propaganda rather than in research."[7] Those who attempt to define terrorism while ignoring political preferences still disagree strongly on the best definition. Some researchers define terrorism based on those who commit the act. Sánchez-Cuenca and De la Calle, for example, define terrorism from an actor-based approach and claim that it is violence perpetrated by insurgents, defined as violent rebel groups that lack territorial control.[8] This argument proposes that those who have established territory are deemed guerrillas and that their corresponding violent actions are referred to as guerrilla warfare.[9] Guerrilla warfare and terrorism both seek to increase violence and gain recognition, but the need to seek and rule over territory is a main goal of guerrillas as part of an effort to disrupt state power, provide a safe haven for recruitment and training, and establish a military capability.[10] This definition is problematic, as it implies that terrorism is committed solely by terrorist organizations, a designation that rarely exists.[11] Tilly explains that although groups which specialize in terror exclusively do form and exist, they are usually unstable and short-lived, whereas it is more common that an assortment of actors adopt terrorism strategies.[12] Most definitions of terrorism thus focus on who the targets of attacks are, which is why this chapter focuses on differing targets to construct varying definitions of terrorism.

Target-based approaches define the perpetrating group as terrorists if they commit a violent act against a particular type of target. This classification is advantageous in that it does not limit observations to activities of underground groups that have a unique ideology or cause.[13] However, the operationalization of terrorism in databases can vary widely based on the target.[14] Most definitions agree that terrorism includes attacks against civilians,[15] but some argue that it should also include government and security targets. Merari for example argues: "In its modern manifestations, terror is the totalitarian form of war and politics. It shatters the war convention and the political code. It breaks across moral limits beyond which no further limitation seems possible, for within the categories of civilian and citizen, there isn't any smaller group for which immunity might be claimed. . . . Terrorists anyway make no such claim; they kill anybody."[16] If terrorists are willing to kill anybody to achieve their goals, as some argue, then all targets should be included in the definition of terrorism. Richards found that 70 of

250 definitions specified that targeting civilians was a necessary condition of terrorism, whereas the remainder of the definitions used more general nomenclature.[17] However, such generalizations can be problematic.

If it is true that terrorism can be utilized against civilians and noncivilians, such as government and security targets, the question arises whether attacks against both of these targets are rooted in the same causes. Goodwin and Crenshaw argue for the existence of selective terrorism and categorical terrorism.[18] Selective terrorism is directed toward specified targets that the perpetrators hold responsible for social or political policies that they oppose. Categorical, or indiscriminate, terrorism is directed toward anonymous targets because of their involvement in a particular religious or ethnic group, nationality, or social class. Presumably, these different constructs of terrorism are administered for different reasons and, therefore, potentially have different causes. Evidence suggests that targets of terrorism are not random and that perpetrators make a rational choice when selecting their target, based on perceived risk,[19] suggesting that different processes may be responsible for targeting different groups. Coding terrorism based on targeting civilians compared to civilians and noncivilians allows us to identify if the different constructs of terrorism align with different causal factors.

## THE CAUSES OF TERRORISM

Much of the empirical quantitative literature has focused on a small set of variables in modeling country-level variance in terrorism. Variables such as regime type, country population, country wealth, discrimination, political rights, and regime durability appear in many analyses of the likelihood of terrorism.[20] Crenshaw and others argue that modern, wealthy, and urban societies create environments that are vulnerable to an increased number of targets and opportunities for attacks.[21] Much of this research also finds that the target country's population significantly and positively predicts transnational terrorism.[22]

A large body of research has shown that political freedom and democracy are related to terrorism in a nonlinear way in that semi-democracies, or countries with intermediate political freedom, are more prone to terrorist attacks, as they do not have the effective defense characteristic of democratic or autocratic societies.[23] Research has also shown that discrimination and oppression are also related to terrorism.[24] To the best of our knowledge, none of these analyses used the same variables from the same data set or varied the sample to examine whether different constructs of terrorism yield different causes.

## DATA AND METHODOLOGY

To assess the differences in explanatory variables in relation to different groups of targets, we use two different measures of terrorism as our dependent variable that are then separated into three sets of target groups. The dependent variable measures include the absolute number of attacks and the number of target fatalities caused by those attacks. Each of these dependent variables is examined with respect to three different target groups, which include all targets (civilian, government, and security targets), civilian and government targets only, and civilian targets only. Thus, six different dependent variables are obtained for each country-year pair: the number of attacks against all targets, the number of attacks against civilian and government targets only, the number of attacks against civilian targets only, the number of all target fatalities, the number of civilian and government target fatalities, and the number of civilian target fatalities.

To measure terrorism we used data from the GTD,[25] as it is the largest terrorism database compiled to date and is the only one that contains information on both international and domestic attacks. Our final sample consists of 158 countries over the period 1972–2011.[26] We use a zero-inflated negative binomial fixed-effects model in our analysis.[27] We analyze commonly identified causes in terrorism literature, and include various characteristics of a country's profile such as political affiliation, economic performance, regime durability, ethnic discrimination, and population. The choice of measurements and hypothesized relationships reflects the discussion in the literature review.

We measure regime type using a combined standardized measure of the Freedom House data set and the Polity IV data set.[28] A higher score corresponds to more democratic regimes.

Our models explore polity in three ways. First, each model examines polity to see if it is significant in the zero-inflated portion of the model. In the GTD, there may be two processes occurring that must be modeled: (1) an absence of occurrences and fatalities may be the result of a country never reporting having been a target of terrorism, or (2) the zero entries could be zero for a country in a specified year, but positive in another time period. Drakos and Gofas find a statistically significant negative relationship between the level of democracy and the zero-always propensities of terrorist attacks.[29] Second, the linear relationship between polity and terrorism attacks and fatalities is explored to see if this relationship changes based on the target group. Third, we examine the nonlinear effect of polity across target groups, since much research has shown that semi-

TABLE 11.1 Dependent Variables

| Target Group(s) | Dependent Variable |
| --- | --- |
| **Civilian** | Attacks |
| | Fatalities |
| **Civilian + Government** | Attacks |
| | Fatalities |
| **Civilian + Government + Security** | Attacks |
| | Fatalities |

democracies are more prone to terrorism than democratic or authoritarian regimes.[30]

Economic performance is measured using the real gross domestic product (GDP) per capita in constant US dollars in the base year 2005 as found in the Expanded Trade and GDP Data.[31] Terrorism literature reveals mixed results related to the linear relationship between economic performance and terrorism severity, so our analyses examine if these mixed relationships are the result of specifying different target groups. These mixed results may also be a result of a nonlinear relationship. Ghatak and Gold find a strong, statistically significant negative relationship between the squared natural logarithm of GDP per capita and the number of domestic terrorism incidents, indicating that middle-income countries are more vulnerable to attacks.[32]

To measure discrimination, we use the Ethnic Power Relations (EPR) data set.[33] The EPR data set identifies all politically relevant ethnic groups for a given country for a given year, and measures their access to political power to determine whether the group is discriminated against. The EPR data set also provides the fraction of the population that each ethnic group constitutes for a given country-year pair. Thus, the percentage of each country's discriminated population for a given year is calculated as a measure of ethnic discrimination. Previous literature has identified a positive relationship between ethnic discrimination and terrorism severity, hypothesizing that marginalized groups may challenge the power using terror tactics, and we explore whether this relationship changes based on the target group.

The regime durability data come from the Polity IV data set[34] and are measured as the number of years since the last regime change, or the number of years that the current regime has been in power. Regime durability is frequently found to be a negative predictor of terrorism, as the longer a current regime stays in power, the more likely the country has the ability to maintain a strong counterterrorism policy.[35]

The natural logarithm of the population is included as a control variable derived from UN statistics.[36] The majority of research finds that the population size of the target country significantly and positively predicts transnational terrorism.[37] Therefore, we are interested in whether this relationship and its strength hold across all target groups.

Finally, a measure of women's rights is included in the full model. Data for the women's rights measure are collected from the Cingranelli-Richards (CIRI) Human Rights data set.[38] This variable was created by obtaining the standardized average of the CIRI women's economic rights index and the CIRI women's political rights index. A higher score indicates more rights.

We created five models to evaluate the different definitions of terrorism and if there were different causal stories for each. Model I examines the base case, which includes the polity z-score, GDP per capita (ln), ethnic discrimination (%), regime durability, and population (ln). Models II and III add the squared counterparts of the polity z-score and the GDP per capita (ln), respectively. Model IV examines these squared variables simultaneously. Model V displays the full model, which includes a variable for women's rights.

## RESULTS

We first examine the absolute number of attacks against a target country as the dependent variable, differentiated by attacks against all targets, attacks against civilian and government targets only, and attacks against civilian targets only. A brief overview of these analyses reveals similar effects of our explanatory factors across all target groups.[39] All measures of polity receive strong empirical support. As hypothesized, across all models and target groups, there is a strong negative relationship between polity and the number of countries that recorded no attacks for a given year, which supports Drakos and Gofas, who hypothesize that this relationship is premised on the fact that democracies have greater press liberties and are not subject to underreporting bias.[40] The linear standardized measure of polity is also positively related to the rate of terror attacks at a statistically significant level across all models and all target constructs. This finding concurs with previous literature proposing that democracies promote more civil liberties and, therefore, can facilitate organization of terror groups, leading to domestic attacks.[41] However, our models temper this finding by uncovering a nonlinear relationship between polity and the rate of attacks across all groups of targets. This relationship suggests that the previous finding stands only up to a certain level of democracy, at which point the rate of terror attacks starts to decline across all groups of targets. A negative non-linear relationship is consistent across all target groups and supports the previous literature finding that countries with intermediate political freedom are most susceptible to terrorist attacks, as they do not have the defense capabilities of pure autocratic or democratic regimes.[42]

In our analyses, GDP per capita is negatively and significantly related to the number of incidents across all target specifications, but is no longer significant after the nonlinear polity relationship is introduced. Although several studies have found that lower economic performance yields higher terrorism rates, they have not properly controlled for political landscape.[43] Our findings support previous literature in revealing that the relationship between economic performance and terror attacks is weak, but we expand on this literature by uncovering that this relationship is weak after controlling for political landscape, and by finding that the relationship is consistent across all target groups. We also examine the nonlinear relationship between the GDP per capita and the number of terror attacks. We find that only when an attack is indiscriminate, or conducted against all targets, does GDP per capita play a prominent role in the decision to target that country.

This finding supports Ghatak and Gold[44] and reveals that in choosing to attack a country indiscriminately, terrorists are most likely to target middle-income countries. This relationship can be attributed to the fact that terrorists in poor countries may not have the money or skill to deploy a successful domestic attack, whereas extremely wealthy countries may be more successful at discouraging terrorism by offering alternative pathways to economic advantage. Therefore middle-income countries may have the perfect mix of characteristics to make them vulnerable targets of an indiscriminate attack. This is the first instance in which we see a difference arise from altering the construction of terrorism definitions.

Ethnic discrimination is consistently and positively associated with terrorism attacks across all models and all target group types. This finding suggests that the overwhelming majority of research that has found weak or nonsignificant relationships between discrimination and the number of terror incidents may simply have utilized the wrong measure of discrimination. Whereas previous literature uses ethnic fractionalization as a proxy for discrimination, the measure used in our analysis accurately captures the friction between different ethnic groups in each country and, therefore, properly examines the relationship between discrimination and terror attacks.

Regime durability is consistently and negatively associated with terrorism attacks across all models and all target groups, supporting Piazza, who found that state failure and political instability had a strong positive relationship with increased terrorism production.[45] Perhaps the less change in political regime, the more content a country's citizens are, so the less likely a group is to express grievances through violent actions.

All models across all target groups found that a country's population is positively and statistically significantly related to terror attacks. Many reasons explain this relationship. First, a more populated country is more likely to have a larger number of political parties, which can yield greater conflict, resulting in terrorism. Second, countries with larger populations may have a more difficult time in stopping groups from organizing terror attacks. Third, a larger population means more people to recruit to conduct terrorist activities. All of these reasons assume that the attack is domestic. However, a large population can be an attractive characteristic for international attacks, as well, as it may result in more physical and psychological damage. Finally, we have shown that the degree to which women's rights are protected in a country is not significantly related to the propensity of terrorist attacks for any subset of targets.

We extended our analysis and comparison of factors that potentially impact different types of terrorism by focusing on the severity of the attacks, rather than the occurrence, as measured by the number of fatalities, across target groups. As with the analysis of the number of attacks, we apply our models to fatalities from attacks against all targets, fatalities from attacks against civilian and government targets only, and fatalities from attacks against civilian targets only. Examination of our output shows some slight difference between target groups with respect to the linear and nonlinear relationship between GDP per capita and fatalities, but statistical significance and relationships of the remaining variables remain consistent across all target groups. However, some variables associated with occurrences of attacks are unrelated to, or have an opposite effect on, severity of attacks.

Polity remains negatively and significantly related to the probability of a country being classified as an always-zero target of terrorism. This relationship remains consistent across all target groups, providing further evidence for underreporting bias. The linear and nonlinear effects of polity in the standard models for terrorism fatalities remain significant across all target groups, and the relationship shows that countries ruled by an almost, but not completely, autocratic regime tend to experience more fatalities than democratic countries. Less democratic countries may not have medical care adequate to minimize the number of fatalities from such attacks, making the outcome more severe for the lower-polity countries. In completely autocratic countries, attacks are less likely, as previously shown, so there would be fewer fatalities in response to fewer attacks. Combining these hypotheses provides a basis for explaining why the fatalities peak in more autocratic regimes.

The way in which the construct of terrorism is operationalized plays a role when examining the relationship between GDP per capita and the number of fatalities. Similar to our analysis on the number of attacks, our findings indicate that the effect of GDP per capita on the number of fatalities is driven by the nonlinear effect of the political institution for indiscriminate and civilian-only targets. However, the nonlinear and linear relationship between GDP per capita and civilian and government-only fatalities is also positive. This relationship indicates that extremely low-income countries and extremely high-income countries have more civilian and government-related fatalities from terrorism than do countries that approach the median GDP per capita. This result can arise from the congruence of two phenomena. Poorer countries may not have the means to treat injuries from terror attacks, and wealthier countries may be more likely to be transparent about fatalities since they have the means to do so. This relationship may be positive only for the civilian and government subset because terrorists may target government officials in retaliation for their country's dearth or their means to attain wealth. Increases in the number of fatalities in such countries may reflect the terrorists' need to send a message to the government.

The effects of minority discrimination and population remain positive and statistically significant across all target groups. Therefore, the findings demonstrate that the odds of terrorism severity increase as the discriminated population increases, and as the population as a whole increases. Women's rights remain insignificant across all target groups. However, null significance of regime durability indicates that although political stability is negatively related to the number of terrorism attacks, it is not related to the severity of terrorist attacks against any target subgroup.

## DISCUSSION AND CONCLUSION

While there have been superheated conversations about the correct definition of terrorism and whether only attacks against civilian targets should be considered terrorism,[46] this topic has not led to an investigation of whether or not different constructs of the target would yield different causes of terrorism. In this chapter, we investigate three different constructions of the definition of terrorism and fail to find a substantial difference between them. The only substantial difference we find between target groups is the impact of GDP per capita on the number of fatalities as an indication of terrorism severity. This relationship could be attributed to terrorists targeting government personnel to fault them for conditions of extreme wealth.

This analysis is just a first exploration of the question. Our research shows that there is utility in aggregating target groups to examine fundamental questions surrounding terrorism. A logical next step would be to analyze the target groups separately to see if causes of terrorism change corresponding to isolated targets. From there, we can identify additional causes unique to each set of targets. Future research can also examine if organizational characteristics of the perpetrating group vary between target groups.

We have found that, overall, different definitions of terrorism do not seem to be generating very different causal stories. This suggests that while the ethical arguments related to how we construct the definition of terrorism are important, the basic explanations of extreme violent attacks at the country level of analysis are simply not that different, regardless of the target. Given the considerable efforts that academics and policy makers have put into drawing strong lines between different kinds of violence, our results raise important questions about whether such delineation between types of political violence is useful from a policy or academic perspective.

## NOTES

1. We should note that while not rejecting the idea of state terrorism, this chapter focuses on nonstate actor terrorism. When we refer to terrorism and the definition of terrorism, we mean nonstate actor terrorism.

2. Jeff Goodwin, "A theory of categorical terrorism," *Social Forces* 84, no. 4 (2006): 2027–46.

3. Victor Asal et al., "Killing civilians or holding territory? How to think about terrorism," *International Studies Review* 14, no. 3 (2012): 475–97.

4. Ibid.

5. Gary LaFree and Laura Dugan, "Introducing the global terrorism database," *Terrorism and Political Violence* 19, no. 2 (2007): 181–204.

6. Asal et al., "Killing civilians or holding territory?"

7. Ariel Merari, "Terrorism as a strategy of insurgency," *Terrorism and Political Violence* 5, no. 4 (1993): 213–51.

8. Ignacio Sánchez-Cuenca and Luis De la Calle, "Domestic terrorism: The hidden side of political violence," *Annual Review of Political Science* 12 (2009): 31–49.

9. Merari, "Terrorism as a strategy of insurgency."

10. Sánchez-Cuenca and De la Calle, "Domestic terrorism"; Merari, "Terrorism as a strategy of insurgency."

11. Anthony Richards, "Conceptualizing terrorism," *Studies in Conflict and Terrorism* 37, no. 3 (2014): 213–36.

12. Charles Tilly, "Terror, terrorism, terrorists," *Sociological Theory* 22, no. 1 (2004): 5–13.

13. Richards, "Conceptualizing terrorism."

14. Asal et al., "Killing civilians or holding territory?"

15. Walter Enders and Todd Sandler, *The Political Economy of Terrorism* (Cambridge: Cambridge University Press, 2011), 3–5.

16. Merari, "Terrorism as a strategy of insurgency," 239.

17. Richards, "Conceptualizing terrorism," 226.

18. Goodwin, "A theory of categorical terrorism," 2027–46; Martha Crenshaw, "The causes of terrorism," *Comparative Politics* 13, no. 4 (1981): 379–99.

19. Todd Sandler and Harvey E. Lapan, "The calculus of dissent: An analysis of terrorists' choice of targets," *Synthese* 76, no. 2 (1988): 245–61.

20. Endlers and Sandler, *Political Economy*, 61–103; James A. Piazza, "Poverty, minority economic discrimination, and domestic terrorism," *Journal of Peace Research* 48, no. 3 (2011): 339–53.

21. Crenshaw, "Causes of terrorism," 381; Jose Tavares, "The open society assesses its enemies: Shocks, disasters, and terrorist attacks," *Journal of Monetary Economics* 51, no. 5 (2004): 1039–70.

22. Tim Krieger and Daniel Meierrieks, "What causes terrorism?" *Public Choice* 147, nos. 1–2 (2011): 3–27; Konstantinos Drakos and Andreas Gofas, "In search of the average transnational terrorist attack venue," *Defence and Peace Economics* 17, no. 2 (2006): 73–93.

23. Krieger and Meierrieks, "What causes terrorism?" 7; Drakos and Gofas, "In search of the average transnational terrorist attack venue," 78.

24. Piazza, "Poverty, minority economic discrimination, and domestic terrorism."

25. National Consortium for the Study of Terrorism and Responses to Terrorism (START), *Global Terrorism Database* (College Park, MD, 2013), http://www.start.umd.edu/gtd.

26. Observations were excluded if the target type was unknown or labeled as a violent political party. Data from 1993 were also excluded, as the GTD provides only marginal estimates for that year. Missing data are recorded as zero attacks/fatalities.

27. For a more in-depth explanation of modeling choice, please contact the authors.

28. Freedom House, *Freedom in the world: Aggregate and subcategory scores* (Washington, DC, 2014), https://freedomhouse.org/report/freedom-world-aggregate-and-subcategory-scores; Monty G. Marshall, Keith Jaggers, and Ted Robert Gurr, *Polity IV Project* (Arlington, VA, 2011), http://www.systemicpeace.org/inscr/p4v2015.xls.

29. Drakos and Gofas, "In search of the average transnational terrorist attack venue," 73–79.

30. Krieger and Meierrieks, "What causes terrorism?" 7; Drakos and Gofas, "In search of the average transnational terrorist attack venue," 73–79.

31. Kristian Skrede Gleditsch, *Expanded Trade and GDP Data* (Oslo, Norway, 2013), http://privatewww.essex.ac.uk/~ksg/exptradegdp.html. We center the data and then evaluate the natural logarithm of the variable to avoid multicollinearity with its squared counterpart.

32. Sambuddha Ghatak and Aaron Gold, "Development, discrimination, and domestic terrorism: Looking beyond a linear relationship," *Conflict Management and Peace Science* (2015): 1–22.

33. Andreas Wimmer, Lars-Erik Cederman, and Brian Min, "Ethnic politics and armed conflict: A configurational analysis of a new global data set," *American Sociological Review* 74, no. 2 (2009): 316–37.

34. Marshall, Jaggers, and Gurr, *Polity IV Project*.

35. Joe Eyerman, "Terrorism and democratic states: Soft targets or accessible systems," *International Interactions* 24, no. 2 (1998): 151–70; Quan Li, "Does democracy promote or reduce transnational terrorist incidents?" *Journal of Conflict Resolution* 49, no. 2 (2005): 278–97.

36. National Accounts Main Aggregate Database, *UN Statistics* (New York, 2014), http://unstats.un.org/unsd/snaama/dnlList.asp.

37. Krieger and Meierrieks, "What causes terrorism?" 10.

38. David L. Cingranelli and David L. Richards, "The Cingranelli and Richards (CIRI) human rights data project," *Human Rights Quarterly* 32, no. 2 (2010): 401–24. CIRI data are available only for 154 out of the 158 countries from the period 1981–2011 examined in the other models, reducing the sample size for the full model.

39. For a more in-depth review of statistical output, please contact the authors.

40. Drakos and Gofas, "In search of the average transnational terrorist attack venue," 73–79.

41. William Lee Eubank and Leonard Weinberg, "Does democracy encourage terrorism?" *Terrorism and Political Violence* 6, no. 4 (1994): 417–35.

42. Ibid.; Krieger and Meierrieks, "What causes terrorism?" 16.

43. Krieger and Meierrieks, "What causes terrorism?" 7.

44. Ghatak and Gold, "Development, discrimination, and domestic terrorism," 1–22.

45. James A. Piazza, "Draining the swamp: Democracy promotion, state failure, and terrorism in 19 Middle Eastern countries," *Studies in Conflict and Terrorism* 30, no. 6 (2007): 521–39.

46. Asal et al., "Killing civilians or holding territory?"

# 12. Analyzing Pathways of Lone-Actor Radicalization: A Relational Approach

Stefan Malthaner and Lasse Lindekilde

In a recent study, Gill, Horgan, and Deckert examined socio-demographic network characteristics and antecedent behaviors of 119 lone-actor terrorists.[1] Surprisingly, they found that many lone actors are not that "alone" but interact with—and are linked to—other individuals, groups, and wider networks and movements in various ways. Of the sample, 33.6 percent had recently joined a larger group or movement engaged in contentious politics; 36.1 percent had family members or close associates who were involved in political violence or crime; 47.9 percent of the "lone actors" interacted face-to-face with members of a wider movement; and 68.1 percent had consumed propaganda issued by a political movement.[2] These numbers are based on reports published by news media, which tend to underestimate the actual extent of social ties due to limited access to primary sources. A picture emerges of lone-actor radicalization as not an entirely individual and isolated process, but as a pathway at least partly embedded in social relationships and shaped by dynamics of interaction—though in ways that might differ from common pathways to joining terrorist groups. This picture is in stark contrast to dominant public constructions and conceptions of lone-actor terrorism, which depict perpetrators of lone-actor terrorism as isolated, social atoms who radicalize alone in front of the computer.

This chapter seeks to develop a relational perspective on analyzing the radicalization of lone-actor terrorists—defined here as individuals threatening to carry out or carrying out acts of terrorist violence who (1) operate as a single perpetrator in the preparation and the execution of the attack, (2) do not belong to a terrorist organization or group, and (3) do not act on direct orders or under the direct influence of a leader or group.[3] The aim is thus an analytical framework that adapts existing relational (network) approaches to the study of processes of lone-actor radicalization by specifying relational factors, forms of social embeddedness, and dynamics of interactions relevant in the case of lone actors. Lone-actor terrorists vary significantly with respect to the degree of social isolation in which they operate and how they interact with other militant activists, radical milieus, or virtual communities during the process of radicalization. Thus, we argue, first, that analyzing relational configurations and their evolution over time offers a way to identify patterns and specific mechanisms of lone-actor radicalization that can serve to distinguish main types of lone actors based on the extent and form of their social embeddedness. Second, we argue that a relational perspective can help us develop a more precise understanding of elements of "lone-radicalization" or "self-radicalization." This may seem paradoxical, but isolation is a fundamentally relational process. By focusing on relational configurations, we offer an analytical framework for the study of lone-actor radicalization, which allows for and sheds light on different constructions of lone-actor terrorism. In particular, we argue that our relational approach moves beyond extant research in the area by showing how various personal characteristics interact with relational configurations in constructing terrorism as a solo activity. Furthermore, the reason we believe that relational pathways are particularly relevant here is that they allow us not only to identify causal dynamics but also to locate points of intervention and interdiction, because social ties are cardinal vectors of intervention and because it is primarily via social relationships that "early warning" signs can be spotted.

The chapter draws on the ongoing research project Preventing Interdicting and Mitigating Lone-Actor Extremist Events (PRIME), and shares its objective to develop a relational approach to lone-actor radicalization.[4] The extensive empirical data on which our analytical model is based includes (1) a detailed medium-N open-source data set of twenty-five cases of lone-actor extremist events in different geographical contexts (United States, Europe, and the Middle East) with a variety of perpetrator characteristics (political-religious orientation, gender) and attack types (attack/failed attack); and (2) five in-depth case studies (three German, two Danish) based on interviews and extensive documentary sources, including restricted court and police files. The ambition of this chapter is thus theoretical, rather than empirical. Further research within the PRIME project will help verify the usefulness of the analytical approach developed here and specify pathways and mechanisms of lone-actor radicalization.

The chapter consists of two main parts. We discuss the way relational approaches have been used in studies on radicalization and revisit some classic works in the social movement studies literature in which the approach was originally developed. Based on this literature, we develop a framework for studying processes of lone-actor radicalization as a relational pathway, specifying several basic, general functions of social ties and a number of particular mechanisms relevant in the radicalization of lone actors.

However, before this a few words on the central concept of "radicalization" are warranted. As pointed out in review articles on the concept of radicalization, there is no standard or even broadly accepted definition of radicalization or, as a consequence, deradicalization.[5] Traditionally, "radical" has primarily been defined in terms of political desires and ends. A "radical" was a revolutionary who wanted to change society fundamentally. This change could be achieved through nonviolent and democratic means or through violent and nondemocratic means.[6] Thus, a "radical" could be a democrat. This is rarely the case in recent conceptualizations. In the late nineteenth and early twentieth centuries, "radical" meant progressive and pro-democratic; today, it mostly means the opposite, as "radical" and the process of "radicalization" are most often defined in terms of violent or undemocratic means. A central perception in many recent definitions is that "radicals" use illegal political violence to achieve political goals, progressive or regressive, and radicalization is, thus, the process of coming to accept political violence as a legitimate strategy of action.[7] This is also the definition we embrace here. Thus, we find it useful to distinguish between "nonviolent radicalism" and "violent radicalism," with the process of radicalization concerning only the latter. When applying the term *radical* as a descriptor of, for example, a "group" in the following analysis, we therefore imply a group that makes use of or legitimates political violence.

## SOCIAL TIES AND NETWORKS

### Relational Approaches in Research on Radicalization and Terrorism

That relationships matter is well established in research on violent radicalism. Numerous studies refer to social ties or relational mechanisms to explain how and why ordinary young people end up participating in acts of extreme violence.[8] In addition to the influence of radical preachers on vulnerable youth, these works emphasize two main relational dynamics: (1) the role of pre-existing personal relationships (friendship and kinship ties) in connecting—and channeling—individuals into radical groups and movements; and (2) the radicalizing effect of small-group dynamics—that is, interactions among members of small, confined cliques of friends that push individuals to adopt more extreme attitudes and exert peer-group pressure to participate in high-risk activism.

To recapitulate how relational approaches have been used in radicalization studies, we take a closer look at the work on jihadist militancy in the West by Marc Sageman, who applies a network perspective on radicalization.[9] Sageman emphasizes and combines mobilization via pre-existing ties and group dynamics in his analysis of jihadist radicalization. He argues that what is special about individuals who joined a terrorist group (in contrast to others with similar beliefs and characteristics who did not) is that "they actually made the link," and he identifies pre-existing friendship or kinship ties as relevant in more than 75 percent of the cases in his database.[10] Feelings of moral outrage and the belief that a war is being waged against Islam, particularly when they resonate with personal experiences, constitute important predispositions, but the step to actually affiliate with jihadist networks is often initiated and facilitated by friendship networks. The process of radicalization then takes place as a "group phenomenon": friendship groups and cliques form around mosques and other meeting places; they form strong bonds that promote intense loyalty and emotional support; and intensive interaction as well as increasing isolation from their social environment draws them closer to radical interpretations.[11] In other words, Sageman connects mechanisms of ingroup deliberation with dynamics of withdrawal, enclosure, and isolation vis-à-vis the members' original networks of families and friends, as well as toward the wider mosque communities. Dense, small networks of friends (cliques or enclaves) thereby play a crucial role in transforming individuals' beliefs and perceptions, their "sense of themselves and their relations," while social ties deepen in a spiral of increasing loyalty, devotion, and self-sacrifice.[12]

Sageman summarizes his own analytical perspective as focusing on the "study of relationships of terrorists in context," which includes "their relationship with each other, their relationship with ideas floating in their environment, and their relationship with people and organizations outside the group."[13] One important contribution of his second book was to add virtual relationships and online groups to his analysis of face-to-face, "offline" relationships.[14] Forms of communication and social ties have been transformed by the Internet, and repeated interactions in online forums can provide a sense of belonging and drive radicalization via dynamics of mutual validation, self-selection of the most radical, the illusion of numbers, and other mechanisms.[15] Sageman emphasizes that it is important to link online with offline networks, but he also mentions that virtual relations may be particularly relevant for lone-actor terrorists: "They appear to be 'lone wolfs' only offline," but are often members of forums and (see themselves as part of) virtual communities.[16]

In sum, what characterizes this approach is an emphasis on the role of social ties in *connecting* individuals to political movements and radical groups, and on the role of interactions and relationships within movements and small groups in *shaping perceptions, beliefs, and ideas.* While dispositions and cognitive receptivity play an important role, motivations and ideas do not necessarily precede involvement in activism, but are gradually adopted and reshaped over the course of a process of engaging and interacting with other activists in radical movements and groups.

Another important relational approach to the study of radicalization is Clark McCauley and Sophia Moskalenko's work on mechanisms of radicalization. Rather than describing typical trajectories, they identify recurrent mechanisms at the individual and group level that, in varying succession and combination, shape and drive processes of radicalization.[17] Among these mechanisms are friendship ties as drivers of membership in radical groups (which corresponds to the pre-existing social ties argument); ingroup and intergroup interaction such as extremity shifts in like-minded groups; increasing group cohesion under threat and isolation; radicalization as a result of competition with rival groups; and the "condensing" effects of repression and persecution on radical groups.[18] This approach is interesting to us because it connects relational dynamics at different levels, particularly the individual and group levels, and connects ingroup interactions with outgroup relations and the group's wider social context.

## The Social Movement Perspective: Micromobilization and Social Ties

Before we develop our framework for analyzing processes of lone-actor radicalization, we briefly revisit some classic social movement studies that originally developed the network approach, which, as we argue, can help to clarify important differences in the functions and types of social ties and contain elements that, so far, have not been applied in research on radicalization.

In their seminal study of the role of social networks in facilitating participation in social movements, Snow, Zurcher, and Ekland-Olson focused on what they called "microstructural avenues of recruitment."[19] They emphasized three elements of recruitment into activism: (1) structural proximity, that is, pre-existing social ties that increase the likelihood of contact with movement activists; (2) availability, that is, the absence of constraining ties that bind individuals to other people, groups, and contexts and could hinder recruitment; and (3) affective interaction with activists, meaning the interpersonal dynamics that set in after a person becomes involved. Snow and colleagues took a close look at types of initial contact, differentiating between different socio-spatial settings in which movements and potential participants come into contact, and different forms of interaction.[20] They also offered a more nuanced understanding of pre-existing social ties by emphasizing that extramovement networks can function as countervailing influences hindering recruitment, and that the extent of this "structural availability" often seems to determine whether an individual becomes an activist or remains in a more passive role.[21] In other words, rather than being a simple conveyor belt to activism, pre-existing social networks often have a quite complex and ambivalent role in processes of radicalization of activism.

Doug McAdam's work on recruitment to high-risk activism shares many of Snow et al.'s premises. McAdam distinguishes between different types of social ties, from informal friendship ties to more formal organizational affiliations, as well as strong and weak ties, which have different functions and implications for the recruitment process.[22] Moreover, he distinguishes between low-risk and high-risk activism, making the point that the two are often consecutive stages of gradual involvement in a political movement or radical group—an argument later emphasized by Wiktorowicz.[23] Low-risk activism may thus "pave the way" and draw people into high-risk activism: it offers tentative, safe forays into new roles, new connections to other activists, and processes of socialization that contribute to the adoption of perceptions, attitudes, norms, and identities.[24] "Recruitment" is thus, as McAdam argues, often a gradual process that includes a cyclical dynamic of integration and socialization, as participation in a broader movement facilitates successive shifts toward higher-risk forms of activism.

Several elements in these works are particularly important when we study radicalization from a relational perspective. Links made via social ties are of course important in establishing initial contact with a movement, and activism within a broader movement or milieu then forms the basis for new ties that connect individuals to higher-risk (and radical) forms of activism. Likewise, socialization may have different phases that gradually "pave the way" for acceptance of more radical beliefs. This latter point—together with the notion of structural (biographical) availability—allows us to develop a more nuanced understanding of "disposition" and "vulnerability" to radicalization. Rather than being a static characteristic of an individual's personality, these conditions have a relational quality and are to some extent a result (and a feature) of an individual's past and present relationships with his or her personal social environment. Dispositions are (also) the result of prior socialization experiences and patterns of biographical availability, and vulnerability can be described in terms of the absence of countervailing and constraining influences, as well as in terms of degrees of social disembeddedness and prior personal conflicts with family and friends, for example. Finally, there are very different pathways to participation and radicalization that, as we argue, can be differentiated based on relational characteristics.

These different approaches form the basis of our endeavor to develop a relational perspective on studying processes of lone-actor radicalization. The relevance of a relational approach to radicalization is underlined by recent works that emphasize the fact that radicalization of attitudes is not identical to radicalization of actions, and that radical beliefs do not predict violent actions.[25] As Randy Borum has emphasized, an understanding of radicalization that focuses exclusively on the transformation of perceptions and beliefs risks implying that radical beliefs are a proxy for terrorism.[26] Relational analysis looks at the way beliefs are transmitted and transformed by social networks and interactions and can thus contribute to a much more precise understanding of how beliefs, actions, and social relationships are intertwined in processes of radicalization. Furthermore, it addresses "differential participation," that is, the puzzle of why some individuals end up participating in acts of violence while others with similar predispositions and social backgrounds do not, and why some act alone.

## A RELATIONAL FRAMEWORK FOR ANALYZING
## LONE-ACTOR RADICALIZATION

The challenge in developing a framework for analyzing processes of lone-actor radicalization from a relational perspective is obvious: To what extent can we transfer insights on processes of radicalization in the context of groups and movements to the radicalization of lone actors? What are the specific mechanisms and relational configurations of lone radicalization that are particular to this type of actor? And finally, how can we analytically link relational dynamics with other causal factors, correlates, and mechanisms?

The basic contention of this chapter is twofold. First, as stated at the outset, "lone actors" are rarely entirely socially isolated, but are to some extent, and at certain points in time, embedded in groups or wider milieus and interact with other activists and virtual communities. Second, a relational perspective can help develop a more precise understanding of elements of "lone-radicalization" or "self-radicalization." As stated above, isolation is a fundamentally relational process. It often results from conflictive processes of interaction, withdrawal, or failure to connect to groups and is defined and shaped by an individual's perceptions of his or her immediate and wider social environment, as well as his or her simultaneous orientation toward more abstract reference groups and virtual communities.

## Social Pathways of Lone-Actor Radicalization

With our focus on social relationships and networks as the social pathways of radicalization, we understand radicalization as a gradual process that progresses through a concatenation of relationship patterns and is shaped by dynamics of interaction. As previous studies have shown, trajectories of radicalization are often initiated by encounters or pre-existing personal ties and are embedded in—and to some extent driven by—interactions within small groups and wider movements or milieus in which perceptions, beliefs, and values are formed and reinforced. Earlier phases and "low-risk" forms of activism can facilitate and "prepare" successive engagement in "high-risk" activism by socializing individuals into adopting ideologies, beliefs, and perceptions and providing opportunities to form new ties with other (more radical) activists. Disposition to violent radicalization may thus be the result of prior socialization experiences.

How can we adapt this perspective to the study of lone actors? What is distinctive about relational pathways of lone-actor terrorists is that most of them do not follow a clear-cut pattern of increasing integration into movements and, consecutively, into radical groups, but rather follow *more complex and discontinuous trajectories, often in the periphery of radical networks.* While they are to some extent socially embedded in radical movements or groups at some point in time, the pathways that lead them to eventually commit a terrorist act on their own are also shaped by *patterns of failed joining, marginal drifting, dropping out, rejection, or impatiently pressing ahead and breaking away* from a reluctant group or milieu. In contrast (or in addition) to the approaches discussed above, which focus on dynamics of steadily increasing integration and participation, we also have to look for relational mechanisms that entail conflict, rupture, and isolation, as well as for elements of *partial or weak social embeddedness.*

As mentioned, our analysis starts from the social pathway of radicalization, but it also aims to link with and study the connection of attitudinal and behavioral dimensions of radicalization. Beliefs are adopted, reinforced, and transformed in social interactions, and decisions to act are often taken in group contexts. However, particularly in the case of lone actors, we also need to consider how an individual's attitudes and personality may shape relations with the social environment, as by, for example, impeding the ability to connect to others and function in a group. Being "alone" may be a choice, even a strategic choice, but it may also be the product of (lacking) social skills and personality traits. For example, a person with a combination of poor social skills and an excessive need for cognitive closure or intolerance of ambiguity may be attracted to milieus where extremist ideas and clear action prescriptions prevail, but may stay in the milieu's periphery and integrate only partially.[27] Likewise, an inability to perspectivate one's own beliefs and actions and relate to their effects on others may push individuals toward settings where divergent lifestyles or opinions are not present, but may also hinder full integration in these milieus. A quest for fundamental life embeddedness has been shown to be connected to radicalization when certain individual risk factors are also present.[28] We add to this that social-psychological characteristics interact with an individual's ability to secure social embeddedness in a group context, and we thereby differentiate between processes of self-radicalization and group radicalization.

## Specifying Types and Functions of Social Ties

A first step in capturing more complex and discontinuous relational processes is to specify different types and functions of social ties, which will provide us with a conceptual toolbox to precisely analyze a broader variety of relational dynamics in trajectories of lone-actor radicalization.

First, we distinguish between *weak and strong social ties.*[29] Strong ties imply prolonged interaction and greater emotional investment, loyalty, and shared values; weak ties imply lower levels of engagement and commitment and may consist of mere superficial contacts based on few encounters. Obviously, rather than representing distinct types, strong and weak ties may be seen to define a continuum with various forms of "medium-strength" ties in-between. Moreover, we distinguish between *face-to-face* and *online interactions* and relationships, but emphasize that both types of ties can differ in strength. Online relationships range from prolonged interaction with the same people in closed online forums to singular, anonymous encounters or passive consumption of another person's messages and contents on the Internet (as a "one-sided" virtual tie). We use the term *affiliative ties* to refer to impersonal relations that indicate a sense of common connection and identification.[30] In this weakest form of relationship, there is no direct communication or other linkage among individuals.

Furthermore, to capture evolving patterns of relational embeddedness, we propose a simple matrix that specifies relationships and interactions with radicalizing settings and radical activists by charting a relational field comprising three main sectors (or "sets of relationships") that, in turn, are

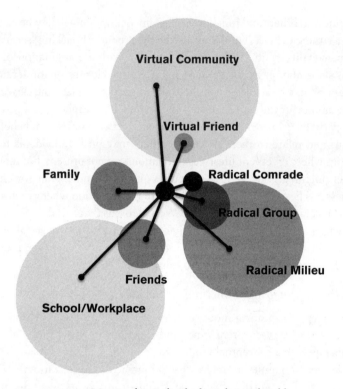

FIGURE 12.1. Matrix of an Individual's Relational Field
Comprising Three Sets of Relationships.

categorized according to strength versus weakness ("strength" including
dimensions such as duration, level of personal closeness and investment,
and intensity of interactions) (see figure 12.1):

1. The *personal social environment:* family relationships, friendship
   groups, and relations in the school, college, or workplace.

2. *Relationships with radicalizing agents and radicalizing settings
   (face-to-face, "real world" relationships):* close relationships with a
   radical mentor or comrade; ties with a small radical group; ties with
   a large radical milieu or movement.

3. *Virtual radicalizing relationships:* direct and prolonged interaction
   with a specific radical activist; belonging to a virtual radical group
   (online forum) that interacts regularly; affiliative abstract ties with a
   wider virtual community.

In figure 12.1, the links to larger circles indicate weak ties, while links to the smaller circles suggest strong ties. Clearly, the main categories of relations can overlap, such as radicalizing family relationships or online and offline relationships with the same people at the same time. Of course, figure 12.1 is a snapshot of an individual's relational field, and we argue that to understand radicalization of lone actors, we need to investigate changes in relational configurations across time.

As discussed above, strong ties are generally considered important for engaging in high-risk activism, whereas weak ties are deemed crucial in establishing connections across a broader movement and in spreading ideas and information.[31] However, for the purpose of this chapter, it seems important to consider a broader variety of *functions* and combinations of weak and strong ties. Drawing on Passy's network approaches to participation in social movements, we differentiate between the *socialization, structural connection,* and *decision-shaping functions* of social ties.[32]

The *socialization function* of social ties refers to the fact that participation is an identification process and that norms and values are adopted, and identities are created and shaped, in social interactions with other activists. Yet social ties also seem to have weaker—but still important—effects on an individual's beliefs and values. Just as a dynamic of tight integration into close social relationships can reshape values and identities, we suggest that weaker ties may play a crucial role in *confirming, reinforcing,* and *sustaining* certain beliefs. Moreover, social ties can point individual processes of religious (or ideological) seeking in a certain direction, without necessarily strongly influencing their content. Finally, socialization and influence on beliefs and identities can occur at different points during a radicalization process, not only in the initial stages.

*Structural connection* corresponds to the role of pre-existing social networks in linking potential recruits to radical movements. Again, we argue that a wider spectrum of connections at different points in time needs to be considered, beyond "first contacts" facilitated by family and friendship ties, including connections formed via weak social ties or chance encounters, and connections formed at different moments along a pathway of radicalization. Thus, social selection is a process.

Finally, the *decision-shaping function* of social ties refers to the fact that social interactions shape more specific and shorter-term perceptions and expectations that influence decision making (in contrast to socialization, which shapes more stable values and norms).[33] However, it also seems important to consider other forms of influencing decisions—particularly decisions to engage in certain forms of action—such as peer-group pressure, notions of loyalty, and emotional commitments. One important way in which social ties shape decision making is by transmitting direct or indirect encouragement of particular actions. Action encouragement cues are often crucial in connecting attitudes and attitude-relevant actions, perhaps especially engagement in costly actions such as political violence.[34] Through ties with online or offline radical milieus or actors, an individual may receive direct action encouragement cues (specific behavioral guidance or suggestions) or indirect cues (e.g., consumption of written, oral, or pictorial material that in a general way encourages certain actions) or be inspired to act by engaging with a modular performance of the behavior in question (e.g., watching people you know or admire perform violence). Lone actors often do not receive direct and specific action encouragement from others to carry out an attack, but are rather, through (weak or affiliative) social ties, exposed to indirect action encouragement cues or modular performance of actions that shape decision making. In a number of cases, emotionally charged action encouragement cues—such as videos, songs, and photos— seem to have been the trigger that connected ideational processes and corresponding actions and, thus, the decision to carry out violence alone.

Finally, it is worth mentioning the *constraining function* of social ties. Alternative personal networks and social ties outside a radical group or setting may exert countervailing influences that prevent further radicalization (e.g., the idea behind radicalization mentoring programs); on the other hand, close personal ties among members of a radical group may also constrain withdrawal or defection. We therefore argue that in addition to the more stable patterns of structural (or biographical) availability mentioned above, we also need to pay attention to sudden changes in constraining patterns of relationships—such as the death of a close family member, the break-up of an engagement, or sudden unemployment—that weaken constraints and clear the way for previously impossible decisions and steps. This is a relational mechanism that McCauley and Moskalenko call unfreezing.[35]

## Mechanisms of "Lone-Actor Radicalization"

To reiterate: the aim of this chapter is to develop an approach for analyzing lone-actor radicalization from a relational perspective, which we hope will enable us to distinguish several main (ideal) types of pathways of lone-actor radicalization based on the extent and form of their social embeddedness, and to identify the specific mechanisms that shape these pathways. Our conceptualization and understanding of causal mechanisms—the building blocks of ideal-typical pathways of lone-actor radicalization—are inspired by the process-and-mechanism approach developed by Doug

McAdam, Sidney Tarrow, and Charles Tilly in social movement studies. Thus, the process of radicalization is broken down into constituting causal mechanisms understood as "delimited changes that alter relations among specified sets of elements in identical or closely similar ways over a variety of situations."[36]

We here take a first step toward specifying relational mechanisms of lone-actor radicalization. As mentioned, the radicalization of terrorist lone actors is not an entirely distinct phenomenon, and many "conventional" mechanisms of group-based radicalization may play a role at various points in the process, including initial contact with radical activists via pre-existing social ties and socialization processes within radical milieus. In addition, we tentatively propose four sets of relational mechanisms that are *specific* to lone-actor radicalization and that shape individual trajectories in particular ways and at particular points in the process:

1. *Mechanisms that account for the lack of closer integration in terrorist groups and extremist networks.* Many lone actors never join a militant group or a radical network, but remain at their margins. It is at this point, in particular, that personal and psychological characteristics of lone actors interact with social mechanisms to create distinct relational patterns.[37] Because of antisocial characteristics, a very withdrawn and indecisive personality (often in combination with depressive episodes), or a pattern of erratic and volatile behavior, individuals refrain from engaging in closer relations with radical groups or are rejected and frozen out by them. A *self-reinforcing dynamic of conflict, rejection, withdrawal, and isolation* can thereby push individuals toward a more isolated pattern of radicalization.

2. *Mechanisms that account for the exclusion or withdrawal from extremist groups.* Some lone actors had been members of militant groups or networks before they carried out their attack individually, but had dropped out or become disconnected from these groups because of internal disputes and rivalries, because the individual was "burnt" due to police investigation, because he or she was injured and could not remain an active member, or because the group disintegrated as a result of pressure from security services. This mechanism of sudden disconnection from a radical group or network—which is also relevant in cases of returned foreign fighters—represents a distinct type of *unfreezing*, which often results in a personal crisis, a search for purpose, or an urge to

continue, through isolated actions, "the struggle" or reconfirm one's identity as a militant activist. Another mechanism within this set is *pressing ahead:* frustration and impatience trigger a break with a reluctant political (or even radical) group or milieu, often after internal conflicts over ideology, strategy, and leadership, and the individual "goes all the way" on her or his own.

3. *Mechanisms that drive or sustain radicalization in situations of isolation or weak embeddedness.* Whether as a result of withdrawal, failed joining, or exclusion, lone actors further radicalize in a situation in which they have only weak or affiliative ties with other radical activists and milieus. Among the mechanisms that contribute to this process are the *dynamic of conflictive interactions and isolation* (confrontations with family members and prior friends, leading to the gradual erosion of these relationships) and the dual process of *virtual integration and withdrawal from personal relations* (mutually reinforcing dynamics of "becoming absorbed" in online activities). *Integration in virtual, online groups,* as well as *ideological reinforcement via weak ties* toward broader radical milieus and *perceived certification via affiliative ties,* can have important socializing functions and help to sustain radical beliefs (interactions with and perceived confirmation from other persons or milieus that partly share an individual's beliefs have a sustaining and reinforcing effect on more radical ideas held by that individual).

4. *Mechanisms that account for the shift from radical attitudes to (lone) terrorist action.* An individual's decision to carry out a violent attack on his or her own may be a more gradual outgrowth of his or her process of radicalization, linked, for example, to dynamics of rejection, isolation, and radicalization. Or it may be the result of a more immediate *reaction to experiences of moral shock, action encouragement cues received via affiliative or weak ties, or sudden opportunities.* In many cases, the sudden loss of constraining social ties, such as losing a job, a fiancé, or a family member, also seems to influence this shift.

Finally, we need to pay particular attention to agency in relational processes, both in the case of lone-actor radicalization and in bottom-up processes of joining radical groups. Conventional network approaches, which emphasize initial contacts established via pre-existing ties, mention that prior convictions and sympathies for a movement may facilitate this connection. However, we might have to consider the fact that processes of more or less individual "pre-radicalization," preceding first contact with other activists or a movement, may prompt an individual to actively seek to establish such contact. In other words, we need to consider the role of *agency* in processes of radicalization, a point that has been overlooked in many studies on radicalization and participation in social movements.[38] Rather than being the passive object of influences and group dynamics, and being "dragged" into radical activism by others (as a "fellow traveler"), some individuals actively look for and engage with particular teachings and ideologies on their own initiative (what Bouhana and Wikström call self-selection),[39] seek contact with other radical activists or groups, and have a central role in building the very networks through which pathways of radicalization progress. In general, but particularly if we want to adapt network approaches to studying the radicalization of lone-actor terrorists, it is important to integrate this element of agency into our analysis. Otherwise, we risk reifying the power of networks and groups over passive individuals in a way that prevents us from understanding trajectories and decisions of individuals preceding their joining a radical group—but also trajectories of lone actors who are at the margins of, after breaking from, or isolated from radical groups and movements.

CONCLUSIONS

This chapter presents a theoretical approach that analyzes processes of lone-actor radicalization as a relational pathway. Drawing on theoretical perspectives developed in the literature on terrorism and political violence, as well as social movement studies, we emphasize that processes of radicalization entail a concatenation of relational constellations and are driven by relational mechanisms, seeking to specify forms of social ties and their functions, over time. We highlight the need to consider how an individual's attitudes and personality may shape relations with her or his social environment, and how weak and medium-strength ties may play a crucial role in confirming, reinforcing, and sustaining beliefs within lone-actor radicalization. Likewise, we have pointed to a number of mechanisms that help account for the shift from radical attitudes (i.e., forms of "nonviolent radicalism") to lone-terrorist action (i.e., a form of "violent radicalism").

Beyond analyzing causal dynamics that shape certain individual pathways, we believe that the approach is capable of capturing different, recurrent radicalization pathways, which can form the basis for distinguishing different types of lone-actor terrorists. Lone-actor terrorists vary significantly with respect to the degree of social isolation and how they interact with other militant activists, radical milieus, and virtual communities during the process of radicalization. One construction of lone-actor terrorism, suggested in this chapter, entails an overall pathway of peripheral drifting in and out of radicalizing milieus without ever really integrating and establishing lasting ties to other radicals. Another construction entails a pathway in which lone actors for various reasons are excluded or withdraw from radical groups they have integrated into. Distinguishing types of lone actors based on patterns of relational pathways is relevant insofar as it identifies different causal dynamics as well as potential points of intervention. Further research is needed to pinpoint mechanisms of lone-actor radicalization and to assess the analytical utility of the proposed approach, to examine how robust or typical the identified causal mechanisms of lone-actor radicalization are, and to explore the extent to which they appear in recurring combinations forming distinct pathways. Our research in the PRIME project leads the way.

## NOTES

The research leading to these results has received funding from the European Research Council under the European Union's Seventh Framework Programme (FP7/2007-2013)/ERC grant agreement no. 608354.

1. Paul Gill, John Horgan, and Paige Deckert, "Bombing Alone: Tracing the Motivations and Antecedent Behaviors of Lone-Actor Terrorists," *Journal of Forensic Sciences* 59 (2014): 425–35.

2. Ibid., 430.

3. This definition excludes individuals who are members of a terrorist group or who act on orders from terrorist leaders, or both, but it allows for varying degrees of "loneness" during processes of radicalization, as well as various forms of social ties and assistance in phases preceding the attack. Following Borum et al., we concede that lone-actor terrorists can be conceptualized more precisely by using a dimensional approach that specifies degrees of loneness, direction, and motivation. See Randy Borum, Robert Fein, and Bryan Vossekuil, "A Dimensional Approach to Analyzing Lone Offender Terrorism," *Aggression and Violent Behavior* 17 (2012): 389–96.

4. This project has received funding from the European Union's Seventh Framework Programme for research, technological development, and demonstration under grant agreement no. 608354.

5. Noemié Bouhana and P.-O. Wikström, *Al Qai'da–Influenced Radicalisation: A Rapid Evidence Assessment Guided by Situational Action Theory*, RDS Occasional Paper 97 (London: Home Office Research, Development and Statistics Directorate, 2011), accessed July 13, 2016, https://www.gov.uk/government /uploads/system/uploads/attachment_data/file/116724/occ97.pdf; Alex P. Schmid, "Radicalization, De-radicalization, Counter-radicalization: A Conceptual Discussion and Literature Review" (ICCT Research Paper, The Hague, 2013), http://www .icct.nl/download/file/ICCT-Schmid-Radicalisation-De-Radicalisation-Counter-Radicalisation-March-2013.pdf (accessed July 13, 2016); Randy Borum, "Radicalization into Violent Extremism I: A Review of Social Science Theories," *Journal of Strategic Security* 4 (2011): 8.

6. Arun Kundani, "Radicalisation: The Journey of a Concept," *Race and Class* 54:2 (2012): 3–25.

7. Anja Dalgaard-Nielsen, "Violent Radicalization in Europe: What We Know and What We Do Not Know," *Studies in Conflict and Terrorism* 33:9 (2010): 797–814.

8. See Edwin Bakker, *Jihadi Terrorists in Europe. Their Characteristics and the Circumstances in Which They Joined the Jihad; An Exploratory Story* (Netherlands Institute of International Relations Clingendael, 2006), www.clingendael.nl/publications/2006/20061200_cscp_csp_bakker.pdf (accessed July 13, 2016); Thomas Hegghammer, *Jihadism in Saudi Arabia* (Cambridge: Cambridge University Press, 2010); Clark McCauley and Sophia Moskalenko, "Mechanisms of Political Radicalization: Pathways toward Terrorism," *Terrorism and Political Violence* 20 (2008): 415–33; Clark McCauley and Sophia Moskalenko, *Friction: How Radicalization Happens to Them and Us* (Oxford: Oxford University Press, 2009); Petter Nesser, "Jihad in Europe. Patterns in Islamist Terrorist Cell Formation and Behaviour, 1995–2010" (PhD diss, University of Oslo, 2011); Peter Neumann and Brooke Rogers, "Recruitment and Mobilisation for the Islamist Militant Movement in Europe" (London: International Centre for the Study of Radicalisation and Political Violence [ICSR], 2007), http://icsr.info/wp-content/uploads/2012/10/1234 516791ICSREUResearchReport_Proof1.pdf (accessed July 13, 2016); Schmid, "Radicalization, De-radicalization, Counter-radicalization"; Marc Sageman, *Understanding Terror Networks* (Philadelphia: University of Pennsylvania Press, 2004); Marc Sageman, *Leaderless Jihad* (Philadelphia: University of Pennsylvania Press, 2008); Quintan Wiktorowicz, *Radical Islam Rising: Muslim Extremism in the West* (Lanham, MD: Rowman and Littlefield, 2004).

9. Sageman, *Understanding Terror Networks*; Sageman, *Leaderless Jihad.* For an introduction, see Dalgaard-Nielsen, "Violent Radicalization in Europe," 801–5.

10. Sageman, *Understanding Terror Networks*, 99, 113.

11. Ibid., 110, 120–21; Sageman, *Leaderless Jihad*, 86–87.

12. Sageman, *Understanding Terror Networks*, 155; Sageman, *Leaderless Jihad*, 86–87.

13. Sageman, *Leaderless Jihad*, 24.

14. Ibid., 84.

15. Ibid., 113–17.

16. Ibid., 122.

17. McCauley and Moskalenko, "Mechanisms of Political Radicalization"; McCauley and Moskalenko, *Friction.*

18. McCauley and Moskalenko, "Mechanisms of Political Radicalization," 421–26.

19. David A. Snow, Louis A. Zurcher Jr., and Sheldon Ekland-Olson, "Social Networks and Social Movements: A Microstructural Approach to Differential Recruitment," *American Sociological Review* 45 (1980): 789.

20. Ibid., 789–90.

21. Ibid., 793.

22. Doug McAdam, "Recruitment to High-Risk Activism: The Case of Freedom Summer," *American Journal of Sociology* 92 (1986): 77–78.

23. Wiktorowicz, *Radical Islam Rising.*

24. McAdam, "Recruitment to High-Risk Activism," 69–70.

25. Clark McCauley and Sophia Moskalenko, "Toward a Profile of Lone Wolf Terrorists: What Moves an Individual from Radical Opinion to Radical Action," *Terrorism and Political Violence* 26 (2014): 69–85.

26. Randy Borum, "Radicalization into Violent Extremism I: A Review of Social Science Theories," *Journal of Strategic Security* 4 (2011): 8.

27. On the concept of intolerance of ambiguity, see Donna M. Webster and Arie W. Kruglanski, "Individual Differences in Need for Cognitive Closure," *Journal of Personality and Social Psychology* 67 (1994): 1049.

28. Preben Bertelsen, "Voldelig radikalisering: Et systematisk overblik over risikofaktorer og en teoretisk model i Tilværelsespsykologiens optik" (Violent radicalization: A theoretical model based on the categorical structure of a taxonomy of risk factors), in *Tværprofessionelt samarbejde om udsatte børn og unge: En studiebog* (Interdisciplinary collaboration around children at risk: A handbook), ed. J.H. Lund (Aarhus, Denmark: Turbine Akademisk, 2016), 129–78.

29. See Mark Granovetter, "The Strength of Weak Ties," *American Journal of Sociology* 20 (1973): 1360–80; Florence Passy, "Socialization, Connection, and the Structure/Agency Gap: A Specification of the Impact of Networks on Participation in Social Movements," *Mobilization* 6 (2001): 173–92; McAdam, "Recruitment to High-Risk Activism."

30. Bruce Bimber, Andrew Flanagin, and Cynthia Stohl, *Collective Action in Organizations: Interaction and Engagement in an Era of Technological Change* (Cambridge: Cambridge University Press, 2012), 90.

31. Granovetter, "The Strength of Weak Ties"; McAdam, "Recruitment to High-Risk Activism."

32. Passy, "Socialization, Connection, and the Structure/Agency Gap."

33. Ibid.

34. On action encouragement cues, see Robert Abelson, "Are Attitudes Necessary?" in *Attitudes, Conflict, and Social Change*, ed. B.T. King and E. McGinnies (New York: Academic Press, 1972).

35. McCauley and Moskalenko, "Mechanisms of Political Radicalization."

36. Doug McAdam, Sidney Tarrow, and Charles Tilly, "Methods for Measuring Mechanisms of Contention," *Qualitative Sociology* 31 (2008): 308.

37. On the incidence of mental health issues among lone actors, see Gill, Horgan, and Deckert, "Bombing Alone."

38. See also Passy, "Socialization, Connection, and the Structure/Agency Gap."

39. Bouhana and Wikström, *Al Qai'da–Influenced Radicalisation*.

# 13. Constructing Cultures of Martyrdom across Religions, Time, and Space

Mia Bloom

> The Tyrant Dies and his Rule is Over; The Martyr Dies and His Rule Begins.
>
> SØREN KIERKEGAARD

To understand the construction of terrorism, we should look to see how certain cultures celebrate martyrdom and convince youth that they can do far more with their death than they could with their life. Children in violent extremist movements, disparagingly referred to in the Western media as "child terrorists," are not born; rather they are made and learn to *want* to be a part of a violent extremist group, either with or without the knowledge and support of their parents and families. Children's involvement in terrorist violence develops over an extended period of time in which youth are exposed to a "culture of martyrdom" and parents are "groomed" to willingly give the extremists access to their children. While the concept of a "culture of martyrdom" is routinely blamed for the proliferation of young operatives used by terrorist organizations, rarely are the elements that comprise a "culture of martyrdom" defined, delineated, or explained in terms of how they are constructed or by whom. This chapter sets out to explain both the tradition of martyrdom and self-sacrifice and how different cultures have embraced the mythology of the martyr. Its purpose is to demonstrate that cultures of martyrdom play a crucial role in fostering an environment in which children grow up wanting to achieve martyrdom while their parents are enthusiastic supporters.

In cases of prolonged ethno-nationalist conflicts, children grow up in extreme conditions of poverty, violence, and institutionalized harassment. As they mature, many children begin their involvement with terrorist movements largely in support roles: throwing stones at demonstrations, serving as lookouts, ferrying messages, or smuggling weapons. The terrorist organizations create separate units for children in order to involve them at a young age and use the youth movements as a testing ground to spot talent. The permissive environment for political violence depends heavily

181

on a culture in which the sacrifice of one's life is considered the highest form of service to one's community—whether the nation or a religious community.

In many of the cases of children involved in militant movements in the Middle East, recruitment occurred via existing kinship and social networks and, notably, through community-centered activities.[1] At puberty, boys leave home and form play and membership peer associations called *shilla* and *dufa'a* groups. The *shilla* is a lifetime membership group that protects the neighborhood. Those children who graduate from high school, university, or a military academy have an additional kinship network based on their year of graduation. These *dufa'a* networks are especially strong and can result in friends radicalizing and mobilizing one another in a cohort.[2]

Children in conflict areas are routinely exposed to violence (from both sides) from a very early age. Exposure to violence alters the child's perceptions of right and wrong and might also impact his or her willingness to participate in violent activities. For example, early trauma and adversity place a child at risk for a variety of negative outcomes, including greater likelihood of engaging in violence.

As scholar Benedict Anderson argues, the soldier who sacrifices himself (as embodied in cenotaphs and tombs of the Unknown Soldier) has become the repository of "the emblems of the modern culture of nationalism. . . . The public ceremonial reverence accorded these monuments precisely *because* they are deliberately empty or no one knows who lies inside them has no true precedents in earlier times."[3] In essence, martyrdom is the process of making one's death by violence meaningful. The martyr exchanges life for something greater and more lasting in the afterlife.[4]

The understanding of the martyr as a *witness* cuts across all religious traditions. The word *martyr* comes from the ancient Greek *martus* or *martys*, meaning "witness." It encompasses those willing to make great sacrifices for the sake of a principle, as well as the suffering or persecution of someone who refuses to renounce his or her beliefs.[5] The martyr defends a principle or a truth that he or she cannot forsake. In some instances, the martyr can be a symbol not just of faith but also of *the nation*, making the individual willing to make a political self-sacrifice equally likely in a religious or secular context. David Cook, in his seminal book *Martyrdom in Islam*, refers to the witness as the most powerful form of advertisement—communicating personal credibility and dedication.[6] The martyr's death is thus heroic and serves a compelling cause. Whereas "suicide is selfish, . . . martyrdom is selfless."[7] For sociologist Diego Gambetta, the notion of the martyr's immolation implies that there exists a community that will benefit in some way from his or her act of self-sacrifice and that the sacrifice is for the greater good.

The environment in which a culture of martyrdom develops is significant. The structural conditions that foster an environment conducive to appreciating violence can be the result of the shared experiences of a people inhabiting a conflict zone. Ethnic groups facing conflict cohere in unique ways, and the experiences of a few are often felt by the many, especially with modern technology and the global media. In particular, we can observe in cases where a dominant group exercises population control tactics, checkpoints, patrols, and searches and seizures, people suffer humiliation. "When ongoing suffering or humiliation is the shared experience of the people, expressions of this pain may come to occupy a central place in the language, narrative, and practice of its culture."[8] Humiliation may be an impetus for resistance. In a situation marked by past humiliation, there is a further dynamic between emotional experiences and those expressions that are permitted. Stearns and Stearns posit *emotionology*, a social element encompassing how norms of different societies shape emotional expression and spatially limit the locations where such expression is permitted. "Such emotionology influences the individual experience of emotion through processes of socialization."[9] It is under these circumstances that a culture of martyrdom thrives and captures the imagination.

According to Farhad Khosrokhavar, there exist both *offensive* and *defensive* forms of religious martyrdom. Whereas defensive martyrdom can be traced back to Christianity during the Roman Empire, offensive martyrdom encompasses sacrificing the self in battle against injustice.[10] The martyr sacrifices him- or herself on behalf of a community, which in turn politicizes suffering (or death) and plays a role in regenerating national resistance. K. M. Fierke, like Mark Juergensmeyer (see chapter 5 in the present volume), sees acts of self-sacrifice as highly *performative*. In essence, martyrdom is "an act of speech" in which the suffering body communicates the injustice experienced by a community to a larger audience.[11] For Benedict Anderson, language is something that the state (center) can impose on the periphery. In essence, historically, one language became dominant (and codified) because print capitalism made any other version of that language all but obsolete. With constructions of culture, we have similar processes at work. Multiple cultures may coexist within the same space. To create a "culture of martyrdom," one needs the participation of state (or proto-state) institutions to support its creation and sustain the message. Cultures of martyrdom may be constructed via children's education, the media (especially programming directed at youth), and the larger supportive community. The media play a necessary role as participants in the performance of violence. "The perform-ance of violence communicates with the enemy" and likewise communicates internally to a larger constituency.[12]

Across a variety of cases, from Northern Ireland to the Middle East and South Asia, the development of a culture of martyrdom explains the under-lying altruistic instinct of self-sacrifice and the desire to help members of one's community. In addition to the altruistic psychological benefits of doing something for one's community, there are tangible rewards for the individual willing to make the ultimate sacrifice. Fame and notoriety are powerful pull factors for vulnerable youth. Wanting to do something important with one's life and achieve notoriety and fame is as appealing for young men as it is for young women across a variety of cultures and cases.

The process of becoming a martyr involves a discernible set of steps, from self-abnegation, praying, and fasting to practicing and preparing for one's death. Early cases of Palestinian suicide bombers included a prepara-tion phase in which the would-be bomber was instructed to lie down in an empty grave to demystify the experience. The preparatory process prior to the "martyrdom operation" involved fasting, praying, and separation from loved ones so that the individual would not change her or his mind at the last minute. As a culture of martyrdom develops and takes root, the need for this extended process of preparation may decrease as youth need less preparation and convincing of the benefits of martyrdom, about which they will already be familiar from embedded symbolism and the not-so-subtle messages all around them about martyrdom's benefits.

Constructing a culture transcends both religious and secular movements that develop a range of symbols, from postcards to stamps to statues dis-playing images of previous (historical) martyrs and utilizing powerful cul-tural symbols. Such symbols add to the emotional resonance of the suffer-ing experienced by those who have resisted oppression. Such symbolism is one of the ways in which the culture of martyrdom emerges. Symbols play an important role in creating resonance with the past, so that people hearken back to a golden age and can link their individual self-sacrifice to a long history of great men (and women) who came before them, thus adding to the historicity of the actions.

Some religions value the willingness to sacrifice oneself for the greater good or for the community.[13] For the early Christian martyrs facing Roman torture and immolation (e.g., Pionius and Polycarp), death was not seen as an ultimate threat or as a "final frontier that needs to be overcome and tamed, though they make it equally clear that neither was it something they actively desired."[14] Gambetta highlights the Buddhist monks and nuns who sacrificed their lives in protest; in Northern Ireland, hunger strikers made the ultimate sacrifice to protest their treatment and classification as common criminals.[15] We tend to assume that a culture of martyrdom is located within the concept of jihad; in fact, we have manifold examples of people's willingness to endure great suffering for a cause in which they believe.

In Tamil ideology, *thatkodai*, or the gift of the self, is the equivalent of Islamic and Christian martyrdom. Gillespie and colleagues establish that *thatkodai* valorized death as the ultimate sacrifice.[16] It is worth noting that Tamils deliberately use the term *thatkodai* rather than *thatkolai*, the word for suicide,[17] in much the same way that Islamic fundamentalists talk of the *shahid* (witness, martyr), while not using *intihar*, the word for suicide, which is strictly forbidden in Islam (as it is in all the major monotheistic faiths). The success of suicide bombing campaigns conducted by the Liberation Tigers of Tamil Eelam (LTTE) were highly correlated with the presence of the *thatkodai* ideology. According to the former head of the LTTE's political wing, S.P. Thamilchelvam, *thatkodai* "is the gift of the self . . . the person gives himself or herself in full."[18] The benefit of the sacrifice extends not just to the individual but also in some instances to his or her extended family (in Islam, the martyr can intercede for seventy of his or her relatives in the afterlife). In the Tamil case, Paul Gill explains, "those who have given themselves to the cause are *mahaveera*, meaning "brave one," and their mother is *veeravati*, or "brave mother."[19]

Precedents for hunger strikers in Ireland can be traced back to the ancient tradition of self-sacrifice in the face of injustice (usually economic) known as *cealachan*, part of the oral legal code of the Brehon Laws. The Brehon Laws provided a means for seeking restorative justice, including sacrifice and the willingness to die on the doorstep of the source of offense.[20] In the Medieval code *Senchus Mor*, fasting (*troscad*) was done in protest against an individual who one believed to have wronged one, and in the tradition of *cealachan* one achieved justice by starving oneself. To recover a debt or address an injustice, the individual most often starved him- or herself on the doorstep of the individual who caused offense or to whom the person owed money. This antecedent forms the basis of the mythology that surrounded the hunger strikers and inspired the patriotism of the 1916 Easter Rising. During this initial phase of Irish nationalism, the hunger strike was used less for economic reasons than as a political weapon. Between 1913 and 1923, more than fifty hunger strikes occurred. In 1923 more than 8,000 political prisoners opposed to the Anglo-Irish Treaty went on a hunger strike, two of whom died before the protest was called off.[21]

The better-known Irish hunger strikes occurred decades later, led by the prisoners at Long Kesh prison, in particular a member of Parliament, Bobby Sands. In 1980–81 Sands led nine men (and three women) in hunger strikes intended to force the British crown to recognize them as political prisoners and not as common criminals.[22] Imprisoned members of the Provisional Irish Republican Army (IRA) went on hunger strikes to voice their opposition to British rule, demand better conditions, and insist on being treated as political prisoners (subject to the Geneva Conventions). Ten died in the process, including Bobby Sands (elected to Parliament during the strike). In interviews with the author, former hunger strikers emphasized that the hunger strike was intended to send a clear message of their willingness to die, but it was not their desired end state. For people who went on strike (both male and female), opposition to injustice was foremost. The willingness to sacrifice themselves in order to improve conditions for their countrymen casts their political acts as altruism in a way that martyrdom does not. Emile Durkheim's analysis provides three distinct types of suicide: egoistic, fatalistic, and altruistic. Altruistic suicide happens under conditions of social integration. The strong social bonds within a community drive the individual to sacrifice for the good of the community.[23]

The hunger strikers were transformed into martyrs "whose acts of self sacrifice were proof that they were acting not out of self interest but political conviction for a just cause, and with undeniable support, both at home and abroad."[24] The reaction within the community was to virtually deify Bobby Sands and the other nine men. Their images were painted along Fall Road and became iconic symbols of British injustice and especially of Margaret Thatcher's unwillingness to compromise and her willingness to let a democratically elected member of the British Parliament die. Parks and streets were named after Bobby Sands in countries around the world. The ten men who died on hunger strike became icons in Irish society, and their influence continues today not only to demonstrate Thatcher's heartlessness in letting Sands die but also as a symbol of continued resistance. Sands's sister eventually became the leader of a dissident offshoot organization—one that sponsors youth groups and camps to train the next generation.

The Buddhist tradition likewise prohibits suicide but allows for self-sacrifice under specific circumstances. In select strains of Buddhism—notably Mahayana Buddhism, predominant in Southeast Asia—elements of other eastern traditions are evident: Taoism, Confucianism, and ancestor worship. Mahayana Buddhism is concerned with social justice and emphasizes active compassion (*karuna*) and benevolence. "While suicide is prohibited in Buddhism, self immolation, if undertaken with proper intention, is in the exceptional case of Bodhisattva, understood as offering a sacrifice to the Buddha that transcends moral precepts."[25]

The immolation of a seventy-three-year-old Buddhist monk, Thich Quang Duc, in Vietnam on June 11, 1964 (along with several other monks and nuns throughout the 1960s) had its roots in the Lotus Sutra. Self-immolation became a form of political protest against foreign occupation, a response to government coercion against the Buddhist faith (and monasteries) and the injustices perpetrated by immoral rulers such as Ngo Dinh Diem. In the Lotus Sutra, self-immolation comprises two meanings. The first is an act of offering, which places it within the framework of sacrifice. In a context of the people's persecution and destruction, the agent sacrifices the self to Buddha in the hope of bringing all living things closer to liberation. The "gan" offering is a communicative act.[26] Not only did hundreds of monks and nuns make this sacrifice, but nine Americans followed suit, including one in November 1965, a Quaker from Pennsylvania named Norman Morrison outside the Pentagon—in full view of Defense Secretary Robert McNamara.[27]

The second meaning, as self-immolation, has continued to punctuate peace movements and even helped sparked the Arab Spring when, on December 17, 2010, a lone Tunisian fruit peddler, Muhammed Bouazizi, provoked outrage with his one act, "igniting weeks of demonstrations that spread across the country and unseated Zine al-Abidine Ben Ali after 23 years of repressive rule."[28] This act was soon emulated by other people in the region.

> In January 2012, five young Moroccan men auto-cremated (the more accurate term; "self-immolation" technically means any form of self-destruction) following a fifty-two-year-old pensioner in Jordan and an elderly woman in Bahrain. The young men belonged to a group called Unemployed Graduates that had been occupying the Ministry of Higher Education building. They followed upon the action of Mohammed Bouazizi, the Tunisian street vendor, whose self-immolation—inspired by the chronic poverty and corruption of his country—helped incite the Arab Spring.[29]

The spread of these acts of self-immolation reflected a sense of helplessness, and the government's repressive reactions fueled the spread of resistance (most Arab countries accused the protesters of being controlled by terrorist factions). The Arab Federation of Psychiatrists did not believe that Bouazizi's self-immolation (or the other copycat protests) had anything to do with "martyrdom fantasies"; rather, it claimed that the suicides were cries for help against powerlessness, desperation, and frustration.

Bouazizi's act was one of protest.[30] Like the Irish tradition of the Brehon Laws and the tradition of Buddhist monks and nuns, it was an act of suicide committed in full public view.

Gambetta distinguishes people who kill both themselves and others (such as suicide bombers) from those who kill only themselves (self-immolation). In essence both commit acts intended to make a public statement about injustice and influence an audience, yet the differences between someone willing to kill him-or herself for a cause (and become a martyr) and those whose success depends on killing others in the process make one an act of protest and the other an act of terror.

Michael Hardt and Antonio Negri identify two opposing images of the martyr: "The one form, which is exemplified by the suicide bomber, poses martyrdom as a response of destruction, including self-destruction, to an act of injustice. The other form of martyrdom, however, is completely different. In this form, the martyr does not seek destruction but is struck down by the violence of the powerful. Martyrdom of this type is a testimony . . . this martyrdom is an act of love."[31]

Like the Greek *martus* or *martys*, the Arabic term for martyr, *shahid*, means "witness," and the Shahada ("There is no god but God and Muhammed is his Prophet") constitutes a testimony of faith and an assertion about the unity of God. In the Sunni Muslim tradition, martyrdom is linked to jihad as the noblest act in testifying for one's faith. David Cook provides as an example the story of the Ethiopian slave Bilal, who was persecuted for his beliefs as a follower of Muhammed. Bilal became a powerful symbol because of his willingness to suffer for Islam.[32] For Shi'a Islam, martyrdom is more closely linked to rituals of suffering, mourning, and redemption.[33] While martyrdom can trace its lineage back to Sunni and Shi'a traditions, the different religious traditions evolved different understandings of the concept of martyrdom until the modern era, when the traditions associated with offensive martyrdom merged the Sunni and Shi'a interpretations. As Fierke observes, "In the twentieth century Sunni revivalists once again highlighted the importance of physical jihad and armed struggle and it became the duty of the individual Muslim to participate in jihad to liberate the land in the case of Muslim territory being occupied by an enemy invader."[34]

There is no greater taboo in Islam than committing suicide. The Holy Qur'an emphatically states, "Do not kill yourselves, for God is merciful to you. If any of you does these things out of hostility and injustice, we shall make him suffer Fire: that is easy for God" (4:29). Babak Rahimi adds, "As noble as it is to die in battle, to die at the enemy's hands in a just cause—so has it been considered shameful to willfully take one's own life."[35]

In the Islamic tradition, suicide and martyrdom were distinct from each other. Suicide (*intihar*) is strictly prohibited in the Qur'an (as it is for all the Abrahamic faiths). In contrast, Al Bukhari notes that martyrdom is an act of devotion to God. Martyrdom as expressed by Islamic militants makes a connection between earthly and divine objectives. The martyr gives up earthly life with the promise of continuing life in paradise.[36]

Beyond religious justification, "cultures of martyrdom" are derived from a variety of secular sources. Organizations turn what are ordinarily mundane and innocent venues into recruitment tools. Among the diverse sources that Chris Huebner lists are rap music, music videos that allegedly entice children to become combatants, comic books about Islamic martyrs, and teen-oriented stories of "classic martyrs," as well as biographical accounts of contemporary martyrs. Statements by children aired on television discussing how they want to become martyrs and statements by political leaders (both religious and secular) extolling the virtues of martyrdom reinforce this message. "Martyrdom," David Brooks observes, "has replaced Palestinian independence as the main focus of the Arab media."[37] As Huebner notes, "The market for martyrs is growing at a striking rate."[38]

A culture of martyrdom provides the context in which parents may willingly provide access to their children and even promote the idea of their making the ultimate sacrifice. The role of families remains highly contentious when they allow violent organizations access to children. There are intense community pressures for families to support their children's acts of martyrdom, regardless of whether they were aware of their children's involvement or genuinely supported it.[39]

Sacrifice and risk—when employed on behalf of the group—become valuable virtues, rewarded by social status. A veritable culture of martyrdom transforms individual risk and loss into group status and benefit, ultimately cycling that status back onto the individual. Thus, a preliminary solution to the problem of terrorism would be to eliminate the positive values associated with martyrdom and shift community acceptance away from violence against civilians.

The state can undercut despair through positive empowerment responses that are divorced from a fundamental refusal to "reward terrorism." The state can reward the community without rewarding the terrorists themselves. Notably, jailing terrorist leaders rather than killing them through targeted assassination might prove a superior strategy,[40] and drain the sea in which the insurgents swim by allowing the domestic population to turn away from the terrorist organizations. While a culture of martyrdom has both tangible and intangible elements, taken together they create powerful incentives for children to aspire to involvement in militant groups and give the impression that the children in fact concede to that involvement. Further, when parents willingly give terrorist groups access to their children, it makes it all the more difficult for children to resist. Given how pervasive the culture of martyrdom is in a variety of societies, it becomes crucial that youth are convinced that their lives matter and that they can affect change in a positive way instead of through their self-sacrifice.

## NOTES

Some material in this chapter has been drawn from Mia Bloom and John Horgan, *Small Arms: The Rise of Children and Terrorism* (Ithaca, NY: Cornell University Press, forthcoming).

This work was supported in part by a MINERVA grant on Grooming the Next Generation: Children and VEOs under the auspices of the Office of Naval Research. The views and conclusions contained in this document are those of the authors and should not be interpreted as representing the official policies, either expressed or implied, of the Department of Defense, the Office of Naval Research, or any part of the US government.

*Epigraph:* Søren Kierkegaard, *The Journals of Kierkegaard,* trans. Alexander Dru (New York: Harper Torchbooks, 1959), 151.

1. L.J. Cantori and I. Harik, eds., *Local Politics and Development in the Middle East* (Boulder, CO: Westview Press, 1984).

2. David J. Anthony, "Political Culture and Participation in Egypt," MA thesis, Naval Postgraduate School, June 1980, https://archive.org/details/politicalculture-00anth_djvu.txt (accessed January 2017).

3. Benedict Anderson, *Imagined Communities: Reflections on the Origins and Spread of Nationalism* (London: Verso, 1991), 50.

4. Jocelyn J. Belanger, Julie Caouette, Karen Sharvit, and Michelle Dugas, "The Psychology of Martyrdom: Making the Ultimate Sacrifice in the Name of a Cause." *Journal of Personality and Social Psychology,* 107:3 (2014): 494–515.

5. Daniel Brown, "Martyrdom in Sunni Revivalist Thought," in M. Cormack, ed., *Sacrificing the Self: Perspectives in Martyrdom and Religion* (New York: Oxford University Press, 2002), 113.

6. David Cook, *Martyrdom in Islam* (New York: Cambridge University Press, 2007), 1.

7. K.M. Fierke, *Political Self-Sacrifice: Agency, Body, and Emotions in International Relations* (Cambridge: Cambridge University Press, 2013), 5.

8. Ibid., 92.

9. Peter Stearns and Carol Stearns, "Emotionology: Clarifying the History of Emotions and Emotional Standards," *American Historical Review* 90:4 (1985): 813–36, cited in Fierke, *Political Self-Sacrifice,* 94.

10. Farhad Khosrokhavar, *Suicide Bombers: Allah's New Martyrs* (New York: Pluto Press, 2005), 6–10, cited in Fierke, *Political Self-Sacrifice,* 10.

11. Fierke, *Political Self-Sacrifice,* 37, 39, 48.

12. Neil L. Whitehead and Nasser Abufarha, "Suicide, Violence, and Cultural Conceptions of Martyrdom in Palestine," *Social Research* 75:2 (Summer 2008): 405.

13. Belanger et al., "The Psychology of Martyrdom," 495.

14. Chris K. Huebner, "Between Victory and Victimhood: Reflections on Culture and Martyrdom," *Direction* 34:2 (Fall 2005): 229, http://www.directionjournal.org/article/?1402#15.

15. D. Gambetta, ed., *Making Sense of Suicide Missions* (New York: Oxford University Press, 2006), chapter 5.

16. Marie Gillespie, Alasdair Pinkerton, Gerd Baumann, and Sharika Thiranagama, "South Asian Diasporas and the BBC World Services: Contacts, Conflicts, and Contestations," *South Asian Diaspora* 2:1 (2010): 3–23.

17. Faisal G. Mohammed, *Milton and the Post-secular Present: Ethics, Politics, Terrorism* (Stanford, CA: Stanford University Press, 2011), 116.

18. Amy Waldman, "Masters of Suicide Bombing: Tamil Guerrillas of Sri Lanka," *New York Times*, January 14, 2003, http://www.nytimes.com/2003/01/14/world/masters-of-suicide-bombing-tamil-guerrillas-of-sri-lanka.html?pagewanted=all.

19. Paul Gill, "A Multi-dimensional Approach to Suicide Bombing," *International Journal of Conflict and Violence* 1:2 (2007): 148, http://ijcv.uni-bielefeld.de/index.php/ijcv/article/viewFile/12/12.

20. Fierke, *Political Self-Sacrifice*, 108.

21. G. Sweeney, "Irish Hunger Strikes and the Cult of Self Sacrifice," *Journal of Contemporary History* 28:3 (1993): 421–37, cited in Fierke, *Political Self-Sacrifice*, 111–12.

22. Interviews conducted by the author, Belfast, Northern Ireland, 2009.

23. E. Durkheim, *Suicide: A Study in Sociology* (New York: Simon and Shuster, 1951), cited in Whitehead and Abufarha, "Suicide Violence and Cultural Conceptions of Martyrdom in Palestine."

24. Fierke, *Political Self-Sacrifice*, 128.

25. Ibid., 162.

26. Ibid., 181.

27. James Verini, "A Terrible Act of Reason: When Did Self-Immolation Become the Paramount Form of Protest?" *New Yorker*, May 16, 2012, http://www.newyorker.com/culture/culture-desk/a-terrible-act-of-reason-when-did-self-immolation-become-the-paramount-form-of-protest.

28. "Peddler's Martyrdom Launched Tunisian Revolution," *Reuter's Africa*, January 19, 2011, http://af.reuters.com/article/libyaNews/idAFLDE70G18J20110119.

29. Verini, "A Terrible Act of Reason."

30. Fierke, *Political Self-Sacrifice*, 219.

31. Michael Hardt and Antonio Negri, *Multitude: War and Democracy in the Age of Empire* (New York: Penguin, 2004), 346, cited in Huebner, "Between Victory and Victimhood."

32. Cook, *Martyrdom in Islam*, 14. Bilal was eventually saved by Abu Bakr and did not die.

33. Fierke, *Political Self-Sacrifice*, 195.

34. Ibid., 196.

35. Babak Rahimi, "Dying a Martyr's Death: The Political Culture of Self-Sacrifice in Contemporary Islamists," paper presented to the Association for the Sociology of Religion, San Francisco, August 14, 2004.

36. Al Bukhari, quoted in Fierke, *Political Self-Sacrifice*, 204.

37. David Brooks, "The Culture of Martyrdom: How Suicide Bombing Became Not Just a Means but an End," *Atlantic*, June 2002, https://www.theatlantic.com/magazine/archive/2002/06/the-culture-of-martyrdom/302506/ (accessed March 26, 2017).

192 / *Mia Bloom*

38. Huebner, "Between Victory and Victimhood."

39. Joyce M. Davis, *Martyrs: Innocence, Vengeance, and Despair in the Middle East* (New York: St. Martin's Press, 2015), 126.

40. Jenna Jordan, "When Heads Roll: Assessing the Effectiveness of Leadership Decapitation," *Security Studies*, 18 (2009): 719–55.

# 14. Introducing the Government Actions in Terror Environments (GATE) Data Set

Laura Dugan and Erica Chenoweth

As the word *terrorism* is loosely conceptualized to include a wide range of behaviors—all of which are considered bad—the question of how governments can stop terrorism naturally follows. Yet counterterrorism, or the response to terrorism, is also murkily conceptualized, though Western nations typically frame it within the context of large-scale military operations that aggressively target terrorist operatives. These actions align with US president Ronald Reagan's 1981 proclamation, "Let terrorists beware that when rules of international behavior are violated, our policy will be one of swift and effective retribution." Indeed, later US presidents followed through on Reagan's threat by bombing Iraq's military intelligence headquarters in 1983, attacking Afghanistan and Sudan with missiles in 1998, and leading wars in Afghanistan and Iraq since the early 2000s. Retribution follows a basic tenet of the US criminal justice system that severe punishment will deter lawbreaking, an idea that appeals broadly to both policy makers and the public.[1] It assumes that human beings—even terrorists—are rational, self-interested actors who seek to minimize personal cost while maximizing personal gain.[2]

The appeal of conceptualizing counterterrorism as aggressive responses to terrorism is unsurprising, especially after unprecedented attacks like those on September 11, 2001, in the United States and the more recent atrocities carried out by ISIS in the Middle East and Europe. People want revenge and will generally support retaliation in the aftermath of an atrocity. President George W. Bush's approval ratings soared when he used phrases like "wanted dead or alive," vowed that the United States would "smoke them out," and told would-be terrorists to "bring it on."[3] The United States public generally supported its military's invasion of Afghanistan, which demonstrated resilience and strength while destroying al-Qaeda training camps. Further, the November 13, 2015, attacks in Paris have increased momentum for building coalitions to stop ISIS through bombing campaigns.

Despite the popularity for retributive counterterrorism, it is unclear that such efforts actually deter terrorism. While al-Qaeda has not orchestrated another attack approaching the magnitude of 9/11 since the United States decimated its camps, its popularity soared after the US invasions in Afghanistan and Iraq,[4] which has inspired some of the deadliest terrorist groups active today, including Boko Haram and al-Shabaab. This suggests that repressive counterterrorism could lead to unexpected backlash. In fact, some have argued that the wars in Afghanistan and Iraq have undermined US legitimacy because of the perceived low value that seemed to be placed on Afghan and Iraqi lives.[5] Others claim that Osama bin Laden's intent behind the 9/11 attacks was to elicit a US response that would kill Muslims and lead to further retaliation.[6] This sort of "jujitsu" strategy is designed to provoke a response to terrorism harsher than the original attack, thereby increasing grievances against the government and strengthening the loyalty of those who follow the terrorist organization.[7]

Some empirical evidence substantiates the concern that repressive counterterrorism could lead to backlash. Evaluations of counterterrorism efforts in Northern Ireland find that repressive policies pursued by the British government to suppress terrorist activity increased rioting and terrorism.[8] Other findings show that despite the immediate success of the repression that the Iranian government undertook during the 1979 Islamic revolution to subdue protests, protests later grew more frequent.[9] Research by Sharvit and colleagues shows increases in Palestinian terrorism after Israel's large-scale military campaign Operation Defensive Shield.[10] Similarly, Argomaniz and Vidal-Diez found that some aggressive responses to Basque terrorism on the part of Spain increased the risk of more ETA (Euskadi Ta Askatasuna) attacks.[11] This evidence suggests that terrorism can emerge as a response to perceived injustices, such as government repression, that inspire groups to mobilize in retaliation.[12] In other words, despite the political appeal of relying on harsh retaliation to deter terrorism, such efforts could fuel more conflict.

Yet we still need to punish lawbreakers, even if such actions fail to deter future attacks. Perhaps other efforts, beyond repression, can effectively reduce terrorism risk. Indeed, governments may have effectively stopped some terrorist attacks through lesser-known actions that fall outside the purview of typical counterterrorism.[13] This chapter argues that the conceptualization of counterterrorism should be broadened to include other acts by governments that might affect terrorists or their constituencies. By broadening how we think of counterterrorism, we can assess the effectiveness of conciliation, target hardening, and campaigns that affect the civilians whom the terrorists purportedly defend.

Of course, in order to assess the effectiveness of government actions, we need data that document what governments do. This chapter describes the process of constructing the Government Actions in Terror Environments (GATE) database that chronicles for select countries a broad set of government actions that are relevant to terrorist conflicts.[14] GATE data have been collected beginning with the year 1988 in Algeria, Canada, Egypt, Israel, Lebanon, and Turkey.[15] GATE data are currently being coded for the United States, and data collection has begun for Afghanistan, India, Pakistan, the Philippines, Sri Lanka, and the United Kingdom. The original six countries were selected first because of their prolonged experience with terrorist violence as well as their inherent interest to the policy community. By combining GATE with data from the Global Terrorism Database (GTD), we can assess the impact that a wide range of government responses to terrorism has had on the incidence of terrorist attacks within these countries.

The remainder of this chapter delineates the process of collecting GATE data, briefly describes the data for several countries, and presents a sample of findings that assess the effectiveness of different strategies for specific conflicts in a subset of countries.

## COLLECTING GATE DATA

This section outlines six steps used in collecting GATE data. The process begins with a thorough review of the terrorist conflicts in each country, including well-known efforts to control terrorism. We then download news stories from open-source databases using broadly defined search terms, and narrow the stories through computer programs so that research assistants can code relevant events.

### Step 1: Downloading News Stories Relevant to the Specific Country

To get a pool of stories from which we extract and code GATE data, the GATE team uses either the Factiva database to download Reuters news stories or LexisNexis to download stories from a broader set of sources. Search terms include portions of the country's name (e.g., Israel*) or keywords of government actors. Reuters news stories have been used for most countries because of its consistent editorial control and its tendency to use a simpler sentence structure and vocabulary than other news sources such as the

*Washington Post,* the *New York Times,* and other international wire services.[16] For the original GATE countries, we used simple search terms to extract tens of thousands of stories from June 1987 through December 2004. The first date marks the beginning of the Reuters archive, and 2004 was specified in the original grant. The following search terms resulted in the reported number of stories: Algeria* 52,575; Egypt* 109,694; Israel* 243,448; Leban* 67,107; Turk* 152,998.

For the United States, there was no simple search term that would indicate that the Reuters news story was relevant to the United States or its nationals. However, because GATE-USA actions were restricted to federal actors, we used search strings that listed relevant federal agencies and their leaders since 1987, resulting in 1,980,197 stories.[17] Because of difficulties in downloading Reuters news stories from Factiva, we used LexisNexis to search for stories from fifteen international and Canadian Anglophone news sources using search terms that mentioned Canada, its provinces, or its capitals. This resulted in 14,757,500 stories.

## Step 2: Extracting the Lead Sentences from the Stories

For the second step, we used a Python program written by Philip Schrodt, the developer of the TABARI (Textual Analysis by Augmented Replacement Instructions) software that we used for step 3, to extract the lead sentences from the downloaded stories. Using the lead sentence instead of the entire article is surprisingly accurate and considerably more efficient.[18] Further, the deeper the text reader goes into an article, the more noise it picks up, reporting inaccuracies. In essence, the lead sentence reports the event, and the remaining article elaborates on the details of the event, including backstories of earlier relevant events.

Once the lead sentences were extracted, they were saved in a text file that is used in the following step.

## Step 3: Extracting Politically Relevant Stories and Coding Key Elements

This step was conducted using the TABARI program, which searches the lead sentences and identifies observations that match the criteria of an extensive set of dictionaries designed to capture international and domestic activity.[19] We used dictionaries that listed nouns, verbs, and formal names and positions of persons from around the globe, focusing especially on persons relevant to terrorism in the specific countries. We supplemented the TABARI team's dictionaries from names extracted from the GTD and other sources. Since TABARI is an automated text-coding program, it also coded the lead sentences based on verb and noun pattern recognition, resulting in codes for each actor, action, and target of the action. We also attached a unique identifier, the date, and the lead sentence to each observation.[20]

## Step 4: Filtering Stories to Include "Only" Those That Match GATE Criteria

GATE events include any action by the government actors that are directed toward terrorist organizations that threaten the country or toward the terrorists' constituencies. For countries where the terrorist constituency is discernable by an ethnic or religious identity (e.g., Palestinian, Kurdish), TABARI codes simplified this process. However, for countries such as Canada and the United States, relevant constituencies share codes with other civilians. Further, instead of having one or two major terrorist threats, Canada and the United States have been targeted by a diverse range of smaller movements, including environmentalist and animal rights extremists, anti-abortionists, right-wing extremists, and al-Qaeda-inspired groups, making it more difficult to identify relevant actions.

For this reason, we used code to remove Canadian and US stories that were clearly irrelevant to the GATE criteria. These include stories in which both actor and target were government entities and those in which other nationalities were represented. However, regardless of the nationality, all targets that are coded as terrorist organizations were kept. Finally, because the US involvement in the Israeli-Palestinian conflict has been cited as a grievance source for Islamic extremists who target the United States, and because we had already downloaded the lead sentences for Israel, we merged into these data all Israeli-Palestinian stories with US involvement. After this filtering process, anywhere from 3,000 to 138,000 stories remained for human coding, depending on the country. This number is especially high for Canada, given the broad range of original sources.

## Step 5: Reviewing Cases by Hand

A set of consistent coding rules was constructed for all GATE countries, with supplemental tasks given to Canadian and US coders to identify the constituency of the different terrorist threats and the relevant location of the action. Also, because Canada and the United States had the largest number of irrelevant stories (for reasons described in step 4), research assistants first reviewed the stories for relevance, marking for removal those that were clearly irrelevant.

During the filtering process described above, we also used the verbs identified by TABARI to autocode where the act falls on a scale from conciliation

TABLE 14.1 Seven-Point Guide for the Conciliatory-Repression Scale

| Value | Description |
| --- | --- |
| **1. Accommodation** | Appeasing or surrendering to adversary |
| | Making full concessions according to opponent's demands |
| | Action required |
| **2. Conciliatory action** | Making material concessions |
| | Taking action that signals intention to cooperate or negotiate with opponent |
| **3. Conciliatory statement or intentions** | Expressing intention to cooperate or showing support |
| | Verbal expression short of physical action |
| **4. Neutral or ambiguous** | No clear moves toward or away from resolution of conflict |
| | Includes all attempts to ask for help from a third party in order to resolve conflicts over Palestinians within the Israeli government |
| **5. Verbal conflict** | Express intent to engage in conflict or threaten violence |
| | Decline to cease ongoing conflict; maintain the status quo during conflict |
| | Short of physical action |
| **6. Physical conflict** | Physical or violent action aimed at coercing opponent |
| | No apparent intention to kill |
| **7. Extremely deadly repression** | Physical action exhibiting intent to kill |
| | Torture or severe violence (such as severe beatings) that could easily kill someone |

to repression, shown in table 14.1. The scale features distinctions in the intensity of the action, as well as the relative placement of the action on a conciliation-repression spectrum, similar to the Goldstein scale.[21] Research assistants evaluated this coding for accuracy. Actions were also autocoded and reviewed for whether, based on the verb pattern, the event was directed toward a discriminate or indiscriminate target. Discriminate actions are those that attempt to single out "guilty" or "suspected" parties from uninvolved parties (e.g., making an arrest). Indiscriminate actions are those that directly affect uninvolved people (i.e., those not suspected of involvement in terrorist activity; e.g., raiding a town). Finally, actions were coded for

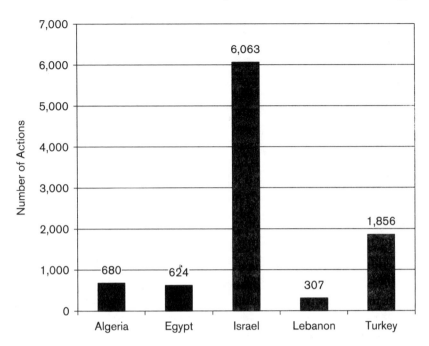

FIGURE 14.1.    Total Number of Government Actions by Country, 1988–2004.

whether they were material or nonmaterial. Material actions are those that involve physical contact between state and nonstate actors, whereas nonmaterial actions are not physical (i.e., typically verbal actions, such as an optimistic statement or a threat).

## Step 6: Cleaning the Final GATE Data Set

After coding, the principal investigators cleaned the final data by (1) reviewing all cases marked for removal,[22] (2) reviewing all cases flagged for review, (3) reviewing all stories marked as including multiple actions, (4) reviewing all stories and removing those marked as duplicates, and (5) looking up the original stories for those marked as missing relevant information needed to complete the coding.

### GATE DATA DESCRIBED

This section provides a brief description of key variables found in the data for completed GATE countries. Figure 14.1 shows the number of government actions relevant to terrorism for each of the five Middle Eastern countries

TABLE 14.2  Percentage of Government Actions That Fall into Each
Type Category

|  | Algeria | Canada | Egypt | Israel | Lebanon | Turkey |
|---|---|---|---|---|---|---|
| **Repressive** | 82 | 59 | 90 | 63 | 72 | 76 |
| **Conciliatory** | 14 | 41 | 9 | 28 | 17 | 9 |
| **Discriminate** | 55 | 37 | 66 | 22 | 48 | 62 |
| **Material** | 70 | 26 | 84 | 64 | 54 | 69 |
| **Political Actor** | 30 | 68 | 22 | 45 | 48 | 33 |
| **Military Actor** | 47 | 12 | 13 | 46 | 31 | 41 |
| **Police Actor** | 9 | 8 | 51 | 4 | 5 | 11 |
| **Judiciary Actor** | 14 | 12 | 15 | 4 | 15 | 14 |

in GATE for the years 1988 through 2004. As we can see, Israel initiated
more than three times the number of actions that Turkey initiated; and the
other three countries initiated fewer than 1,000 reported actions over the
seventeen-year period covered by the data. Despite the large differences
across these countries, the documented 307 actions by the Lebanese government are still more than what has been previously available for a single
country.

GATE-Canada is excluded from this figure because its years range from
1985 to 2013. It includes 7,612 actions. We expect that GATE-USA will be
much larger than the others as there are already more than 3,000 GATE
actions from the Clinton administration alone.

We now look within the government actions and examine the percentage distributions based on the type of actions across several dimensions:
repressive versus conciliatory, discriminate versus indiscriminate, material
versus nonmaterial, and type of actor. Table 14.2 presents the percentage of
actions that fall into each category. Actions are marked as conciliatory when
their code in the Conciliatory-Repressive Scale (shown in table 14.1) is
marked 1, 2, or 3. Conversely, actions are marked as repressive when their
code is marked 5, 6, or 7. When considering the percentage of discriminate
versus indiscriminate cases and material versus nonmaterial, we present
only the percent discriminate and material because each has only two possible outcomes (i.e., percent indiscriminate = 100 − percent discriminate).
We include both the percent repressive and conciliatory because a subset of
cases is considered neutral (item 4 in table 14.1), making the sum of the
percent repressive added to the percent conciliatory less than 100.

When we examine the percentage of actions that are repressive or conciliatory, we notice two things. First, all six countries are more likely to resort to repressive than conciliatory actions, ranging from 59 percent to 90 percent. Also apparent is that Egypt is much more likely to rely on repressive tactics than the other countries, whereas Canada and Israel appear to be more open to trying conciliatory tactics. This difference may be due to the nature of the conflicts in each country. Canada has no primary terrorist conflict, and the primary conflict in Israel is with Palestinian terrorist organizations, which have a large civilian constituency. These figures suggest that Canada and Israel may have made explicit efforts to accommodate the needs of the aggrieved. In contrast, in Egypt the primary terrorist activity occurred in the mid-1990s when a variety of Islamist groups launched an internal war against Hosni Mubarak's regime. These acts were accompanied by massive increases in repression, while conciliatory acts remained virtually nonexistent. Indeed, when they did occur, conciliatory acts generally consisted of prisoner releases of accused Islamists or members of the Muslim Brotherhood. However, the Egyptian regime and Egyptian terrorists generally met violence with violence during this period of high conflict.

When we consider the distribution of discriminate actions across countries, some interesting differences emerge. Here, Israel and Egypt mark the endpoints of the range, with Israel having the fewest relative discriminatory acts (22%) and Egypt having the most (66%). The low percentage of discriminate actions by the Israeli government suggests that it did not distinguish between Palestinian civilians and Palestinian terrorists. In contrast, Algeria, Turkey, and Egypt seemed to target their actions at specific suspects without involving innocent civilians. The distribution of material actions ranges from 26 percent in Canada to 84 percent in Egypt. In fact, Canada is the only country that is more likely to make intangible gestures than take tangible actions. This is likely because a large portion of the Canadian actions are related to setting policy that might appease or enrage the constituencies of extremists. In contrast, the large percentage of material actions in Egypt suggests that it is the most aggressive of the GATE countries.

Finally, when we consider the primary actors of government actions, we see that Egypt once again stands out. For the other five countries, in combination the military and politicians implemented around 80 percent of the actions. In Egypt, over half of terrorist relevant actions are perpetrated by police. This makes sense in the Egyptian system, because under Hosni Mubarak the 500,000-strong police force was the primary body charged with maintaining internal security. In Israel, Turkey, and Algeria, the military represented the plurality of actions, with politicians following close behind. In Canada and Lebanon this trend is reversed: politicians claimed the most actions, with the military following close behind.

We now compare the number of conciliatory and repressive actions to the number of terrorist attacks in Israel and Turkey. Figure 14.2 presents two bar graphs (one for each country) that depict repressive actions with the black bars and conciliatory actions with the gray bars; both are measured by the scale for government actions on the left side of the graph. Terror attacks are shown by the solid black line, and its scale is shown in the right axis of each graph. For brevity, only two countries were selected; the other comparisons are available upon request.

Turning first to the Israeli case, shown in the top graph, we see that during the First Intifada (1987–93), the Israeli government employed persistently repressive action, which it later combined with conciliatory action culminating in the Oslo Accords (September 1993). It seems that terrorist violence dropped when both types of actions were being taken. During the Second Intifada (2000–2005), the Israeli government acted with a record high frequency of repressive actions. In fact, when we look closer at the types of actions during that period, we discover that most actions were extremely repressive with the intent to kill (scale 7). While this figure does not tell us whether governments must use repression to stop terrorism, it does suggest that less repressive means, as were used during the First Intifada, might also be promising in reducing terror attacks.

Turning next to Turkey, shown in the bottom graph, we first point out that the differences in the scales show that Turkey experienced more terrorist attacks (right scale) than its government made relevant actions (left scale). This is important because we see that terrorism increased in Turkey sooner and faster than its repressive responses. Terrorism also peaked earlier in Turkey, with 516 attacks in 1992; while repressive actions continued to rise, peaking later, in 1997, with 201 acts. This shows that despite the decline in terrorist violence, Turkey persisted with aggressive counterterrorism strategies for at least five more years. While this figure suggests that Turkey's strategy may have effectively reduced terrorism, without a more sophisticated statistical analysis, like the one described below, any conclusions are merely speculative.

## ASSESSING EFFECTIVENESS BY USING GATE DATA

Dugan and Chenoweth use GATE-Israel data to assess the effectiveness of discriminate and indiscriminate conciliatory and repressive actions by

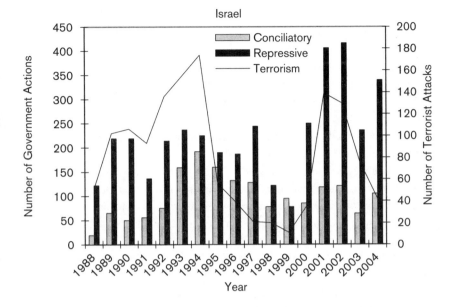

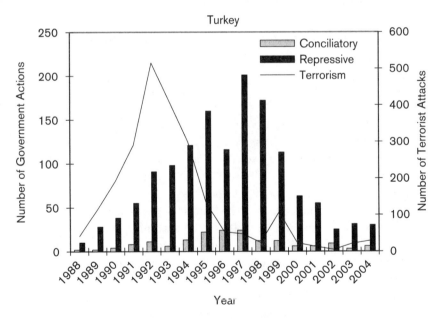

FIGURE 14.2.  Terrorist Attacks and Conciliatory and Repressive Government
Actions in Israel and Turkey, 1988–2004.

Israel directed toward Palestinians.[23] That study uses generalized additive models (GAM) and negative binomial regressions to estimate the effects of government actions in one month on the number of Palestinian terrorist attacks during the following month. The key findings are that when significant, repression is associated with more terrorism (backlash) and conciliation is associated with less terrorism. These findings are especially strong for indiscriminate actions and during the Second Intifada. Figure 14.3 presents the GAM models for conciliatory and repressive indiscriminate actions during the Second Intifada.

Preliminary findings of GATE data for other countries have shown similar results. For the remaining Middle Eastern countries, repression either is ineffective or is associated with more terrorism; and conciliation either is ineffective or is associated with less terrorism. More nuanced analysis from Canada and the United States suggests that different constituencies respond differently to conciliation and repression. A preliminary analysis of actions relevant to right-wing constituencies in the United States during the Clinton years suggests that discriminate repression (i.e., deterrence) is effective in reducing terrorism, while indiscriminate conciliation is associated with more extremist violence. Analysis of GATE-Canada data suggests that al-Qaeda-inspired extremism was very sensitive to actions by the Canadian military in Afghanistan.

## CONCLUSION

This chapter has two main purposes. First, it urges readers to reconsider how we can conceptualize counterterrorism to include more nuanced behavior by governments that could elicit a reaction from terrorist organizations or their constituencies. By expanding how we construct counterterrorism, we are better able to develop insight into what works and what does not work in different contexts. As the findings from the United States show, deterrence might work in specific circumstances, even if it often fuels conflict elsewhere. Further, when we widen the portfolio of possible interactions between governments and vulnerable populations, it becomes less important to define defiant or violent acts as terrorism. In general, governments can behave in a myriad of ways to reduce the risk of violence regardless of how it is conceptualized.

The chapter's second purpose is to introduce the GATE database. While this collection process requires many resources, the findings thus far demonstrate the importance of continued efforts. We are currently working with programmers to develop less burdensome strategies to collect GATE data and expect to be able to produce findings more quickly.

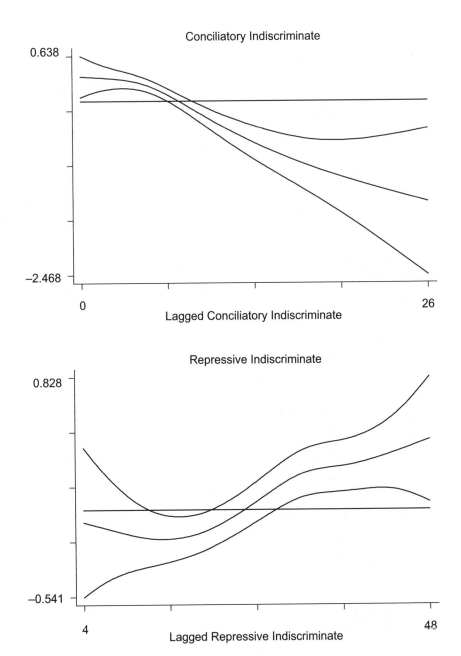

FIGURE 14.3.   Effects of Israeli Actions on Palestinian Terrorism during the Second Intifada.

NOTES

1. Cesare Beccaria, *On Crimes and Punishment* (1764; reprinted, Boston: Branden Books, 1983).

2. Laurence H. Ross and Gary LaFree, "Deterrence in Criminology and Social Policy," in *Behavioral and Social Science Knowledge: Discovery, Diffusion, and Social Impact* (Washington, DC: National Research Council, 1986); Raymond Paternoster, "The Deterrent Effect of the Perceived Uncertainty and Severity of Punishment: A Review of the Evidence and Issues," *Justice Quarterly* 4 (1987): 173–217.

3. "Bush: Bin Laden 'Wanted Dead or Alive,'" *CNN* (September 17, 2001); Brian Knowlton, "Terror in America: 'We're Going to Smoke them Out'; President Airs His Anger," *New York Times* (September 19, 2001); "Bush: 'Bring On' Attackers of U.S. Troops," *Associated Press* (July 2, 2003).

4. Assaf Moghadam, *The Globalization of Martyrdom: Al Qaeda, Salafi Jihad, and the Diffusion of Suicide Attacks* (Baltimore: Johns Hopkins University Press, 2008).

5. Adam Roberts, "Counter-terrorism, Armed Force, and the Laws of War," *Survival* 44 (2002): 7–32; Shirley V. Scott and Olivia Ambler, "Does Legitimacy Really Matter? Accounting for the Decline in US Foreign Policy Legitimacy following the 2003 Invasion of Iraq," *European Journal of International Relations* 13 (2007): 67–87.

6. Daniel Benjamin and Steve Simon, *The Next Attack: The Failure of the War on Terror and a Strategy for Getting It Right* (New York: Times Books, 2005).

7. Clark McCauley, "Jujitsu Politics: Terrorism and Response to Terrorism," in Paul R. Kimmel and Chris E. Stout (eds.), *Collateral Damage: The Psychological Consequences of America's War on Terrorism* (Westport, CN: Praeger, 2006), 45–65.

8. On rioting, see Kathleen Peroff and Christopher Hewitt, "Rioting in Northern Ireland: The Effects of Different Policies," *Journal of Conflict Resolution* 24 (1980): 593–612; Robert White, "From Peaceful Protest to Guerrilla War: Micromobilization of the Provisional Irish Republican Army," *American Journal of Sociology* 94 (1989): 1277–1302. For the increase in the incidence of terrorism, see Gary LaFree, Laura Dugan, and Raven Korte, "The Impact of British Counterterrorist Strategies on Political Violence in Northern Ireland: Comparing Deterrence and Backlash Models," *Criminology* 47 (2009): 501–30.

9. Karen Rasler, "Concessions, Repression, and Political Protest in the Iranian Revolution," *American Sociological Review* 61 (1996): 132–52.

10. Keren Sharvit, Arie W. Kruglanski, Mo Wang, Xiaoyan Chen, Lauren M. Boyatzi, Boaz Ganor, and Eitan Azani, "The Effects of Israelis Use of Coercive and Conciliatory Tactics on Palestinian's Use of Terrorist Tactics, 2000–2006," *Dynamics of Asymmetric Conflict* 6 (2013): 22–44.

11. Javier Argomaniz and Alberto Vidal-Diez, "Examining Deterrence and Backlash Effects in Counter-terrorism: The Case of ETA," *Terrorism and Political Violence* 27 (2015): 160–81.

12. R.J. Brym and B. Araj, "Suicide Bombing as Strategy and Interaction: The Case of the Second Intifada," *Social Forces* 84 (2006): 1969–86; B. Araj, "Harsh State Repression as a Cause of Suicide Bombing: The Case of the Palestinian-Israeli Conflict," *Studies in Conflict and Terrorism* 31 (2008): 284–303.

13. Laura Dugan and Erica Chenoweth, "Moving beyond Deterrence: The Effectiveness of Raising the Benefits of Abstaining from Terrorism in Israel," *American Sociological Review* 77 (2012): 597–624.

14. Erica Chenoweth and Laura Dugan, "Rethinking Repression: Evidence from Israel," paper presented at the American Political Science Association annual

meeting, Washington, DC, September 2010; Laura Dugan and Erica Chenoweth, "Government Actions in Terror Environments (GATE): A Methodology That Reveals How Governments Behave toward Terrorists and Their Constituencies," in V. S. Subrahmanian (ed.), *Handbook of Computational Approaches to Counterterrorism* (New York: Springer, 2013), 467–88.

15. GATE data for Algeria, Egypt, Israel, Lebanon, and Turkey currently end in 2004, but are being updated to 2012. GATE-Canada is available through 2013.

16. Philip A. Schrodt and Deborah J. Gerner, "Validity Assessment of a Machine-Coded Event Data Set for the Middle East, 1982–1992," *American Journal of Political Science* 38 (1994): 825–54.

17. These include the National Counterterrorism Center (NCTC), National Security Agency (NSA), Federal Bureau of Investigation (FBI), Department of Homeland Security (DHS), Central Intelligence Agency (CIA), President, Department of State, Department of Treasury, Department of Defense, Department of Justice, Department of Transportation, Federal Aviation Administration, Executive Office of the President, Senate Committee on Terrorism and Homeland Security, and Senate Committee on Crime and Terrorism.

18. Philip A. Schrodt, "Twenty Years of the Kansas Event Data System Project," unpublished manuscript (University of Kansas, 2006).

19. Ibid.

20. Because LexisNexis used many sources without unique identifiers, unique identifiers were added later.

21. Joshua S. Goldstein, "A Conflict-Cooperation Scale for WEIS Event Data," *Journal of Conflict Resolution* 36 (1992): 369–85.

22. For the United States and Canada the review of removals was done only for a subset of cases.

23. Dugan and Chenoweth, "Moving beyond Deterrence."

# 15. The World versus Daesh

## Constructing a Contemporary Terrorist Threat

Scott Englund and Michael Stohl

In the span of two weeks in early November 2015, Daesh[1] claimed the lives of nearly four hundred unarmed civilians of more than a dozen nationalities on two continents. The series of assaults in Paris and Beirut and in the sky over the Sinai Desert ran counter to contemporary assessments and conventional wisdom about the organization. On November 13, 2015, the day two suicide bombers killed almost fifty in Lebanon, and the day before three teams of terrorists killed almost two hundred in Paris, President Barack Obama, during an interview on CBS News, assured the world that the threat posed by Daesh had been contained. Indeed, even a week prior, US and, according to a CNN online report on November 4, 2015, British intelligence agencies were only cautiously accepting the claim of responsibility by Daesh for downing the Russian charter Metrojet flight 9268 as "possible." Further, it was argued, the core leadership in Syria and Iraq only loosely governed its affiliated "province" in Sinai, and Daesh seemed focused on securing and expanding its self-proclaimed "caliphate."

The threat posed by Daesh in its present incarnation developed rapidly, but how it has been understood has traveled a wide arc, from President Obama's infamous "jayvee team" analogy[2] to claims, even prior to November 2015, that Daesh posed an "existential threat" to the West in general and the United States in particular, as asserted by British prime minister David Cameron on the BBC on June 29, 2015. Both of these extremes are dangerously inaccurate; President Obama failed to appreciate how "local power struggles" could metastasize into a transnational threat, and Prime Minister Cameron underestimated the resiliency of Western civilization and the liberal legal traditions that underpin European governments. In both of these perspectives, Daesh is a unique entity, separate from, and something to be compared to, the existing Islamist terrorist threat al-Qaeda. Indeed, as Daesh grew in the chaos of the Syrian civil war, it was frequently characterized as being "too radical" even for al-Qaeda, which, according to a February 3, 2014, *Washington Post,* disavowed any connection with Daesh. In another sense, Daesh may be seen as a continuation of that same terrorist organization, born in Peshawar, Pakistan, in 1988 as a means of managing the foreign *jihadis* who came to Afghanistan to fight the Soviets. Lack of coordination between the core al-Qaeda leadership and the leaders of its associates in Iraq during the US occupation, and intentional ambiguity on the part of the early Islamic State in Iraq, make it difficult to trace this lineage with certainty.[3]

In this chapter, we describe the dominant constructions of terrorism that Daesh represents and argue that although each of these constructions could accurately describe part of the threat posed by Daesh, all are distinguishable facets that require different responses. Three dominant constructions of Daesh as a threat have developed, and have moderated slightly since the Paris attack. First, Daesh is the Caliphate, a quasi-state existing across the political frontiers of Iraq and Syria. Second, Daesh is a "Trojan Horse," a threat hidden among refugees or among returning fighters traveling on Western passports. Finally, the new dominant construction is Daesh as the new source of transnational terrorism. Of course, Daesh is all of these in part; each construction contains some truth. These three constructions could be thought of as three facets of a singular phenomenon. In the first section of this chapter, we define these three dominant constructions using news media and official statements made by policy officials and testimony before legislative committees. Collectively these definitions represent the dominant constructions as presented by media outlets and political elites. After these three constructions are described, the principal policy responses as stated by senior political leaders are compared. Finally, by comparing the dominant constructions of Daesh to the principal policy responses to it, we can discuss how well policy does or does not match the threat as described.

## DAESH AS A STATE

It is impossible to analyze the rise and success of the so-called Islamic State[4] without considering the US invasion of Iraq in 2003 and the subsequent Sunni insurgency that, at its crest in 2007, was claiming one thousand Iraqi civilians every day, according to some estimates. The ill-conceived de-Baathification order and dissolution of the Iraqi Army under the Coalition Provisional Authority left tens of thousands of Sunni Iraqi men unemployed, marginalized, and armed. For their own part, when the Sunni political leadership boycotted the 2004 elections for a constitutional convention and interim parliament, they made their political impotency official and durable. With the country awash in caches of small arms and explosives, the insurgency quickly became a serious security concern for the occupying US and coalition forces.

When the Syrian conflict began in 2011, fighters formerly active with al-Qaeda in Iraq (AQI) began to move into northern Syria at the urging of Ayman al-Zawahiri, spiritual leader of al-Qaeda.[5] By that time, all the original leaders of the insurgency against coalition forces in Iraq had been killed, and AQI (now known as the Islamic State in Iraq) was led by Abu Bakr al-Baghdadi, the present leader of Daesh. In Syria, a popular uprising, much like others in the "Arab Spring," was overrun by Sunni *jihadi* groups. These groups began to occupy towns and enforce compliance with their own version of Islamic *sharia* law. The restoration of order was, at first, welcomed by local populations. However, the multiplicity of groups with their own allegiances often found themselves fighting one another rather than the Assad regime, adding another level of complexity to the increasingly sectarian Syrian civil war.[6] If the collapse of the Syrian state created room for maneuver for AQI, then the withdrawal of the last of the US military forces from Iraq, and the continued sectarianism of the Iraqi government under Prime Minister Nuri al-Maliki, opened opportunity for a return to Iraq.

Since it declared itself the new Islamic Caliphate in June 2014, Daesh has frequently been described as a newer, more terrifying version of known threats, as retired general John M. Keane testified in the House Foreign Affairs Committee:

> ISIL (Daesh) is the new face of the Al Qaeda and the larger radical
> Islamist movement. ISIL has already accomplished what the 9/11 Al
> Qaeda only dreamt about, but forfeited, when they over reached and
> attacked the American people. As we know, ISIL in 3 short years has
> managed to take control of a vast swath of territory, essentially villages,
> towns and cities from East of Aleppo in Syria through the Iraq/Syria
> border, rendering that border non-existent, to Anbar province in Iraq,
> west of Baghdad, to Mosul.

These assessments are attributed to the rapid battlefield successes enjoyed by Daesh in the spring and summer of 2014, through which it obtained territory, weapons, ammunition and equipment, and a steady income from taxes, the sale of oil, and criminal activity.

In addition to the constructions noted above, Daesh has also been defined both as a terrorist organization and an insurgency, sparking some disagreement among elites. In January 2015 a White House spokesperson made the following distinction in explaining why a prisoner exchange with the Taliban in Afghanistan was permissible, but similar arrangements were not acceptable with respect to Daesh in Syria and Iraq: "The Taliban is an armed insurgency, ISIL is a terrorist group, so we don't make concessions to terrorist groups." Criticizing this characterization, Audrey Kurth Cronin argued in *Foreign Affairs* that when President Obama defined Daesh as "a terrorist organization, plain and simple," he was precisely and completely mistaken. She asserted that the organization "hardly fits that description, and indeed, although it uses terrorism as a tactic, it is not really a terrorist organization at all." She concluded that, "if ISIS is purely and simply anything, it is a pseudo-state led by a conventional army."[7]

As a quasi-state, Daesh has become a highly visible construction of contemporary terrorism. Indeed, like many states and insurgencies, Daesh uses terrorism to coerce the populations under its control, thereby maintaining authority without having to reach every person unfortunate enough to live where Daesh is now the government. What Daesh represents in Syria and Iraq is not entirely settled among the media and political leaders. It is probably best understood as an insurgency, or quasi-state, that can effectively employ both conventional military tactics and terrorism as a means of advancing its political objectives. More important, the fact that it holds territory and owns a significant logistical and weapons capacity makes it a convenient target for military reprisal. Punishing Daesh as it operates in Syria and Iraq has gained much greater support since its recent successes in sponsoring transnational terrorism.

## DAESH, SPONSOR OF TRANSNATIONAL TERRORISM

Just as Daesh is frequently described as surpassing the Taliban, in the size of its territory or the effectiveness of its governance, or exceeding al-Qaeda in its material wealth, it is also being constructed as the new chief exporter of international terrorism, surpassing, even perhaps hastening the end of, its progenitor al-Qaeda. As the London *Guardian* described it in June 2015: "ISIS has not simply eclipsed al-Qaida on the battlefields of Syria and Iraq, and in the competition for funding and new recruits. According to a series of exclusive interviews with senior jihadi ideologues, ISIS has successfully launched 'a coup' against al-Qaida to destroy it from within. As a consequence, they now admit, al-Qaida—as an idea and an organisation—is now on the verge of collapse."[8] The argument is that although al-Qaeda as an organization remains an active promoter of violence (just two weeks after the violence in Beirut and Paris, al-Mourabitoun and gunmen of al-Qaeda in the Islamic Maghreb murdered nearly twenty in a hotel in Bamako, Mali) it is a declining force in the wider jihadist movement.

An effective media campaign has been directly linked to Daesh's ability to export violence. The argument runs, if it can use propaganda to project a positive image and pacify the areas it controls, Daesh will have the institutional capacity to turn its attention to exporting violence. A Reuter's opinion piece warns against this "nice" side of Daesh:

> Thousands of peace-loving people live in Islamic State–occupied areas and are fed a steady stream of positive propaganda: Islamic State members feeding the poor, and hosting ice cream socials, carnivals, and tug-of-war contests. Islamic State is trying—and in some areas, succeeding—in winning hearts and minds. Left unchecked, its public support will grow, making the group more difficult to defeat in the long run and giving it the space it needs to conduct future attacks like those in Paris and Beirut.[9]

In this particular case, effectiveness in propaganda is presented as automatically parlayed into an effective terror campaign abroad.

Daesh has been fairly consistently described as an effective propaganda machine, surpassing both its contemporary rivals and its predecessors in its sophistication and reach. The organization's capacity to produce slick, attractive messages has been the subject of government hearings and studies and well documented in news media. What changed recently was that with recent high-profile attacks, Daesh has elevated its status in the media and among elites as the premier exporter of transnational terrorism. As the "new al-Qaeda," it has captured the attention of a startled public, which, entranced by a steady diet of information provided by media outlets, demands action from political leadership.

## DAESH, THE "TROJAN HORSE"

Before the escalation of violence in 2015, an important construction of the threat posed by Daesh was the possibility that "Westerners" (presumably from Western Europe, North America, and Australia) who traveled to the war zone in Syria and Iraq could return on their national passports and bring with them the skills and will to carry on the jihad at home. Media accounts have carried diverse official government statements to this effect in both the United States and Europe.

Matthew Olsen, the director of the US National Counterterrorism Center (NCTC) was quoted in the *New York Times* as saying, "Syria has become really the predominant jihadist battlefield in the world. . . . The concern going forward from a threat perspective is there are individuals traveling to Syria, becoming further radicalized, becoming trained and then returning as part of really a global jihadist movement to Western Europe and, potentially, to the United States."[10] In a September 2014 hearing, the director of the Federal Bureau of Investigation testified before the US House of Representatives' Committee on Homeland Security: "Foreign fighters traveling to Syria or Iraq could, for example, gain battlefield experience and increased exposure to violent extremist elements that may lead to further radicalization to violence; they may use these skills and exposure to radical ideology to return to their countries of origin, including the United States, to conduct attacks on the Homeland."[11]

After the early-November 2015 violence, especially the attacks in Paris, the "hidden danger" construction shifted notably toward the "Trojan Horse" analogy, according to which committed extremists would infiltrate the tragically large flows of refugees fleeing violence in Syria and Iraq. Posing as refugees themselves, these terrorists would use a humanitarian crisis to deliver violence to the heart of Western Europe and North America.

Fueled in part by a supercharged partisan environment associated with the longest US presidential election season in history, taking a hard line against a potential threat from incoming refugees proved a safe way to earn approval from a population historically hesitant to receive refugees. To illustrate, in November 2015 the Gallup organization published a retrospective on public opinion on this issue covering fifteen crisis points in the twentieth century. In only two instances did the majority of US residents support accepting refugees: in 1999, allowing refugees from the Kosovo crisis and, in 1979, a slim majority agreeing that "Indochinese or 'boat people' would be welcomed in your community." Over 70 percent of those polled were opposed to President Harry Truman's call in 1946 to allow additional refugees displaced by the Second World War; in 1939 only 26 percent supported government plans to accept Jewish children fleeing Nazi Germany.[12]

Constructed as a threat that can reach beyond its territory in Syria and Iraq, Daesh can both sponsor and inspire violence indirectly and, through trained fighters traveling on their own Western passports, on visas, or as refugees. This construction has undergone some transformation, first, in the form of Europeans and Americans returning from the battlefields of Syria and Iraq to wage a clandestine war at home; second, as a "Trojan Horse" with violent men hidden among the refugees flowing into Europe and eventually the United States; and finally, as individuals taking advantage of relaxed visa requirements. Regardless of the vector, this construction presents the least likely danger, but is an ongoing intelligence challenge.

## POLICY RESPONSE: THE WORLD VERSUS DAESH

In spite of this proliferation of constructions, the most visible solution to the problem of Daesh has remained the same: bomb their positions in Syria and Iraq. After the attacks in Paris in November, the president of France, François Hollande, told the French Parliament: "France is at war. . . . These attacks were war. It was an attack against our values, against our youth and our way of life." After conceding that a bomb, likely planted by a Daesh-affiliated group, brought down the Russian Metrojet charter flight over the Sinai Desert on October 31, President Vladimir Putin of Russia said, "We will find them at any place on this planet and punish them." According to reporting from US National Public Radio on November 26, 2015, France and Russia agreed to cooperate against Daesh. As related by President Putin, he and Hollande "agreed on a very important issue: To strike the terrorists only, Daesh and the jihadi groups only, and not to strike the forces and the groups that are fighting against the terrorists. And we are going to exchange some information about that: what can be struck, and what must not be struck."[13] On the same day, according to the *Washington Post*, Putin went further to say, "We are ready to cooperate with the coalition which is led by the United States."[14] As of November 29, British prime minister David Cameron was preparing for a vote to expand his country's aerial bombardment campaign to include targets inside Syria. For its part, the United Nations Security Council, in Resolution 2249, called upon all UN member states with the capacity to do so, "to take all necessary measures, in compliance with international law . . . to redouble and coordinate their efforts to prevent and suppress terrorist acts committed specifically by ISIL, also known as Da'esh as well as ANF, and all other individuals, groups, undertakings, and entities associated with Al Qaeda . . . and to eradicate the safe haven they have established over significant parts of Iraq and Syria."

Declaring "war" on the perpetrators, however named, is an often used rhetorical device to demonstrate resolve, and it did not begin with the series of attacks in November 2015. France's prime minister declared war on "Islamic Extremism" after the January 2015 attack against the *Charlie Hebdo* editorial offices in Paris; the president of Tunisia declared that a state of war existed between Daesh and his country after the June 2015 murder of nearly forty tourists at a beach resort in Sousse, Tunisia. In the wake of that same attack, in which the majority of victims were Britons, Prime Minister David Cameron told Parliament that a state of war existed between Great Britain and ISIS, according to reporting by *The Guardian*.[15]

Semi-retired journalist Tom Brokaw, who anchored NBC's nightly news program for twenty-two years and hosted all three of NBC's major news programs, ended the Sunday, November 22, *Meet the Press* program by commenting: "I don't want this broadcast to end without all of us dealing with the new reality. We're at war; this has changed—Paris has changed the place of America in this war against ISIS and it is now a war. The president's, what I would call, 'benign neglect' about the continuing expansion of ISIS, the more sophistication of it all the time, has to come to a halt."[16] Although the details on levels of commitment reveal a wide range of responses, at a minimum, political and media elites advance the "war" and "victory" frames, and focus on intensifying the air campaign against Daesh, with increased international coordination.

## TERRORISM OR INSURGENCY?

Daesh has been defined both as a terrorist organization and as an insurgency. The fact that Daesh seems to defy definition among sensible, well-intentioned observers raises the possibility that it could represent different things to different audiences. Ross Harrison has aptly suggested that this is in fact part of the problem: "ISIS represents a threat with three different faces. To the United States and its Western allies, it is a terrorist organization. However, for Arab states, ISIS represents an insurgency without political boundaries that threatens the survival of countries. . . . When examined from a regional perspective, ISIS represents the spearhead of a broader movement threatening to sunder the Arab political order that has existed since the end of World War I."[17] As Daesh has now recently regained attention as a terrorist organization, and since Western political leaders are calling for redoubled action against it, it should be helpful to clearly differentiate between terrorism and insurgency.

According to the 2006 United States Army Counterinsurgency (COIN) Field Manual 3–24, an insurgency is "an organized movement aimed at the overthrow of a constituted government through the use of subversion and armed conflict." Putting the matter in other terms, the manual goes on to say that an insurgency is "an organized, protracted politico-military struggle designed to weaken the control and legitimacy of an established government, occupying power, or other political authority while increasing insurgent control." Therefore, as defined by the US government, an insurgency is an effort organized with the goal of militarily overthrowing an existing political order and eventually replacing that order with something new.

Terrorism, on the other hand, is violent political speech. What distinguishes terrorism from other forms of violence (even asymmetric warfare) is that the death and suffering of the immediate victims of violence is intended as a means to some other end. The terror group is not particularly interested in its victims; rather, its audience consists of the survivors and people who might be in a position to give the terrorist group what it wants. The goal of terrorism is to induce compliant behavior on the part of the audience to violence. Terrorism is coercion—I hit him to get you to do what I want.

While terrorism is almost universally condemned, its violent acts can also be mislabeled as such for political purposes, because terrorism generates such impassioned condemnation. It is important that we carefully distinguish between terrorism and other violent acts, because the response to terrorism involves communication as well as security (police or military) strategies and actions. Terrorists seek through their acts of violence (whether perpetrated or threatened) to create fear or compliant behavior, or both, in a victim or a wider audience, or both, for the act or threat. Not all violent acts are terrorism. What distinguishes the terrorist act is that the violence is directed at an audience beyond the victim(s), and that is the main purpose of the violence. That is, terrorism is communicatively constituted violence, and it is the action, not the actor, that makes a particular act terrorism. The violence that occurs in the context of a pitched battle is thus not generally considered terrorism.

Insurgencies can employ terrorism as a tactic—in fact, they often do so in order to undermine the people's confidence in the government that the insurgency is trying to overthrow. Terrorism is also employed by insurgent groups to coerce support from a population. But it is important to maintain the distinction: terror is a tool, a means of communication. It is defined not by who commits a particular act, but by the intention of the act itself. Insurgencies have broad politico-military objectives that include radically altering a political system. This is what Daesh is attempting to do. Indeed, by erasing the established borders between Iraq and Syria and replacing the legitimately constituted governments in the territory it holds, this is precisely what it has done. The mere fact that one can refer to "it" on a map and say that "it" governs in any practical sense immediately distinguishes Daesh from traditionally defined terror groups such as al-Qaeda or the Provisional Irish Republican Army.

## COUNTERTERRORISM AND COUNTERINSURGENCY

Traditional counterterrorism strategies are not effective against insurgencies. Although counterterrorism and counterinsurgency strategies are often employed together, they are very different approaches with different assumptions about the application of lethal force and the role of the local population. Counterinsurgency strategies involve a long-term commitment to the goal of driving a wedge between insurgent forces and the population. Ultimately, counterinsurgent forces need to win popular support and legitimacy for local political leadership. Tactically, counterinsurgency means applying the least amount of force necessary, trading short-term force protection and security for long-term cooperation and trust. Counterinsurgency operations would be problematic, at best, in the Syria-Iraq theater.

In contrast, counterterrorism operations, militarily speaking, are often conducted from a distance, relying on intelligence-driven precision application of munitions. Even a well-planned counterterrorism missile strike that causes collateral damage can ruin counterinsurgency operations designed to build trust and cooperation. "Rather than being mutually reinforcing," Michael Boyle argues, "they [such strikes] may impose tradeoffs on each other, as counterterrorism activities may blunt the effectiveness of counterinsurgency approaches and vice versa." Yet, Boyle continues, this conclusion is largely ignored among political elites: "At the political level, . . . the effects of the conflation of counterterrorism and counterinsurgency are perhaps more serious. . . . To treat every terrorist threat through the lens of counterinsurgency is to commit the US to undertaking countless state-building missions abroad, often with limited prospects of success. To treat every insurgency as the potential incubator of a future terrorist threat is a recipe for overextension, distraction and exhaustion."[18]

Hunting and killing key leaders in terrorist organizations and insurgencies has been an important element of US counterterrorism and counterinsurgency operations. The effectiveness of these "decapitating blows" is not a settled issue. Robert Pape argues that these sorts of campaigns are rarely successful.[19] Criticizing the limited scope and strict definitions of "success" found in previous studies of "decapitation" effectiveness, Patrick Johnston concludes that leadership decapitation, "1.) increases the chances of war termination; 2.) increases the probability of government victory; 3.) reduces the intensity of militant violence; and 4.) reduces the frequency of insurgent attacks."[20] These "high-value targets" (HVTs) are routinely killed through a variety of means; working through a target deck can provide convenient metrics and a sense of progress, but these operations do not always lead to strategic gains over the long run. "Too often," Matt Frankel notes, "HVT campaigns are plagued by poor intelligence, cause unnecessary collateral damage, spur retaliatory attacks, and in many cases, yield little to no positive effects on the insurgent or terrorist group being targeted."[21] These HVT campaigns are most successful when carried out by local forces, and least successful when led by occupying or colonial powers; they are best employed against a highly centralized organization and as but one part of a much larger strategy.[22]

Counterterrorism policy is more than simply the prevention of future violence and the elimination of potential terrorist actors, two objectives that clearly must be at the heart of any successful strategy. The strategy must also consider the appropriate communicative response to acts that do occur, to both prepare the public for the occurrence of such attacks and respond to the audience's reactions to the acts when they occur. Terrorists use their violence to communicate fear to the target audience and also wish to convince them that the authorities can no longer protect those who are targeted. The authorities' tasks are not limited to the prevention of attacks but also include the apprehension of the terrorists and taking actions that make it less likely that a future attack will succeed. At the same time, authorities must also persuade the public to subjectively believe that they are more secure and create confidence and trust that they are not only making them more secure but are doing so in a manner consistent with societal expectations. Failing to make the public more secure, or failing to make the public perceive that they are secure, amounts to a victory for the terrorist. As a process, failing to make the public believe it is safe and that the political authorities are doing all that they should in a manner consistent with societal norms often presents more of a threat to the political system than particular security lapses. Moving beyond a particular state border to the regional or global level immediately increases the number of audiences that the terrorist and the state address and thus increases the difficulty of the communications necessary to engender trust and the perception of security, as well as the sense that the actions taken are both legitimate and necessary.

The day after the United States bombed targets in Libya in retaliation for that state's sponsorship of an attack on a Berlin nightclub that killed two US service members and one Turkish woman and injured 229 others, on the floor of the US Senate, Senator Mark Hatfield (R-Ore.) voiced a minority assessment of the previous day's military action: "The vast moral gulf which once separated us from the terrorists was narrowed yesterday.... Take another look at those bleeding children before you delight over the precision of the rockets, my colleagues. Tell them you are not sure the policy will work, but it sure did feel good."[23] In spite of years of attack and counterattack, there exists no coherent, long-term US policy on how to effectively counter terrorism. How bad does terrorism have to be before threats of retaliation are carried out? When and whom should we attack?

How will we know? How many innocent lives lost is an acceptable number? What will be gained by retaliation? Will we deter terrorism, or will we simply "feel better" to have acted, however futilely? What possibility exists that our retaliation will, as the French learned in Algeria in 1959–62, fuel further resentment that may incite future violence?

## CONCLUSION

The complexity presented by the Syrian-Iraqi problem demands careful study. Daesh presents a multifaceted terror threat that requires a multifaceted response. Daesh has been constructed as a quasi-state with a conventional military capacity; as an inspirational propaganda machine, recruiting fighters from around the world and encouraging others to wage their jihad wherever they are; and as a clandestine threat, hidden among refugees, or as battle-tested soldiers returning from the front lines in Syria and Iraq to carry on the fight at home. Bombing Daesh fighters in Raqqa will not make Parisians more secure; killing individual Daesh leaders is not likely to liberate Mosul; screening refugees more carefully will not solve the crisis that displaced them. The best-planned aerial bombing campaign may demonstrate resolve and is a highly visible retributive act, but it is likely to inspire violence far from the target of that campaign. Absent a coherent strategy that appropriately addresses each potential threat, uncoordinated efforts will very likely be counterproductive. When Cronin criticized President Obama in *Foreign Affairs* for mistaking Daesh for a "terrorist organization," when it is, in her mind, clearly a quasi-state with a conventional military, she did not take that analysis far enough. If Daesh is a state, then it can employ terror as other states arguably have; terrorism is not defined by the actor, but by the intent behind the action. Thus "degrading and ultimately destroying" a state, as Daesh pretends to do in Syria and Iraq, is fundamentally separate from protecting people in faraway places from a real, albeit remote, threat of terrorist violence posed by Daesh.

## NOTES

1. The name Daesh represents the Arabic acronym for the so-called Islamic State. We use this name for the organization commonly referred to as the Islamic State in Iraq and the Levant (ISIL) or the Islamic State in Iraq and al-Sham (ISIS).

2. President Obama's full statement: "The analogy we use around here sometimes, and I think is accurate, is if a jayvee team puts on Lakers uniforms that doesn't make them Kobe Bryant. I think there is a distinction between the capacity and reach of a bin Laden and a network that is actively planning major terrorist plots against the homeland versus jihadists who are engaged in various local power struggles and

disputes, often sectarian." As quoted in: David Remnick, "Going the Distance, on and off the road with Barack Obama," *New Yorker*, January 27, 2014, http://www.newyorker.com/magazine/2014/01/27/going-the-distance-david-remnick.

3. William McCants, *The ISIS Apocalypse: The History, Strategy, and Doomsday Vision of the Islamic State* (New York: St. Martin's Press, 2015), chapter 1.

4. Daniel Byman, *Al Qaeda, The Islamic State, and the Global Jihadist Movement* (New York: Oxford University Press, 2015), 163–64. Byman counts nine different possible names, translations, and other variants for this organization over its relatively short existence. The name Al-Qaeda in Iraq (AQI) typically refers to the pre-2011 organization that operated largely in Iraq; and the name ISIS or ISIL, or the Arabic Daesh, to the post-2011 organization that operates in Syria, Iraq, and elsewhere.

5. Ibid., 166.

6. Patrick Cockburn, *The Rise of the Islamic State: ISIS and the New Sunni Revolution* (London: Verso, 2015), chapter 1.

7. Audrey Kurth Cronin, "ISIS Is Not a Terrorist Group," *Foreign Affairs* 94 (2015): 98.

8. Ali Younes, Shiv Malik, Spencer Ackerman, and Mustafa Khalili, "How Isis Crippled al-Qaida; The Inside Story of the Coup That Has Brought the World's Most Feared Terrorist Network to the Brink of Collapse," *The Guardian*, June 11, 2015.

9. Jacqueline Lopour, "The Scariest Thing about Islamic State? Its Kinder, Gentler Side," *Reuters*, November 26, 2015, http://www.reuters.com/article/idUS328865418620151127 (accessed March 18, 2017).

10. Eric Schmitt, "Worries Mount as Syria Lures West's Muslims," *New York Times*, July 28, 2013, A1.

11. "Worldwide Threats to the Homeland," statement of James B. Comey, Director, Federal Bureau of Investigation, Department of Justice, before the Committee on Homeland Security, House of Representatives, September 17, 2014, http://docs.house.gov/meetings/HM/HM00/20140917/102616/HHRG-113-HM00-Wstate-ComeyJ-20140917.pdf (accessed March 18, 2017).

12. Frank Newport, "Historical Review: Americans' Views on Refugees Coming to U.S." (blog post), November 19, 2015, http://www.gallup.com/opinion/polling-matters/186716/historical-review-americans-views-refugees-coming.aspx (accessed March 26, 2017).

13. Avie Schneider, "Russia, France Agree to Cooperate in the Fight against ISIS," National Public Radio, November 26, 2015, http://www.npr.org/sections/thetwo-way/2015/11/26/457526125/russia-france-agree-to-cooperate-in-the-fight-against-isis (accessed March 18, 2017).

14. Andrew Roth and Karla Adam, "Moscow Is Ready to Coordinate with the West over Strikes on Syria, Putin Says," washingtonpost.com, November 26, 2015.

15. Patrick Wintour and Emma Graham-Harrison, "Tunisia Attack: David Cameron Pledges 'Full Spectrum' Response to Massacre," *The Guardian*, June 29, 2015, https://www.theguardian.com/uk-news/2015/jun/29/tunisia-attack-david-cameron-pledges-full-spectrum-response-to-massacre (accessed March 18, 2017).

16. *Meet the Press*, November 22, 2015, NBC News, http://www.nbcnews.com/meet-the-press/meet-press-november-22-2015-n467821 (accessed March 18, 2017).

17. Ross Harrison, "Towards a Regional Strategy Contra ISIS," *Parameters* 44 (2012): 37.

18. Michael Boyle, "Do Counterterrorism and Counterinsurgency Go Together?" *International Affairs* 86 (2010): 353.

19. Robert A. Pape, "The Strategic Logic of Suicide Terrorism," *American Political Science Review* 97 (2003): 1–19.

20. Patrick Johnston, "Does Decapitation Work? Assessing the Effectiveness of Leadership Targeting in Counterinsurgency Campaigns," *International Security* 36 (2012): 47–79.

21. Matt Frankel, "The ABCs of HVT: Key Lessons from High Value Targeting Campaigns against Insurgents and Terrorists," *Studies in Conflict and Terrorism* 34 (2011): 18.

22. Ibid.

23. 132 Cong. Rec. S7483–S7484 (April 15, 1986).

# Conclusion

*Understanding How Terrorism Is Constructed*

Scott Englund, Michael Stohl, and Richard Burchill

The violence witnessed in 2015–16 has at times defied categorization and challenged the way we understand political violence. In Orlando, Florida, a lone gunman with murky motives killed forty-nine people in an LGBTQ nightclub. During the rampage, the shooter pledged allegiance to the so-called Islamic State (ISIS, ISIL, or Daesh), a terror group with which he had never had direct contact; incongruously, he had also been sympathetic to Hezbollah, a group antithetical to ISIS.[1] In Nice, France, a heavy-drinking, pork-eating Tunisian truck driver mowed down eighty-four people and critically injured more than one hundred others attending French Independence Day festivities; known for a violent temper, he was not religious, but ISIS claimed him as one of its own.[2] Acts of terrorist violence can be planned and logistically supported directly by known terror groups, as in Paris in November 2015, or conducted by individuals who are merely "inspired" by a shared ideology, with no direct contact or support from terror groups abroad. The variance in the scale of violence, the complexity of methods used, and the amount and kind of central planning forces analysts to question fundamental definitions and concepts, making it difficult to understand and explain the phenomenon we observe. In this environment, understanding the terrorist act or crafting a coherent response to acts of terrorism is difficult at best, muddled and ineffective at worst.

Coming to grips with the variance in scale and complexity of the methods that terrorists use has proven to be a major challenge for governments around the world. There is no question that the threat of terrorism has changed how we go about our day-to-day lives, from security at airports, to the organization of public events, to the work of police and security forces around the world. While it appears governments have been undertaking substantial efforts to respond to the threat of terrorism, these efforts do not appear to be preventing acts of terrorist violence. Throughout this volume we see the power that different constructions of terrorism have on understanding the nature of the threat, the actors who employ it, and responses to it. The contributors, coming from across the social sciences and humanities and building upon positivist and critical epistemologies, all demonstrate the importance of considering how the problem of terrorism is constructed. While they differ and would, no doubt, argue vigorously with one another about the relative power of their own construction and the utility it brings to understanding the problem and response, three clear themes emerge within the chapters.

First and perhaps most important, there can be negative consequences of both politicizing and polemicizing the definition of terrorism and responses to it. Second, at the heart of generating support for counterterrorism policies is the audience to political violence and to ensuing counterterrorism violence, and it is important to understand the political dynamics and social settings in which governments and terrorists compete for support and commitment. Third, it is important to understand how counterterrorism choices (both violent and nonviolent responses) are constructed in the context of the political dynamics and their consequences.

## CONSTRUCTING A POLITICALLY NEUTRAL DEFINITION OF TERRORISM

"A problem well stated," American inventor Charles Kettering is purported to have said, "is a problem half solved."[3] Applied here, a clear definition of terrorism is logically necessary to studying it. As a political act, the word *terrorism* is itself subject to political manipulation. At the international level, states have agreed to counterterrorism strategies pursued through the United Nations, but still cannot agree on a clear definition of terrorism. States may benefit from defining terror in such a way as to exclude themselves from the class of potential terrorists. Political actors within a government apparatus might benefit from defining terrorism in such a way that includes their political or ideological opponents. Lisa Stampnitzky initiates the discussion of politicizing the definition of terrorism by asking three questions that structure the problem: First, who is the enemy? Second, when is violence legitimate? Finally, what is political? Often in an attempt to delegitimize the political opposition, she argues, terrorism is defined by the enemy associated with terrorism rather than by a set of objective criteria. Ruth Blakeley reminds us that states use the terrorism label to delegitimize opponents and justify violence against them and that states can employ terrorism as a means to effect desired political outcomes. David Schanzer also points out that labeling serves the purpose of eliminating the discussion of the political context that might assist in understanding the choice of violence and opposition that led to the attacks.

John Mueller and Mark Stewart note that terrorism, as tracked by global databases, outside of war zones has generated only two hundred to four hundred deaths per year. Much of the violence now commonly defined as terrorism would, before 9/11, have been considered in the context of insurgency or civil war. The consequence, they argue, is that the deaths attributed to terrorism have created a discourse concerned with an existential threat rather than the much more contained (though still deadly) threat that actually exists. Rachel Levin and Victor Asal argue that it is the violence, not the label, that should be the focus of our concern. However, as is clear from the discussion offered by Blakeley, Stampnitzky, and Mueller and Stewart, in the highly politicized context in which terrorism is normally discussed in the media and by policy makers, changing the discourse has proven problematic at best.

## CONSTRUCTING RESPONSES TO TERRORISM

The polemical use of the term *terrorism* and the politicization of the discussion concerning what to do about it not only threatens our ability to understand the threat that terrorism poses but also negatively impacts our collective ability to construct and understand the effectiveness of possible responses. An ill-conceived definition of a particular threat, or one that has been molded for use to achieve political gain, will result in the misapplication of security resources. This fact is becoming more and more prominent in state responses as threats are vividly described by political leaders but those condemnations are then followed by no substantive efforts to understand how and why individuals and groups have chosen to use violence as a political strategy. Overstating a threat needlessly increases public anxiety. Misapplying countermeasures leads to inefficiency and inevitably results in breaches in security. Ineffective and inefficient responses erode public confidence. Therefore, at the heart of good counterterrorism is an accurately described threat.

Richard Burchill and Richard Falk each discuss how defining terrorism in different ways has affected the use of laws and the rule of law in responses to terrorism. Burchill argues that beyond the troubling conclusion that more law does not increase counterterrorism effectiveness, the problem is that the law also becomes a lesser tool in the promotion of the feeling of security that the law should provide. Falk builds on the consequences of favoring a war-fighting counterterrorism strategy over a law enforcement approach. In the context of fighting a war on terrorism, an escalation in violence, with the attendant diminishment of the rule of law, human rights, and civil liberties, is more easily accepted, whereas in a law enforcement paradigm these same concepts are elemental. A multifaceted threat, as Scott Englund and Michael Stohl note, requires a multifaceted response. For example, retaliating with military action in Iraq and Syria for attacks in Paris and Brussels is not likely to do much good in disrupting transnational terror threats by nonstate actors. Indeed, such a response most likely also exacerbates problems within Iraq and Syria. Counterterror activity that is mismatched to the threat is inefficient and counterproductive. Yet continually the perception of the threat and the issue of how best to respond to it remain disconnected. This disconnect is not necessarily due to a lack of knowledge, but has more to do with a lack of understanding of the wider context in which terrorist violence occurs.

## CONSTRUCTING TERRORISM IN ITS POLITICAL CONTEXT

Just as important as constructing a politically neutral definition of terrorism, and matching appropriate policy responses to well-defined threats, is understanding the political context in which terrorist violence occurs. Even terror groups with similar motivating ideologies each act within a particular political environment and seek their own political solutions to localized political problems. The political context in which terrorist violence occurs logically includes state responses to terrorism. Thus, understanding terrorism is as much an introspective process as it is a task of understanding the motives and commitment of those who employ terrorist violence. Mark Juergensmeyer contends that it is the "performative" aspects of the violence, transmitted primarily by television, that create the act's power and the need to respond to it. Benjamin Smith and his coauthors maintain that the media play a significant role in the transmission and construction of the understanding of terrorism and consequently how the public (and public officials) thinks about the construction of counterterrorism choices and policies. Seeking to construct a common, popular understanding of new terror threats, states, the media, and others employ familiar, though inappropriate, frames that can obscure, rather than clarify. Smith et al. argue that the power of media frames structures not only what we think about when we think about threats and the organizations that employ them, but how to respond.

Terrorism is often thought of as a means for the weak to coerce the strong. However, terrorism can also be understood as an act of violence meant to stir up anger and incite a response. Clark McCauley argues that anger, not fear, is the more likely response; anger reactions are associated with more aggressive responses to attack and with overreactions. In this form of "jujitsu politics," a relatively smaller, weaker terror group uses the weight and power of the state against itself, inciting an overreaction that is likely to build political support for the group's cause. Richard Falk echoes Juergensmeyer's and McCauley's concerns with attacks on symbolic targets and "spectacular" events that will spread fear and arouse anger and therefore create responses that are overreactions in both the military-security and political-legal arenas. These overreactions engender threats to civil liberties, democratic norms, and reactions to refugees and difference itself. In addition, as Laura Dugan and Erica Chenoweth stress, it is often conciliatory, rather than repressive, policies (the latter of which also produce backlash) that are associated with less terrorism.

Anthony Richards examines the counterterror strategies employed by the United Kingdom and finds that overreactions tend to blur the distinction between extremist views and extremist actions. This runs the risk that those who hold extreme or radical views but do not engage in violence are not considered potential partners in dissuading support for or engagement in terrorist actions. Mia Bloom and Stefan Malthaner and Lasse Lindekilde make clear the importance of relational ties and socialization for understanding the willingness both to belong to a group that employs violence and to use violence against others. They echo the conclusions of Richards, making clear the importance of distinguishing different pathways to violence and of distinguishing between acts of violence and terrorism on one hand and political opposition and radicalization on the other.

## THE WAY AHEAD

The ancient calculation "Kill one, frighten ten thousand," attributed to fifth-century BCE writer Sun Tzu, has been magnified by ubiquitous mass and social media that potentially allow millions of people to bear witness to an incident of violence thousands of miles distant. In spite of a revolution in communication and the increased lethality of individual attacks, the underlying relationships between violent actors, their victims, those who witness violence, and those responsible for preventing violence remain the same. In the aftermath of a violent attack there is an understandable demand for authorities to protect an affected population and provide improved security in the future. The resulting fear and anger drive calls for a retaliatory response. As our authors consistently argue, these responses are often counterproductive, due to the lack of an appropriate understanding of the events and their wider context. States have to respond, but responses tend to be more short-sighted in approach, concerned more with the immediate situation than with wider contextual issues over both time and space. Perhaps a major factor in this failure to respond appropriately is the challenge terrorist violence poses to states and societies. An effective response to terrorism should include initiatives and actions that cut across government ministries and departments and require coordinated acts within and between states. Effective responses need to incorporate an understanding of what motivates people to violence, how these motivations then become organized into acts, and how these acts are carried out. This is not easy to do. Terrorism and the use of political violence may appear to the public and policy makers to be simplistic acts carried out by bad people. The reality is most often far more complex, and terrorist acts cannot be prevented simply by eliminating a few "bad people," but rather require multifaceted approaches for prevention and response. And because the causes and opportunities for terrorism are highly complex, governments need to do more to move beyond overly emotional, politicized responses that too often attempt to present the problem as a simple issue of "us" versus "them."

A singular concern is the militarization of the US response to the September 11, 2001, attacks and the consequences of that decision. It is worth noting that prior to 9/11 the predominant response to terrorism in most democratic nations was the responsibility of the criminal justice system. Fifteen years after 9/11, despite all the criticisms of the "War on Terror" metaphor, war fighting dominates counterterrorism discussions and continues to influence criminal justice and political responses. The objective of war is the destruction of enemy forces, yet, if a threat comes that has no regular formations and "inspires" as much as it "directs," war fighting on its own may be insufficient. At best, a hybrid approach that applies lethal force consistent with the principle of proportionality in the context of a modern legal framework is needed. More work needs to be directed toward understanding why states have responded in the ways that they have, and more careful (and nonpartisan) analysis of the successes and failures of those responses are required. As the contributors to this collection make clear, the current constructions of terrorism often fall short of these necessary attributes.

An interesting element of counterterrorism debates concerns managing (or containing) versus defeating terrorism. As many of our contributors note (in addition to their dissent from this characterization), the post 9/11 threat of terrorism has often been described as existential. If contemporary terror threats are indeed "existential," this conflict is a fight in which one must kill or be killed. In a fight for one's very survival, anything is permitted; moral and legal constraints become unreasonable fetters that literally cost lives. In response to such an existential threat, war fighting, by military, police, or security forces, becomes the only appropriate response. Framed in this way, liberal societies can either abandon (temporarily) some of their cherished civil protections or face annihilation. The potential costs of framing a threat as existential are therefore daunting. With respect to surveillance, privacy, and the protection of human rights, there are significant trade-offs that must be carefully considered. Such a debate can benefit only from applying frames that provide the widest variety of responses. The war construction has not only altered the approach to terrorism abroad but also transformed the legal system at home. It is impossible to demonstrate that the war-fighting approach has been more effective than the previous law enforcement approach in either containing or defeating terrorism, but it is clear that the public is far more concerned about terrorism than should be warranted (outside war zones) because "terrorism" has not been fully defeated. This further demonstrates the complexities of constructing our understandings of terrorism and appropriate responses and of their impact on the public's perception of security.

If, however, the conversation can be altered for the purpose of exploring possible responses, and if terrorism is viewed as a manageable security threat, it is possible to discuss how to best manage that threat and work toward attainable objectives such as secure and tolerant societies, rather than attempting to completely eliminate the threats of terrorism, either real or perceived. How can states and societies respond to changes in the construction of counterterrorism? Does the war-fighting approach fruitlessly restrict the range of options available to security practitioners, and do legal structures offer any helpful alternatives?

Contemporary terrorism threats are a continuation of an ancient calculation according to which violence can alter behavior. Fear, anxiety, and anger can be powerful motivators. At the same time, the lethality of individual actors and the diffusion of violent ideologies, combined with ubiquitous, high-speed, high-definition communication, present an unprecedented security challenge. This combination of continuity and change presents a compelling and vitally important analytical puzzle. At the very heart of the problem is defining what it is that we are studying. A good definition makes it more likely that a coherent response can be crafted, and current experiences make clear we do not have good definitions or coherent and effective responses. Fixing terrorism in its political context, which logically includes security responses to it, is as much about introspection as it is about understanding the means and motives of those who choose terrorism to advance their cause.

The work presented in this volume approaches this complex analytical problem from a variety of disciplines, applying different methods, and though differences can be found, surprising agreement exists. Although this collection of essays, and the larger Constructions of Terrorism project, do not presume to give the final answer to definitional questions, they advance the discussion of a topic that is central to many of our contemporary political debates and unfortunately occupies considerable space in the news media. In that environment, it is vitally important for analysts to continually challenge existing paradigms, question apparently foregone conclusions, and offer sensible alternatives, and all of this thought and deliberation should be based on methodologically rigorous and theoretically sound research.

## NOTES

1. "Omar Mateen, Twice Scrutinized by F.B.I., Shows Threat of Lone Terrorists," *New York Times*, June 13, 2016, http://www.nytimes.com/2016/06/14/us/politics/orlando-shooting-omar-mateen.html.

2. "Moment of Silence Turns into Outcry against Government after Nice Attack," *New York Times*, July 18, 2016, http://www.nytimes.com/2016/07/19/world/europe/nice-france-attacker.html?_r=0.

3. Quotes.net (STANDS4 LLC, 2016), s.v. "Charles F. Kettering," http://www.quotes.net/quote/40299 (accessed July 20, 2016).

# Contributors

VICTOR ASAL   Professor of Political Science and Chair of Public Administration at the University at Albany, State University of New York.

RUTH BLAKELEY   Professor of International Relations, University of Kent. She is Codirector of The Rendition Project.

MIA BLOOM   Professor of Communication at Georgia State University, Atlanta. She conducts ethnographic field research in Europe, the Middle East, and South Asia.

RICHARD BURCHILL   Director of Research and Engagement at TRENDS Research and Advisory, Abu Dhabi, United Arab Emirates.

ERICA CHENOWETH   Professor and Associate Dean for Research at the Josef Korbel School of International Studies, University of Denver.

LAURA DUGAN   Professor in the Department of Criminology and Criminal Justice, University of Maryland.

SCOTT ENGLUND   Nonresident Fellow with TRENDS Research and Advisory and Postdoctoral Research Fellow at the Orfalea Center for Global and International Studies, University of California, Santa Barbara.

RICHARD FALK   Fellow at the Orfalea Center for Global and International Studies, University of California, Santa Barbara, and Albert G. Milbank Professor Emeritus of International Law at Princeton University.

ANDREA FIGUEROA-CABALLERO   Doctoral candidate in the Department of Communication at the University of California, Santa Barbara.

MARK JUERGENSMEYER   Professor of Sociology and Global Studies at the University of California, Santa Barbara.

RACHEL LEVIN   Graduate student in Criminal Justice at the University at Albany, State University of New York.

LASSE LINDEKILDE Associate Professor in the Department of Political Science, Aarhus University, Denmark.

STEFAN MALTHANER Research Fellow at the Hamburg Institute for Social Research, Germany.

CLARK MCCAULEY Research Professor of Psychology at Bryn Mawr College, Bryn Mawr, Pennsylvania, and a lead investigator with the National Consortium for the Study of Terrorism and Responses to Terrorism.

JOHN MUELLER Professor of Political Science at Ohio State University and Senior Fellow at the Cato Institute in Washington, DC.

ANTHONY RICHARDS Reader in Criminology in the Royal Docks School of Business and Law at the University of East London.

DAVID H. SCHANZER Associate Professor of the Practice at the Sanford School of Public Policy, Duke University, and Director of the Triangle Center on Terrorism and Homeland Security.

BENJAMIN K. SMITH Doctoral candidate in the Department of Communication at the University of California, Santa Barbara.

LISA STAMPNITZKY Lecturer in Politics at the University of Sheffield.

MARK G. STEWART Professor of Civil Engineering and Director of the Centre for Infrastructure Performance and Reliability at the University of Newcastle, Australia.

MICHAEL STOHL Director of the Orfalea Center for Global and International Studies at the University of California, Santa Barbara. He is Professor of Communication, Political Science, and Global and International Studies at UCSB.

# Index

Note: Locators in italics (e.g., *96*) indicate figures or tables.